T0176065

Knitting the Semantic Web

Knitting the Semantic Web has been co-published simultaneously as *Cataloging & Classification Quarterly*, Volume 43, Numbers 3/4 2007.

Knitting the Semantic Web

Jane Greenberg, PhD
Eva Méndez, PhD
Editors

Knitting the Semantic Web has been co-published simultaneously as *Cataloging & Classification Quarterly*, Volume 43, Numbers 3/4 2007.

Routledge
Taylor & Francis Group

LONDON AND NEW YORK

Transferred to Digital Printing 2008 by Routledge 2008
2 Park Square, Milton Park, Abingdon, Oxon, OX14 4RN
711 Third Ave, New York NY 10017

Routledge is an imprint of the Taylor & Francis Group, an informa business

First issued in paperback 2012

First published by

The Haworth Information Press®, 10 Alice Street, Binghamton, NY 13904-1580 USA

The Haworth Information Press® is an imprint of The Haworth Press, Inc., 10 Alice Street, Binghamton, NY 13904-1580 USA.

Knitting the Semantic Web has been co-published simultaneously as *Cataloging & Classification Quarterly*®, Volume 43, Numbers 3/4 2007.

The development, preparation, and publication of this work has been undertaken with great care. However, the publisher, employees, editors, and agents of The Haworth Press and all imprints of The Haworth Press, Inc., including The Haworth Medical Press® and Pharmaceutical Products Press®, are not responsible for any errors contained herein or for consequences that may ensue from use of materials or information contained in this work. With regard to case studies, identities and circumstances of individuals discussed herein have been changed to protect confidentiality. Any resemblance to actual persons, living or dead, is entirely coincidental.

The Haworth Press is committed to the dissemination of ideas and information according to the highest standards of intellectual freedom and the free exchange of ideas. Statements made and opinions expressed in this publication do not necessarily reflect the views of the Publisher, Directors, management, or staff of The Haworth Press, Inc., or an endorsement by them.

Cover design by Kerry E. Mack.

Library of Congress Cataloging-in-Publication Data

Knitting the Semantic Web / Jane Greenberg, Eva Méndez, editors.
    p. cm.
    Co-published simultaneously as Cataloging & classification quarterly, volume 43, numbers ¾.
    Includes bibliographical references and index.
    ISBN-13: 978-8-7890-3591-2 (hbk)
    ISBN-13: 978-0-415-54156-5 (pbk)
    1. Semantic Web. 2. Libraries and the Internet. I. Greenberg, Jane. II. Méndez, Eva. III. Cataloging & classification quarterly.
ZA4240.K58 2007
025.04–dc22

                                                                              2006038232

Knitting the Semantic Web

CONTENTS

PART II: SEMANTIC WEB PROJECTS AND PERSPECTIVES

ABOUT THE AUTHORS

Daniel Brickley, BSc <danbri@foaf-project.org> is an independent Semantic Web developer. He worked for six years as a member of the World Wide Web Consortium (W3C) team, where he helped establish the Semantic Web activity. He served as co-chair of the RDF Core Working Group, edited the RDF Schema standard, and directed the SWAD-Europe project which provided support to the growing Semantic Web community. He retains an involvement with W3C, but is now focussed on research and commercial work that uses Semantic Web infrastructure, and on the development of the FOAF (Friend Of A Friend) project.

Adam Constabaris, MA, MA <adamc@email.unc.edu> is a programmer and systems architect for the Knowledge Management group at the University of North Carolina at Chapel Hill. He received an MA in Philosophy from the University of British Columbia in 1995 and an MA in Philosophy from UNC-Chapel Hill in 1998. Adam is responsible for the exploration and implementation of new framework technologies and programming methodologies to facilitate information exchange across campus.

D. Grant Campbell, PhD <gcampbel@uwo.ca> completed his BA in English at the University of Toronto in 1982. He completed his MA in English at Queen's University in Kingston, Ontario in 1986, and his PhD in English at Queen's in 1989. After teaching at University of Toronto for one year, he took a break from academia to work at the North York Public Library from 1990 to 1995. He received his MISt in Library and Information Studies from the Faculty of Information Studies at University of Toronto, and in 1997 was the Coordinator of the Cataloguing Internet Resources Project at FIS. He taught at Dalhousie University from 1997 to 1998, and since 1998 has been teaching in the Faculty of Information and Media Studies at the University of Western Ontario, where he holds the position of Associate Professor. His research interests include resource description and classification in both traditional and non-traditional contexts; the design of electronic text; the Semantic Web; the design of electronic consumer health information; and information architecture.

Mike Graves, MSLS <gravm@email.unc.edu> is a technical editor for the Knowledge Management group at the University of North Carolina at Chapel Hill. He received his MSLS from UNC-Chapel Hill in May 2003. His main work focuses on incorporating Semantic Web technologies into the daily operations of a large organization. Current projects include using FOAF to model organizational structure, delivering event metadata through Microformats, and encouraging the reuse of common vocabularies with SKOS.

Corey A. Harper, MSLS <charper@uoregon.edu> is a metadata librarian at the University of Oregon Libraries. He provides system administration for the University's Institutional Repository, Scholars' Bank, and plays a lead role in building digital collections. He received his MSLS from the University of North Carolina, Chapel Hill in May 2002. He participates in the Dublin Core Metadata Initiative (DCMI) and is currently serving as 2005-2006 chair of the Pacific Northwest Chapter of the American Society of Information Science & Technology (ASIS&T). In 2004, Harper was recognized as one of Library Journal's "Movers and Shakers." His work interests include library automation, emerging technologies, programming, authority control, and digital preservation.

Johannes Keizer, PhD <Johannes.Keizer@fao.org> oversees FAO's scientific documentation and related activities, including the international AGRIS network of openArchive data and service providers. His group has launched various initiatives in the last few years toward a Semantic Web supporting FAO's subject area, namely the Agricultural Ontology Service (AOS) initiative and the AgMES (Agricultural Metadata Element Set) initiatives. Johannes Keizer holds a PhD in Biology from the University of Mainz. Prior to joining FAO in 2000, he was a researcher in biochemistry at the Italian High Health Institute and then as Free Lance Consultant for Management of Scientific Data. He lives in Rome.

Anita C. Liang, PhD <linguist@sdf.lonestar.org> is currently a Senior Specialist in Application Development at Perot Systems, Inc. working on enterprise architecture design in health information systems. She worked as an ontology expert from 2003 to 2005 in the AGRIS/CARIS Documentation Group at the Food and Agricultural Organization. During her tenure there, she was involved in numerous projects, both within and outside of FAO, concerned with Semantic Web technologies, most notably, with the conceptualization, design, and implementation of the Agricultural Ontology Service. She provided support in the form of ontological engineering, domain modeling, database (re)design, terminology development, natural language processing, and knowledge representation. Dr. Liang holds a PhD in linguistics from the University of California, Berkeley. Prior to joining FAO, she was a computational linguist working in Washington, DC, on question-answering software.

Charles McCathieNevile, BA <chaals@opera.com> Chief Standards Officer at Opera Software, is a Web standards and information architecture expert, with a special interest in accessibility and usability. Before joining Opera in 2005, McCathieNevile spent six years with the World Wide Web Consortium (W3C), putting his extensive experience with IT accessibility and hypertextual networks to use, as well as participating in the SWAD-E (Semantic Web Advanced Development-Europe) project. He also serves as the vice president of Fundación Sidar, a non-profit organization working in Iberian languages to improve Web standards and accessibility. McCathieNevile holds a degree in Medieval History from the University of Melbourne in Australia. His current research interests include usable security for the Web, extending the reach of the Web to devices and regions where it hasn't worked well until now.

John Michon, MD <micho001@mc.duke.edu> is on the faculty of the Department of Ophthalmology at the Duke University School of Medicine. After his clinical training at the University of Illinois, Johns Hopkins University, and the University of Southern California, he earned a master's degree in biomedical informatics from Stanford University. His research interests focus on the application of information technology to biomedicine. A major goal is to allow computers to perform routine inference over large biomedical databases in order to save human attention for more important tasks such as imagination, intuition, and creative thinking. Besides his work in knowledge representation and information semantics, he also does research in systems biology, a field that seeks to predict the behavior of cells and organs in health and disease based on their underlying molecular components.

Alistair Miles, MSc, MA Cantab. <A.J.Miles@rl.ac.uk> is a research associate at CCLRC Rutherford Appleton Laboratory. He holds a degree in Natural Sciences from Cambridge University. Alistair joined CCLRC in 2002, and participated in the Semantic Web Advanced Development for Europe (SWAD-Europe) project, co-ordinating the SWAD-Europe Thesaurus Activity. He is a member of the W3C Semantic Web Best Practices and Deployment Working Group, and has co-ordinated the SWBP-WG "Porting Thesauri" Task Force. Alistair is strongly motivated by issues relating to practical deployment of Semantic Web technologies, and is an editor of several W3C Working Drafts, including the SKOS (Simple Knowledge Organisation System) Core Guide and the Best Practice Recipes for Publishing RDF Vocabularies.

José R. Pérez-Agüera, MSc <jose.aguera@fdi.ucm.es> is Assistant Professor in the Department of Software Engineering and Artificial Intelligence of the University Complutense of Madrid in Spain. In 2002, he received the bachelor degree in Early Modern History from the University Complutense of Madrid. Later, in 2004, he received the DEA (Advanced Studies Diploma–a kind of Research Master Degree) in Library and Information Science and in 2005 received the DEA (Master) in Computer Science. Currently, he is working for his PhD in Computer Science in the University Complutense of Madrid. His research interests include information retrieval on the Web using natural language processing techniques and the Semantic Web paradigm.

G. Philip Rogers, MA <gerogers@email.unc.edu> is a Senior Business Analyst in Instructional and Information Systems (IIS) at UNC's School of Public Health and also a Doctoral student in Information Science at UNC. Gershom's research interests include applying IT processes, infrastructure, and tools to help solve major Public Health and Library/Information Science research challenges, metadata interoperability, Semantic Web/Web 2.0, Business Intelligence/Knowledge Management, Content Management, Agile Project Management, and use case-driven business analysis and requirements elicitation.

Thomas Severiens, Dipl.-Phys. <severiens@mathematik.Uni-Osnabrueck.DE> studied Physics at the Carl-von-Ossietzky University Oldenburg. In 1995 he started to develop PhysNet. After graduating, together with some colleagues he founded the Institute for Science Networking

Oldenburg (ISN). Since 2004 he is working as a lecturer in Information Engineering and as a researcher at the University of Osnabrück. He is one of the chairs of Dublin-Core Working Group "Tools" and was a member of W3C Working Group "XQuery" from 2001 until 2005. His research interests include the development of distributed library systems, user oriented scientific information portals, strategies for long-term preservation of the scientific research output, and development tools for full-text semantics.

Gauri Salokhe, MEng <Gauri.Salokhe@fao.org> is Information Management Officer, AGRIS/CARIS Documentation Group, FAO, United Nations. She holds BEng in Industrial Engineering and MEng in Information Management. She is currently working on an initiative that aims to bring coherence to the information management standards in the Agriculture domain. She has been extensively involved in the creation of an exchange format for metadata for agricultural document-like information resources. Currently, she is working on semantic standards related issues, including domain ontologies and metadata ontologies for the agricultural domain. She is involved in the enhancement of AGROVOC, the multilingual agricultural thesaurus used worldwide as a standard for document/resource indexing and information retrieval purposes. She collaborates with internal and external FAO partners on issues pertaining to management of metadata on various types of information resources, providing training when necessary. She has been involved in the production of coursework, for the distance learning materials (Information Management Resource Kit on "Management of Electronic Documents").

Margherita Sini, MSc <Margherita.Sini@fao.org> after several years of work in International Organizations and private small and medium companies on software development, computer training, GIS and collaboration on EU-Funded projects, is currently working in FAO as an Information Management Specialist. A major part of her work involves working on information resources description and discovery systems, bibliographical and information systems, metadata schemas, thesauri, and development of domain specific multilingual ontologies. She is primarily working on the Agricultural Ontology Service (AOS) initiative and she is one of the main actors in the development of the AGROVOC multilingual thesaurus.

Joseph I. Tennis, PhD <jtennis@interchange.ubc.ca> is an assistant professor at the School of Library, Archival and Information Studies of the University of British Columbia, Canada. Dr. Tennis received his BA in Religious Studies from Lawrence University, his MLS, and Specialist degree in Library and Information Science in Book History from the School of Library and Information Science at Indiana University. He received his PhD from the University of Washington in 2005. He is involved in the InterPARES 2 research project on authentic digital records in electronic systems. He is a member of the DCMI Usage Board, and his research interest include: classification theory; interaction with, and management of classificatory structures; functional analysis of metadata; and comparative studies of knowledge organization practices.

Christian Thiemann, BSc <mail@christian-thiemann.de> worked for Oldenburg Research and Development Institute for Information Technology Tools and Systems (OFFIS) during high school. After his mandatory military service, he worked for the Institute for Science Networking Oldenburg (ISN) in PhysNet project (2003-2005). Since fall 2003 he studies Physics at the Georg-August-University Göttingen. In 2005/2006 he studied at the University of California in San Diego. He also has been a member of the working group on Physics of Transportation and Traffic at the University of Duisburg-Essen and is currently a member of the "Traffic Modelling and Econometrics" working group at the Dresden University of Technology. His research interests include cellular automaton models of freeway traffic, computational physics, and computer science in general.

Barbara B. Tillett, PhD <btil@loc.gov> is Chief of the Cataloging Policy and Support Office (CPSO) at the Library of Congress and Acting Chief of the Cataloging Distribution Service. She currently serves as the Library of Congress representative on the Joint Steering Committee for Revision of the Anglo-American Cataloguing Rules, chairs the IFLA (International Federation of Library Associations and Institutions) Division IV on Bibliographic Control, and leads the IFLA work towards an International Cataloguing Code and a Virtual International Authority File. In addition she leads the worldwide initiative within IFLA to update and replace the 1961 "Paris Principles," which are the foundation of nearly every cataloging code used in the world today. Her publications have focused on cataloging theory and practice, authority control, bibliographic relationships, conceptual modeling, and library automation. Dr. Tillet has received several awards, including the Margaret Mann Citation in 2004, recognizing her many contributions in the areas of cataloging and classification.

Stuart L. Weibel, PhD <weibel@oclc.org> has worked in OCLC Research since 1985, during which time he has managed projects in the area of automated cataloging, automated document structure analysis, electronic publishing, persistent identifiers, and metadata. He was a founding member of the International WWW Conference Committee (IW3C2) and has also served on program and organizational committees for the Internet Society, the European Conference on DLs, the Joint Conference on DLs, and the International Conference on Asian DLs. Work with Eric Miller in the Internet Engineering Task Force working group on Uniform Resource Names led to the development of the PURL system at OCLC. From 1995 until 2005 he led the Dublin Core Metadata Initiative (DCMI), an international consensus building activity that develops and supports cross-disciplinary resource discovery standards. Weibel spent the 2006 calendar year at the University of Washington (iSchool) where he studied persistent identifiers and Web 2.0 issues as they relate to libraries. His thoughts and photographs are irregularly recorded at: http://weibel-lines.typepad.com.

ABOUT THE EDITORS

Jane Greenberg, PhD, is Associate Professor in the School of Information and Library Science, University of North Carolina at Chapel Hill (SILS/UNC-CH); Director of the SILS Metadata Research Center; and recently was awarded a Frances Carroll McColl professorship. Professor Greenberg's research and teaching focus on metadata and classification problems. She is the Principal Investigator for the Memex Metadata (M^2) for Student Portfolios project, sponsored by Microsoft Research and UNC's Information Technology Services. She serves on the Dublin Core Metadata Initiative (DCMI) Advisory Board and is Co-Chair of the DCMI Tools Working Group. She frequently serves on national and international digital library and metadata conference program committees, and was Program Co-Chair of the 2003 Dublin Core conference. Dr. Greenberg was the Principle Investigator of the AMeGA (Automatic Metadata Generation Applications) project and the Metadata Generation Research (MGR) project, collectively sponsored by Microsoft Research, OCLC Online Computer Center, and the Library of Congress. Professor Greenberg earned a master's degree in Library Science from Columbia University and a doctorate in Library and Information Science from the University of Pittsburgh.

Eva Méndez, PhD, is Associate Professor in the Library and Information Science Department, University Carlos III of Madrid, where she has been teaching and researching since March 1997. She holds a doctorate in Information Science from the same University, awarded in the academic year 2001-2002 as the outstanding thesis of the year in her field. She is a member of the Dublin Core Metadata Initiative (DCMI) Advisory Board and served as Co-Chair of the International Conference on Dublin Core and Metadata Applications (Vocabularies in Practice) held in Madrid in 2005. Her research focuses on Semantic Web technologies applied to digital information systems and services, with an emphasis on metadata standards and other vocabularies. In addition to the DCMI, Dr. Méndez has served on many conference and workshop program committees worldwide. She has also served as an advisor on information practice and policy in countries in the European Union and Latin America. Dr. Méndez was Fulbright-EU Research Scholar at University of North Carolina at Chapel Hill, School of Information and Library Science, Metadata Research Center, during the academic year 2005-2006.

Introduction:
Toward a More Library-Like Web
via Semantic Knitting

Jane Greenberg
Eva Méndez

Over the last five years, the library community's attention to the Semantic Web has progressed at a creeping pace. More recently–within the last year–the Semantic Web appears to be gaining greater attention by information professionals looking for answers to manage the complex world of the Web. This development is perhaps best explained by Paul Miller's (2005; 2006) stimulating and thought provoking notion of "Library 2.0" inspired, in part, by Tim O'Reilly's (2005) highly influential *"What Is Web 2.0."* Part of Miller's central thesis is that the rich untapped structured data sources which libraries possess need to be exposed and mined. He believes the 21st century library is *obligated* to expose its rich data and provide a new level of service, information access, and knowledge discovery for the good of its users and citizens at large. Miller's Library 2.0 integrates with the foundation ideas and evolution of the Semantic Web, and invites librarians to think outside the box and actively engage in the development of the Semantic Web. This special volume demonstrates that librarians and other information professionals, including people involved in information intensive work (e.g., medical doctors), are taking Miller's advice and building a more library-like World Wide Web (Web) through what we call "semantic knitting."

[Haworth co-indexing entry note]: "Introduction: Toward a More Library-Like Web via Semantic Knitting." Greenberg, Jane, and Eva Méndez. Co-published simultaneously in *Cataloging & Classification Quarterly* (The Haworth Information Press, an imprint of The Haworth Press, Inc.) Vol. 43, No. 3/4, 2007, pp. 1-8; and: *Knitting the Semantic Web* (ed: Jane Greenberg, and Eva Méndez) The Haworth Information Press, an imprint of The Haworth Press, Inc., 2007, pp. 1-8. Single or multiple copies of this article are available for a fee from The Haworth Document Delivery Service [1-800-HAWORTH, 9:00 a.m. - 5:00 p.m. (EST). E-mail address: docdelivery@haworthpress.com].

Available online at http://ccq.haworthpress.com
© 2007 by The Haworth Press, Inc. All rights reserved.
doi:10.1300/J104v43n03_01

THE SEMANTIC WEB AND UNDERLYING PRINCIPLES

The Semantic Web represents Berners-Lee's initial idea of the Web, and is defined as "an extension of the current Web in which information is given well-defined meaning, better enabling computers and people to work in cooperation" (Berners-Lee et al., 2001). In more conventional terms, Connolly (1998) explains that the Semantic Web will relieve him from the "bane of my [his] existence" of performing mundane tasks that he knows a computer can perform for him (e.g., searching for a doctor who accepts his health insurance plan).

The Semantic Web requires that information bearing entities on the Web be tagged with machine-processable meaning (semantic metadata) in a standard way. The standardization will enable the exchange, use, and reuse of information. Tagging entities with ontological or other standard values will result in a semantically knitted network that can support computational activities and provide people with services efficiently. A fundamental component to this activity is the development, registration, and sharing of metadata schemas and ontologies.

Koivunen and Miller (2001) identify the following principles to guide Semantic Web development:

1. *Everything can be identified by URIs (Uniform Resource Identifier).* People, places, things, and attributes about these entities can all be identified with an URI.
2. *Resources and links have types.* Identifying relationships such as "is version of," "has subject," and "is author" make data machine processable.
3. *Partial information is tolerated.* There is no limit on the encoding of entities (resource, links, and relationships).
4. *There is no need for absolute truth.* Truth of information on the Web cannot be guaranteed, but Semantic Web agents will be able to determine what information is trustworthy via context.
5. *Evolution is supported.* The Semantic Web is organic, and new information can be added to older information.
6. *Minimalist design.* The goal is to standardize no more than is necessary; "When we use the Semantic Web technologies the result should offer much more possibilities than the sum of the parts."

Although these principles emphasize the simplicity of the Semantic Web, they are only valuable if there is a means by which they can be achieved. Concrete examples demonstrating these principles are needed to motivate Semantic Web development. This volume contributes to this need by presenting Semantic Web foundations, projects, and philosophical ideas.

STATUS OF THE SEMANTIC WEB

We teach in the area of organizing information and digital content and data management. We encourage students to read about the Semantic Web, explore Semantic Web developments, and think critically about the Semantic Web's future. At times we are challenged when discussing the Semantic Web, particularly when students and colleagues ask: "Where is it [The Semantic Web]?" "Can I see the Semantic Web in operation?" and "What about privacy issues?" Our replies to such questions generally unfold in the following order: Semantic Web development is underway with enabling technologies and standards, such as the Resource Description Framework (RDF), Web Ontology Language (OWL), Friend Of A Friend (FOAF), and the newest language Simple Knowledge Organizations System (SKOS). We also point to RSS (RDF Site Summary/Really Simple Syndication), which incorporates RDF and has had a global impact on the Web-based news syndications. These technologies provide the technical backbone required to form the Semantic Web's infrastructure. These technologies have also motivated the development of Semantic Web tools and projects (Table 1) helping to form an infrastructure that allows information to be digested and used in new ways as envisioned by Berners-Lee.

Notwithstanding Semantic Web progress (e.g., Table 1), it would be incorrect to say that these developments support a mature Semantic Web. In other words, when asked if the Semantic Web currently supports agents scheduling personal appointments or planning a vacation to Hawaii, we reply "no." We can, however, look at online calendaring applications and travel services, such as Expedia.com, and see semantic components that could be harvested for Semantic Web development. Despite these developments, current Semantic Web limitations have led to criticism (Marshall, 2004; Shirky, 2003). Criticism is useful for addressing current shortcomings and planning the next step in developing a Semantic Web. The downside of criticisms is that they often fail to note where important progress has been made.

What is important and stands as evidence of major progress is the wide range of communities with a growing interest in information standards, data interoperability, and open information. Never in our time

TABLE 1. Examples of Semantic Web Tools and Projects

Semantic Web Tools	Semantic Web Projects
Annotea: http://www.w3.org/2001/Annotea **Annozilla:** http://annozilla.mozdev.org/ **FOAF RDF vocabulary:** http://xmlns.com/foaf/0.1/ **ORACLE:** http://www.oracle.com/technology/tech/semantic_ technologies/index.html **RDFPic:** http://jigsaw.w3.org/rdfpic/ **Swoogle:** http://swoogle.umbc.edu/ **Tabulator (SW Browser):** http://dig.csail.mit.edu/2005/ajar/ajaw/tab.html http://widgets.opera.com/widget/5053	**APAIS (Australian Public Affairs Information Service) Thesaurus:** http://www.nla.gov.au/apais/thesaurus/ **Biocomplexity Thesaurus of the National Biological Information Infrastructure:** http://thesaurus.nbii.gov/portal/server.pt **FAO Thesaurus:** http://www.fao.org/aims/ag_intro.htm **MusicBrainz:** http://musicbrainz.org/ **NCI Thesaurus:** http://www.mindswap.org/2003/CancerOntology/ **Physnet:** http://www.physnet.de/PhysNet/ **Semantic Web Environmental Directory:** http://www.swed.org.uk/swed/index.html

has there been a more universal interest in producing structured, standardized information. The idea of the Semantic Web initiative will, at the very least, help many more initiatives to benefit from standardized organization and access to information. We conclude then, that the Semantic Web is being knitted. We may not create one big knitted snug blanket, although the number of Semantic Web projects is growing, and they can be knitted together via standards for more powerful computing operations than previously possible.

PURPOSE OF THIS VOLUME

The overall purpose of this special volume is to explore the Semantic Web initiative. More specifically, the goals are to:

- Bring together a series of articles by leaders in library and information science, computer science, and information intensive domains, who are exploring the Semantic Web and playing a significant role in its development.
- Provide librarians and other readers with a greater understanding of the Semantic Web.
- Aid librarians/information professionals is discovering the role they may play developing, growing, and maintaining the Semantic Web.

Library science is a cross-domain discipline that has always involved experts from a variety of disciplines (e.g., library science, computer science, and people with topical subject expertise). One reason for this is that libraries can be found with collection holdings documenting any discipline. Another related reason is that a library can be found serving nearly any type of client. The Semantic Web needs librarians and informational professionals not only because of their experience and expertise with standards and bibliographic control, but their experience and expertise as information custodians for the last several hundred years (Greenberg, 2006). In short, we have edited this special volume because we firmly believe that librarians can play a significant role in developing the Semantic Web.

WHY **KNITTING** *THE SEMANTIC WEB?*

We have chosen to present the articles in this volume in the context *knitting* for the following reasons:

- Knitting means to interlock or join closely. Garments and fabrics are produced by interlocking single strands of yarn, broken bones heal through knitting, and a close-knit relationship is generally a supportive and positive relationship. A *knitted Semantic Web* will result in a more powerful and robust Web.
- Several monographs published about the Semantic Web draw upon tasks relating to the craft of knitting. For example, there was first "weaving" the Web (Berners-Lee, 1999), followed by "creating" (Hjelm, 2001), and "spinning" (Fensel, 2003).
- A simple "knit-purl" stitch (knitting) is used to create simple to quite complex and sophisticated designs. Similarly, simple semantics underlying the Semantic Web intend to support simple to complex and sophisticated operations.
- Knitting permeates many strata–from the men who knit on Taquile Island, Lake Titicaca, Peru, and knitting cooperatives all over the world (Greenberg, 1996), to recent faddish "knit-ins"[1] and knitting celebrities.[2] The Semantic Web is applicable to all citizens.

FRAMEWORK FOR THIS VOLUME

Knitting the Semantic Web is arranged into two parts. Part I addresses Semantic Web foundations, standards, and tools; and Part II presents Semantic Web projects and perspectives.

Part I begins with a foundation article by Campbell discussing how Foucault's *The Birth of the Clinic* serves as a pattern for understanding the paradigm shifts represented by the Semantic Web. This work is followed by McCathieNevile and Méndez's work on RDF, its expressive power, and its ability to underlie the new Library catalog card of the 21st century. Harper and Tillett then explore Library of Congress controlled vocabularies and their value and application for developing the Semantic Web. Next, Miles and Pérez-Agüera introduce the newest Semantic Web language, Simple Knowledge Organization System (SKOS), which is for representing controlled structured vocabularies, including thesauri, classification schemes, subject heading systems, and taxonomies. This work is followed by Tennis' presentation of a conceptual framework and a methodology for managing scheme versioning in the Semantic Web. Part I concludes with Rogers' review of semantic tools and technologies that libraries and other knowledge-intensive organizations can use for building Semantic Web projects.

Part II of this volume begins with an article by Severiens and Thiemann presenting their RDF triples database, Physnet, a Semantic Web portal service for physics. This article is followed by Michon's article on the value of Semantic Web technologies in biomedicine and his work, which is grounded in RDF. Michon, a medical doctor, also identifies several important roles that library and information scientists can play in developing a more powerful biomedical information infrastructure in the context of the Semantic Web. Next is an article by Liang, Salokhe, Sini, and Keizer presenting the intellectual processes and technical specifications for developing the United Nations, Food and Agriculture's ontology. This work is followed by a piece by Graves, Constabaris, and Brickley introducing the Semantic Web's Friend Of A Friend (FOAF) vocabulary specification, and also presenting a real world case study of FOAF for solving specific identity management problems in an information technology department at a University. Greenberg then presents a deductive analysis on the applicability of primary library functions (collection development, cataloging, reference, and circulation) to Semantic Web development. The last article is a perspective piece by Stuart Weibel, founder of the Dublin Core Metadata Initiative, one of the most significant programs bringing together members of the library and Semantic Web communities. In this concluding article, Weibel provides a personal perspective on libraries and the Semantic Web in the context of social bibliography.

CONCLUSION

Librarians have the intellectual knowledge and skills required to work with Semantic Web enabling technologies (e.g., XML, RDF). We do not need to be computer programmers to do this, as there are many tools available to aid our use of these standards (see the Rogers contribution). What is important is that we are experts in developing information standards, and, most importantly we have the most sophisticated skills and experience in knowledge representation. In sum, if librarians transfer their skills to the semantic knitting required for a Semantic Web, we can help build a better Web.

ACKNOWLEDGEMENTS

The Editors would like to acknowledge all of the authors for their contributions to this volume. The Editors would also like to thank Sandy Roe, Teri Devoe, and the *CCQ*'s Editorial Board for their support of this special volume. The Editors would also like to thank the Fulbright Program for support that allowed Eva Méndez to work as EU Research Scholar at the SILS Metadata Research Center, University of North Carolina at Chapel Hill, over the last year to complete this book.

NOTES

1. The Big Knit In: http://www.knitin.co.uk/; Anglicare Knit-in 2006: http://www.abc.net.au/perth/knitin/default.htm.
2. Celebrity Knitters . . . Look Who's Knitting: http://www.worldknit.com/celebrityknitters.html.

REFERENCES

Berners-Lee, T. (1999). *Weaving the Web: The Original Design and Ultimate Destiny of the World Wide Web by Its Inventor*. San Francisco: Harper.

Berners-Lee, T., Hendler, J., and Lassila, O. (2001). The Semantic Web. *Scientific American*, 284(5): 34-43. Also available at: http://www.sciam.com/article.cfm?articleID=00048144-10D2-1C70-84A9809EC588EF21.

Connolly, D. (1998). *The XML Revolution*. World Wide Web Consortium: http://www.w3.org/People/Connolly/9810xn.html.

Fensel, D., Wahlster, W., Lieberman, H., and Hendler, J. (Eds.) (2003). *Spinning the Semantic Web: Bringing the World Wide Web to Its Full Potential*. Cambridge: MIT Press, 2003.

Greenberg, J. (2006). Advancing Semantic Web via Library Functions. *Cataloging & Classification Quarterly*. 43(3/4): 203-225.

Greenberg, M. (1996). Bolivia: Women's Knitting Cooperative. *South American Explorer Issue*, 45: 8-15.

Hjelm, J. (2001). *Creating the Semantic Web with RDF: Professional Developer's Guide*. New York: John Wiley & Sons.

Koivunen, M., and Miller E. (2001). W3C Semantic Web Activity. E. Hyvönen (Ed.). *Semantic Web Kick-Off in Finland: Vision, Technologies, Research, and Applications*. Helsinki Institute for Information Technology (HIIT), Helsinki, Finland. May 19, 2002, pp. 27-43. Also available online at: http://www.cs.helsinki.fi/u/eahyvone/stes/semanticweb/kick-off/proceedings.pdf, and http://www.w3.org/2001/12/semweb-fin/w3csw.

Marshall, C. (2004). *Taking a Stand on the Semantic Web*. Texas: Center for the Study of Digital Libraries: http://www.csdl.tamu.edu/~marshall/mc-semantic-web.html.

Miller, P. (2005). Web 2.0: Building the New Library. *Ariadne*, 45: http://www.ariadne.ac.uk/issue45/miller.

Miller, P. (2006). Coming Together around Library 2.0: A Focus for Discussion and a Call to Arms. *D-Lib Magazine*, 12(4): http://www.dlib.org/dlib/april06/miller/04miller.html.

O'Reilly, T. (2005). What Is Web 2.0: Design Patterns and Business Models for the Next Generation of Software. *O'ReillyNet*: http://www.oreillynet.com/pub/a/oreilly/tim/news/2005/09/30/what-is-web-20.html.

Shirky, C. (2003). *The Semantic Web, Syllogism, and Worldview*. [First published on the Networks, Economics, and Culture mailing list.]: http://www.shirky.com/writings/semantic_syllogism.html.

PART I:
SEMANTIC WEB FOUNDATIONS, STANDARDS, AND TOOLS

The Birth of the New Web:
A Foucauldian Reading
of the Semantic Web

D. Grant Campbell

SUMMARY. Foucault's *The Birth of the Clinic* serves as a pattern for understanding the paradigm shifts represented by the Semantic Web. Foucault presents the history of medical practice as a 3-stage sequence of transitions: from classificatory techniques to clinical strategies, and then to anatomico-pathological strategies. In this paper, the author removes these three stages both from their medical context and from Foucault's

Funding for this research has been provided by a generous research grant from the Social Sciences and Humanities Research Council of Canada. The author gratefully acknowledges the assistance of Robin Hepher.

[Haworth co-indexing entry note]: "The Birth of the New Web: A Foucauldian Reading of the Semantic Web." Campbell, D. Grant. Co-published simultaneously in *Cataloging & Classification Quarterly* (The Haworth Information Press, an imprint of The Haworth Press, Inc.) Vol. 43, No. 3/4, 2007, pp. 9-20; and: *Knitting the Semantic Web* (ed: Jane Greenberg, and Eva Méndez) The Haworth Information Press, an imprint of The Haworth Press, Inc., 2007, pp. 9-20. Single or multiple copies of this article are available for a fee from The Haworth Document Delivery Service [1-800-HAWORTH, 9:00 a.m. - 5:00 p.m. (EST). E-mail address: docdelivery@haworthpress.com].

Available online at http://ccq.haworthpress.com
doi:10.1300/J104v43n03_02

historical sequence, to produce a model for understanding information organization in the context of the Semantic Web. We can extract from Foucault's theory a triadic relationship between three interpretive strategies, all of them defined by their different relationships to a textual body: classification, description, and analysis. doi:10.1300/J104v43n03_02 *[Article copies available for a fee from The Haworth Document Delivery Service: 1-800-HAWORTH. E-mail address: <docdelivery@haworthpress.com> Website: <http://www.HaworthPress.com> © 2007 by The Haworth Press, Inc. All rights reserved.]*

KEYWORDS. Semantic Web, Foucault, classification, discourse analysis

INTRODUCTION

The emergence of file-sharing networks, folksonomies, weblogs, instant messaging, RSS feeds, and other next-generation Web tools presents fresh challenges to libraries and other organizations devoted to organizing and providing access to information. These tools, increasingly classified as the "Web 2.0," promise to create a new environment in which the Web serves as a platform offering services rather than software: services that place the user in control of the data through an architecture of participation, data mixing, and the harnessing of collective intelligence (O'Reilly 2005). Libraries, with their traditional emphasis on documents organized according to internationally-produced and centrally-administered standards of description and classification, seem to be the antithesis of this exciting new user-centered environment. Instead of controlled vocabularies and classification schemes, the Web 2.0 offers folksonomies: user-centered tagging systems that classify tags into data "clouds." Instead of documents, the Web 2.0 offers BitTorrent, which breaks files into pieces and then reassembles them, and file sharing systems that enable one to download individual data files and shuffle them according to individual needs and whims.

This has happened before. Online databases initially promised to do away with controlled vocabularies; metadata initiatives initially promised to do away with library cataloguing. In earlier cases, libraries survived, not by ignoring the new innovation, but by negotiating a fresh role for themselves in relation to these innovations. Online databases generated a need for rigorously-designed thesauri (Williamson 1996, 156); metadata systems gave rise to the adaptation of cataloguing principles to serve metadata application profiles, such as the Dublin Core's Library Application Profile (Clayphan & Guenther 2004); information architects found a new use for principles of faceted classification (Rosenfield & Morville 2002). As libraries face a new generation of Web users and Web tools, the questions remain the same as for previous changes:

- What facets of the new information environment would be most receptive to collaboration with libraries and information professionals?
- What specific skills and tools in the library environment would be most useful, if reinvented for this new context?

The author has argued elsewhere (Campbell & Fast 2004, 382) that the Semantic Web initiatives of the World Wide Web Consortium offer the closest and most reasonable link between the emerging Web environment and library services. Envisioned by Tim Berners-Lee as the next step in the Web's evolution, the Semantic Web offers a pyramid of information standards that would enable information to be machine-understandable as well as machine-readable. The Semantic Web will utilize semantic markup (XML), a standard for describing resources (Resource Description Framework), methods of reconciling differences in namespaces (ontologies), and methods of certifying authenticity through digital signatures. If fully realized, this new network will enable intelligent agents to extract documents on-the-fly that directly answer users' individual questions: "Now we can imagine the world of people with active machines forming part of the infrastructure. . . . Search engines, from looking for pages containing interesting words, will start indexes of assertions that might be useful for answering questions or finding justifications" (Berners-Lee 2002, xvii).

The presence of W3C representatives at important conferences such as the Dublin Core Workshop and the meetings of the American Society for Information Science and Technology suggest that the skills of librarianship and information management are a key component of the Semantic Web. Creating machine-understandable data that enables agents to draw inferences and extract data correctly requires disambiguation, recognition of context, vocabulary control, and categorization. Librarians know how to do this, and the World Wide Web is eager to draw on the library community's skills.

Nonetheless, we know from experience that when skills and tools migrate into new environments, they change. Post-coordinate thesauri designed for use in online databases are far different from the *Library of Congress Subject Headings*; the Dublin Core metadata set is a far cry from the *Anglo-American Cataloguing Rules*. Libraries are already finding ways to adapt their powers of description to Semantic Web needs; OCLC's Connexion service transforms MARC records into RDF Dublin Core records. But we need to understand how these adaptations will change the basic concepts underlying information organization and description, and how those changes will have an impact on our traditional practices of bibliographic control.

This paper attempts to establish a theoretical frame for comprehending this transition, by drawing on the archaeological theory of Michel Foucault. In particular, I will argue that Foucault's analysis of clinical diagnosis in *The Birth of the Clinic* (1963) provides a triadic model of three different principles of description and diagnosis; these three principles, when extracted both from the historical context and from Foucault's insistence on a historical progression, provide a useful understanding of the relationship between bibliographic control in libraries and resource description on the Semantic Web.

BACKGROUND: *FOUCAULT'S* BIRTH OF THE CLINIC

The Birth of the Clinic marks Foucault's first major work in his "archaeological" period: a period that also produced *The Order of Things* (1966) and *The Archaeology of Knowledge* (1969). LIS researchers frequently use *The Archaeology of Knowledge*, which questions, on a more general level, the ways in which discourse is produced within communities according to surfaces of emergence and institutional places which sanction authoritative statements. This is very useful for analyzing how libraries get trapped in their own discursive formations (Radford 2003, 16), or for analyzing how our conceptions of knowledge are based on pre-conceptual underpinnings (Hannabuss 1996, 87). *The Birth of the Clinic*, however, offers special advantages, in that it analyzes changes in knowledge development within a specific relationship–that of doctor and patient–which can translate more easily to the relationship between the information professional and the information user.

In *The Birth of the Clinic*, Foucault uses a close analysis of French medical texts in the late eighteenth and early nineteenth centuries to demonstrate a transition in the conceptualizations of medical diagnosis: a transition from diagnosis based on classification to diagnosis based on patient observation, and then to diagnosis based on dissection and anatomo-clinical theory. At the risk of missing Foucault's entire point (that discourse is historically and culturally situated), I propose to extract this transition both from its historical context and from Foucault's sequence. Instead, I will argue that information organization can be classified according to the simultaneous presence of these three factors in a triadic relationship of classification, description, and analysis, each of which maps to a different facet of the Semantic Web.

KNOWLEDGE THROUGH CLASSIFICATION

In the eighteenth century, Foucault argues, doctors diagnosed disease by abstracting it from the patient's body and assigning it a place in a grid of resemblances and differences. Understanding emerges from the spatial dimensions of the classification as "picture," similar to that of the genealogical tree:

> This organization . . . defines a fundamental system of relations involving envelopments, subordinations, divisions, resemblances. This space involves: a 'vertical,' in which the implications are drawn up–fever, 'a successive struggle between cold and heat,' may occur in a single episode or in several; . . .; and a 'horizontal,' in which the homologies are transferred– . . . what catarrh is to the throat, dysentery is to the intestines. (Foucault, 5)

As with traditional classification schemes, medicine in this stage relies for its work upon an external construct, similar to a classification schedule, which takes subjects and sets them into relationships of hierarchy and differentiation, relationships that exist apart from the appearance of the subjects in documents.

Like library classification schemes, with their principles of order, their standard subdivisions, tables of wide application and defined facets, the taxonomies of disease in the eighteenth century produce "a space in which analogies define essences. The pictures resemble things, but they also resemble each other" (Foucault, 6). And in both library and medical classifications, "the form of the similarity uncovers the rational order" (Foucault, 7). The structure of the ordering system enables knowledge discovery by revealing meaningful relationships.

On the Semantic Web, the classification principle exists most prominently in the need for ontologies: web-based tools for resolving different conceptions and usages of terms. Ranging in complexity from simple glossaries to complex tools capable of representing numerous types of relationship, ontologies serve the conventional purposes of controlled vocabularies and classification schemes; they can resolve different namespaces, recognizing synonymous terms in different domains and provide a basis for site navigation and support (McGuinness, 179). In addition, they also provide opportunities for other, more sophisticated actions, such as consistency checking, completing a user's query in a logical fashion, interoperability support, validation of data, and supporting structured, comparative, and customized search (McGuinness, 181-84). Most of these uses imply that knowledge can be removed from its specific context, to some degree, and classified, mapped to other domains, and used to facilitate information and knowledge discovery.

KNOWLEDGE THROUGH SYMPTOMS

In the early nineteenth century, Foucault argues, a new clinical approach to diagnosis and treatment supplanted the traditional classificatory approach. This clinical method places a much greater emphasis on symptoms as they occur in the patient: "There is no longer a pathological essence beyond the symptoms: everything in the disease is itself a phenomenon" (Foucault, 91). Where classification for Foucault is essentially pictorial, the clinical method rests on a linguistic description of the symptoms and what they connote; clinical method, therefore, alternates between observing and explaining, between the gaze and language. For instance, the doctor observes the patient's symptoms, as always. But instead of classifying those symptoms against a pictorial hierarchy of relationships, the physician now describes those symptoms verbally, and in so doing, reveals the intrinsic causal relationships within the confines of the individual patient. The doctor achieves this method through an exhaustive description, based on "a statutory form of correlation between the gaze and language":

> It is in this exhaustive and complete passage from the totality of the visible to the over-all structure of the expressible . . . that is fulfilled at last that significative analysis of the perceived that the naively geometric architecture of the picture failed to provide. It is description, or rather, the implicit labour of language in description, that authorizes the transformation of symptom into sign and the passage from patient to disease and from the individual to the conceptual. (Foucault, 114)

Library cataloguers create exhaustive descriptions, expressed in a standardized language and structure established by the International Standard Bibliographic Descriptions (ISBDs) and specific cataloguing codes such as the *Anglo-American Cataloguing Rules* (AACR). These descriptions involve using the specific features of the document to describe and represent the abstract features; the material manifestation, with its title page, preliminaries, and other metadata, becomes the basis for a description that does justice to the work, or the content contained within the carrier. The process involves more creativity than most people realize: "Cataloging appears to be routine work so long as one believes that the materials *just have* a regular structure which can be trivially read off. But on inspection, it appears that this regular structure is the *output* of the work of catalogers, not the input" (Levy 1995). The structure which Levy detects in bibliographic records rests upon the assumption that documents are entities with concrete attributes. Providing access to these documents requires correctly transcribing those attributes in a standard order, and then subjecting some of them (known as access points) to processes of disambiguation and normalization.

The Semantic Web rests more explicitly upon a principle of utterance. At its core lies the realization that we assess documents and their usefulness by saying things about them: "this document is about physics; that document is by William Shakespeare." If automated agents are to assess Web resources properly, those statements need to be readable by the agents, as well as by human beings. The World Wide Web Consortium has developed the Resource Description Framework (RDF) as a standard means of describing Web resources. RDF casts these statements as triples, containing a subject, predicate, and object; the subject is the resource being described, the predicate indicates the property being described, and the object indicates the value of the property. A Web page by Grant Campbell, therefore, could have a triple as presented in Example 1.

Like the early clinicians in Foucault's history, the Semantic Web aims to achieve complex and useful interpretation by a careful scrutiny of attributes as they appear within or upon a specific entity. Like the spi-

EXAMPLE 1. An RDF Triple Declaring the Creator of a Web Resource

Subject	http://www.webpage.org/gcampbell.htm
Predicate	http://purl.org/dc/elements/1.1/creator
Object	"Grant Campbell"

ders in current search engines, semantic agents will gain access to Web documents and analyze them. With RDF, however, the analysis will extend beyond word frequencies to analyze not just the attributes of documents but the relationships between documents (Passim 2004, 22). Furthermore, RDF allows for rigorous language control at multiple levels; namespaces can be used to specify metadata elements and values from multiple metadata sets, with ontologies mapping relationships between multiple vocabularies.

KNOWLEDGE THROUGH ANATOMO-CLINICAL THEORY

For Foucault, anatomo-clinical practice, or pathological anatomy, is an extension of the initial transition from classification to clinical diagnosis. Pathological anatomy studies disease in the body, as does the practice of clinical diagnosis; but it does so at the level of tissues: "[Doctors] begin . . . to work on the physical surface of the body, and not on the body as a set of abstract, *readable*, phenomena. Their gaze penetrates, it becomes active" (During 1992, 48). Scientists like Bichat in his *Traité des membranes*, examined not the body as a whole unit but the muscles and tissues:

> Bichat imposes a diagonal reading the body carried out according to expanses of anatomical resemblances that traverse the organs, envelop them, divide them, compose and decompose them, analyse them, and, at the same time, bind them together. It is the same form of perception as that borrowed by the clinic from Condillac's philosophy: the uncovering of an elementary that is also a universal, and a thehodical reading that, scanning the forms of disintegration, describes the laws of composition. (Foucault, 129)[1]

Bibliographic control in libraries has traditionally focused on the monograph and serial levels of description: the book, as a discrete bibliographic unit, or the journal as a discrete collection of incremental volumes. Occasionally, however, libraries stray into analysis: describing and cataloguing individual chapters or volumes of a book, or finding concise ways of summarizing the presence of one work within a larger work. And periodical indexes provide descriptions of articles within journals. Effective access sometimes means breaking the link between the physical unit and the bibliographic unit and recognizing that the most meaningful unit of description is not necessarily the most easily identified physical item.

The Semantic Web is providing even more technologically-sophisticated means of dissecting information "bodies" as they have been traditionally conceived. One chief function of RDF is to "describe relationships between bits of data" (Passim 2004, 22). This will enable web agents, not just to retrieve documents, but to assemble documents on the fly by collecting excerpts from Web sites, and by querying databases and encoding the results. This places the Semantic Web on a continuum with other Web tools that function on principles of dissection and recombination: BitTorrent and other file sharing programs, that not only dissect the "album" into songs, but also files and programs into shared and transferable bits that can be reassembled; folksonomies, which enable blog entries and items to be organized and combined in various ways; RSS feeds, that aggregate multiple entities together.

Unlike library catalogues, the Semantic Web will have a much looser connection to formal "documents," in the form of books, Web pages, and other digital resources. It will succeed not by reassembling the parts as they originally were, but by reconfiguring them in ways that specifically meet the user's needs. By taking classification (in the form of ontologies and taxonomies) and description (in the form of RDF) below the document level into the realm of databases and granular data, and making it possible to recombine data at this granular level, the Semantic Web is giving technology a more "invasive" role than it has traditionally played. The extra inferential power gained by the machine-readable semantic metadata will be used to extract relevant data from multiple sources in multiple formats to produce customized answers to specific questions.

DISCUSSION

Using Foucault to understand the relationship between libraries and the Semantic Web would seem to violate the very premises of Foucault's theory. Foucault grounded his treatment of medical practice at the turn of the nineteenth century upon close reading of historical evidence, in an effort to illuminate a specific historical process, one characterized "not as a progressive heaping-up of discoveries, but as a series of shifts or breaks" (During 1992, 44). Removing his three stages, not only from their historical context but from their historical sequence, puts Foucault's discourse analysis to very questionable use: it robs his historical method of history, and of the discontinuities that form a central part of his theories. However, there are distinctive advantages, if not for Foucault studies, at least for information studies.

Libraries have experienced revolutionary changes in cataloguing methods and procedures over the years, but very rarely have innovations completely supplanted their predecessors. Books continue to coexist alongside other media; MARC records have survived the appearance of RDF and Dublin Core; Google has not yet replaced library catalogues; nor has Google Scholar yet replaced periodical databases. Libraries must hold differing approaches in balance, and Foucault's analysis of medical discourse provides us with a useful model for a triadic relationship, in which three differing perspectives maintain a more or less constant presence (Figure 1).

Both library cataloguing and the Semantic Web, therefore, work by triangulating different perspectives and different methods. Just as libraries use controlled vocabularies to compensate for the weaknesses of classification systems and vice versa, so too does the Semantic Web use a variety of tools: URIs, XML, RDF, RDF Schema, metadata schemes, namespaces, and ontologies. This use of overlapping, complementing methods and standards is perhaps the most compelling point of connec-

FIGURE 1. A Triadic Relationship, in Clinical Medicine, Library Catalogues and the Semantic Web

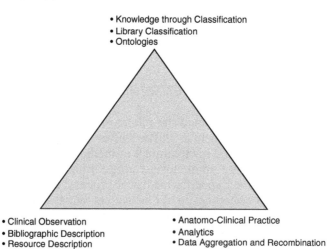

• Knowledge through Classification
• Library Classification
• Ontologies

• Clinical Observation
• Bibliographic Description
• Resource Description

• Anatomo-Clinical Practice
• Analytics
• Data Aggregation and Recombination

tion between the library community and the World Wide Web Consortium. It represents, in both communities, a commitment to providing information access at a far more sophisticated and variegated level of service than most tools currently emerging as the Web 2.0.

In addition, the Semantic Web resembles traditional bibliographic control in its stubborn commitment to research. It reveals this commitment through a model of expansion: while XML tags and RDF namespaces need not be particularly precise or complex, they can become precise and complex if necessary. Like Charles Cutter's Expansive Classification, the Semantic Web can adopt multiple levels of complexity, depending on the need, from unqualified Dublin Core elements up to highly qualified and precise descriptors.

Because of this connection, the Semantic Web may well be the library community's best ally in its effort to redefine itself in the new Web environment. Well-designed and well-described Web resources can be harvested and used in concert with bibliographic records (Campbell & Fast 2004); bibliographic records in RDF format can be integrated with other records in other formats; the development of ontologies could revitalize interest in traditional classification. The network of protocols and standards emerging from the World Wide Web Consortium could dramatically widen the library community's access to other experts in different disciplines, making their specialized knowledge electronically available to supplement and enhance library records.

CONCLUSION

Foucault, in *The Birth of the Clinic*, was concerned with ruptures in our ways of thinking; he saw history not as a continuous stream but as a series of breaks, ruptures, and discontinuities. Libraries have a close relationship with the Semantic Web precisely because both communities strive to contain these breaks and ruptures, and to incorporate disparate voices and perspectives into their information systems. Both systems anticipate the need for rigorous precision in information design, to satisfy rigorous demands from information users. Both systems attempt to attain this precision by triangulating different ways of thought and analysis, in hopes that the chorus of methods and tools will provide the best possible support to the highest possible demands.

NOTE

1. This approach received popular expression in the 1860s with the character of Dr. Lydgate in George Eliot's *Middlemarch*: the ambitious physician inspired by Bichat to undertake research to discover the fundamental human tissue.

REFERENCES

Berners-Lee, Tim. "Foreword." *Spinning the Semantic Web: Bringing the World Wide Web to Its Full Potential*. Ed. Dieter Fensel et al. Cambridge: MIT Press, 2003: xi-xxiii.

Campbell, D. Grant & Karl V. Fast. "Academic Libraries and the Semantic Web: What the Future May Hold for Research-Supporting Library Catalogues." *Journal of Academic Librarianship* 30 (2004): 382-390.

Clayphan, Robina & Rebecca Guenther. *Library Application Profile*. Dublin Core Metadata Initiative: 2004. [http://www.dublincore.org/documents/2004/09/10/library-application-profile/].

During, Simon. *Foucault and Literature*. London: Routledge, 1992.

Foucault, Michel. *The Birth of the Clinic: An Archaeology of Medical Perception*. Trans. A.M. Sheridan Smith. New York: Pantheon, 1973.

Hannabus, Stuart. "Foucault's View of Knowledge." *AsLib Proceedings* 48 (1996): 87-102.

Levy, D. 1995. Cataloging in the Digital Order. *Digital Libraries '95: The Second Annual Conference on the Theory and Practice of Digital Libraries*. Austin, Texas: 11-13 June, 1995. [http://csdl.tamu.edu/DL95/papers/levy/levy.html].

Manola, Frank & Eric Miller. *RDF Primer*. World Wide Web Consortium, 2004. [http://www.w3.org/TR/rdf-primer/].

MGinnis, Deborah L. "Ontologies Come of Age." *Spinning the Semantic Web: Bringing the World Wide Web to Its Full Potential*. Ed. Dieter Fensel et al. Cambridge: MIT Press, 2003: 171-194.

O'Reilly, T. "What is Web 2.0: Design Patterns and Business Models for the Next Generation of Software." *timo'reilly.com* 09/30/2005. [http://www.oreillynet.com/pub/a/oreilly/tim/news/2005/09/30/what-is-web-20.html].

Passim, Thomas B. *Explorer's Guide to the Semantic Web*. Greenwich: Manning, 2004.

Radford, Gary P. "Trapped in Our Own Discursive Formations: Toward an Archaeology of Library and Information Science." *Library Quarterly* 73 (2003): 1-18.

Rosenfeld, Louis & Peter Morville. *Information Architecture for the World Wide Web*. 2nd ed. Cambridge: O'Reilly, 2002.

Williamson, Nancy. "Standards and Rules for Subject Access." *Cataloging & Classification Quarterly* 21 (1996): 155-176.

doi:10.1300/J104v43n03_02

Library Cards for the 21st Century

Charles McCathieNevile

Eva Méndez

SUMMARY. This paper presents several reflections on the traditional card catalogues and RDF (Resource Description Framework), which is "the" standard for creating the Semantic Web. This work grew out of discussion between the authors after the Working Group on Metadata Schemes meeting held at IFLA conference in Buenos Aires (2004). The paper provides an overview of RDF from the perspective of cataloguers, catalogues, and library cards. The central theme of the discussion is resource description as a discipline that could be based on RDF. RDF is explained as a very simple grammar, using metadata and ontologies for semantic search and access. RDF has the ability to enhance 21st century libraries and support metadata interoperability in digital libraries, while maintaining the expressive power that was available to librarians when catalogues were physical artefacts. doi:10.1300/J104v43n03_03 [Article copies available for a fee from The Haworth Document Delivery Service: 1-800-HAWORTH. E-mail address: <docdelivery@haworthpress.com> Website: <http://www.HaworthPress.com> © 2007 by The Haworth Press, Inc. All rights reserved.]

KEYWORDS. RDF, resource description framework, Semantic Web, vocabularies, catalogues, library cards, bibliographic control, metadata interoperability

[Haworth co-indexing entry note]: "Library Cards for the 21st Century." McCathieNevile, Charles, and Eva Méndez. Co-published simultaneously in *Cataloging & Classification Quarterly* (The Haworth Information Press, an imprint of The Haworth Press, Inc.) Vol. 43, No. 3/4, 2007, pp. 21-45; and: *Knitting the Semantic Web* (ed: Jane Greenberg, and Eva Méndez) The Haworth Information Press, an imprint of The Haworth Press, Inc., 2007, pp. 21-45. Single or multiple copies of this article are available for a fee from The Haworth Document Delivery Service [1-800-HAWORTH, 9:00 a.m. - 5:00 p.m. (EST). E-mail address: docdelivery@haworthpress.com].

INTRODUCTION: REMEMBERING LIBRARY CARDS

The 20th century presented many significant changes, but one central feature remained constant, and would last until the end of, but not beyond, the entire century. In our own university libraries, very far away one from another (University of Melbourne in Australia and University of León in Spain) when we first arrived as students in the 1980s-1990s they still held pride of place, the central object you saw as you entered, taking up the main space of the ground floor. Big, wooden, familiar, box after box held drawer after drawer filled with catalogue cards. Authors, Titles, Subjects, and classification codes served to order the infinite cards of 11.5×7.5 cm (4.5×3 inches) with a small hole punched at the bottom where a rod was inserted to keep them in order.

Those cards held the secrets of the library. Each one contained information about a book (or perhaps a map, a vinyl record, or even a video-cassette, because they were already modern libraries). The modern librarians would have to make several cards for every book, and then organize them one by one, following alphabetic criteria and different rules. There might be several more that were indexed by subject. A hundred years of history had given them personality, from the hand-written cards in copperplate that we learned to appreciate and decipher in equal measure, to the typewritten cards with their letters not quite straight, and the ultra-modern printed cards that came out of a specific kind of software for printing the cards or even directly from the computerized catalogue, and into the boxes just for completeness in the transition.

As late as the mid-1990s those cards were the best of all catalogues. The computer catalogue was faster, but not yet complete. Many of the important facts were reduced to one giant set of notes at the end of the computer record. A shame, because the cards in the box held rich descriptions, cross referencing each other and pointing to trails of investigation just waiting for the curious.

It is fair to say that the computer system in use at the time was not the best available in the world. And it should be noted that the "librarian" on duty was often simply a student, making some relatively easy money by working in a place they more or less knew, close by, with only the briefest of introductions to the systems they were expected to use. A true librarian could be expected to know how to catalogue a collection, how to ensure that the cross references were all correct and correctly entered, that the work was listed according to the appropriate subjects. And a true librarian might also have gone to the card catalogue looking, checking the information against what was there already.

The catalogue, then, was made to produce reliable results, to display differences between books and cards, to bring together what has to be together, to present meaningful choices and to locate what users want. Modern catalogues, as we move into the 21st century, want to do the same. But in automatic cataloguing and database systems, catalogue data has to be encoded in well-defined ways, which requires a data format. Systems used a variety of formats, sometimes proprietary and not always homogeneous. What was needed for communication between systems was an exchange format; particularly, a machine readable cataloguing format. It had to contain a large number of fields, typically structured into subfields. The content of the fields, however, was governed by the cataloguing rules. The format was and will be a container, and different containers may be used to communicate the same content. Nowadays, these containers could be MARC21, XML (Extensible Markup Language), or even RDF (Resource Description Framework) (Méndez, 2005) in a more semantic Web. We will devote this paper to the value of using RDF for libraries, after the era of catalogue cards has really passed.

In the world of library cards, there were separate physical catalogues for authors and titles, subjects and situation codes. In the world of library OPACs, there were always combined formal and subject access points in the same database if not generally in the same index. However, in the world of WebPACs and the WWW, bibliographic information from the catalogues still largely remains buried within the "hidden Web"–and that, as long as different layers of information remain blended in bibliographic records, the non-librarian world probably is better off without these thousands of identical bibliographic records pointing simply to different items or manifestations (Gradmann, 2005). Furthermore, an important amount of our current library users never have searched in a card catalogue and they have though searched a lot in all kind of search boxes on Internet/Web search engines.

At the end of the last century, all the Librarianship and Information Science (LIS) research had a prospective tone, as if digital information management changed completely and all the librarians waited for a kafkaesque mutation into computer scientists. Now, entering the 21st century we have realised that the user's needs are basically the same, even though users are more autonomous. Information professionals, librarians, and specialised cataloguers are learning to adapt their skills in processing of books to a technological processing of "resources."

Traditional cataloguing blends the main elements: tangible documents, processes (bibliographic description, content analysis–mainly indexing and abstracting), and products, which are fruits of this activity (typically bibliographic records collected as a catalogue). Resource description implies: documents like information objects, the creation–automatic or manual–of information about the attributes of those objects (metadata), making metadata records and metadata repositories (Table 1).

THE WEB: OUR BIGGEST EVER LIBRARY?

With the growth of Internet and, in particular, the success of the World Wide Web, the myth of the "universal library" from Borges has been revived in many scholarly and philosophical discussions. That dream of a library where the whole of human knowledge would be accumulated has been seen to come closer to fruition with the Web. Every once in a while we see a paradigmatic new project or a new birth of the *universal library*.[1] Attempts to create universal libraries, from the mythical Library of Alexandria, failed in previous centuries. In the 21st century knowledge is not perceived as a solid structure any more. The universal library is still a utopia despite the Web. Notwithstanding, the Semantic Web and the technologies used in its construction let us dream again of universal access to knowledge, which in a more modern and technological way we would call something like: "interoperable access to distributed digital knowledge."

TABLE 1. Traditional Cataloguing Elements vs. Electronic Resources Organization

	TRADITIONAL CATALOGING	ELECTRONIC RESOURCES ORGANIZATION
OBJECT	Books/documents	Resources/DLOs (Document-Like Objects)
PROCESS	Bibliographic Description	Resource based metadata/Descriptive Metadata Creation
	Classification	Subject based metadata*/Specific vocabularies
PRODUCT	Bibliographic Record	Metadata Record
	Catalogue/OPAC	Metadata Repository
	Technical processes	**Technological processes**

*Ahmed, Kal et al. (2001) made this distinction between *resource based metadata* and "subject based metadata." Resource based metadata are those metadata used for cataloguing and identification, used to associate specific properties and their values, and the traditional example is the library catalogue record giving its title, author, publisher, etc. On the other hand, *subject based metadata* are the metadata which represents subjects and their interrelationships and also usually designates specific information resources as belonging to these subjects; this kind of metadata implies specific vocabulary construction and encoding such us ontologies, thesauri, or topic maps.

But while there are many smart librarians, working in libraries great and small, and managing information in ways that a 19th century librarian might not recognize, there is more information being produced. It has been claimed that at the beginning of the 21st century the Web allowed more information to be published in a single year than there had ever been published in human history until that year. Publishing to a large audience is no longer the preserve of the wealthy, the large publishing house, or the highly motivated pamphleteer. Anyone with access to the Internet (somewhere between a quarter and a half or so of the world's population, although it is difficult to measure) can publish persistent documents or "document-like objects," as the post-modern "text" has become known in a digital world.

The number of librarians graduating this year will not exceed the total number of librarians who have ever lived and worked before. Their traditional work is increasingly being done by students or neophyte librarians with relatively little training, or by authors themselves who may have no formal training. The rise of "tagging" or personal tagging to produce "folksonomies" shows a kind of catalogue being constructed in a chaotic way by people whose average training in the use of ontologies and subject thesauri is vanishingly close to zero. To make the most effective use of this information requires being able to determine some kind of order. Folksonomies pursue an ancient technique for organising libraries by natural language description as a modern approach to organising the Web, but rely on the ability to look up tags much faster than in a physical library. WikiPedia,[2] the radical worldwide open encyclopaedia project, can be an enormously valuable resource to a town too far off the beaten track to be visited by an encyclopaedia salesman, but the traditional approach of getting experts to write articles is replaced with a process that allows anyone to add information. A lot of "instant librarians" are indexing in free language their photos on Flickr,[3] their resources on del.icio.us,[4] etc., and a lot of authors are, creating Web sites, digital information, electronic resources, or even encyclopaedias.

On the other hand, information professionals have been discussing about digital libraries, virtual libraries, global libraries, universal libraries, etc., for more than eight years. Because of their virtual nature, professionals have fallen to the temptation of equating the World Wide Web itself to a giant digital library (Brisson, 1999), and metadata, as the technical basis of processing in digital libraries, increased the interest on cataloguing, even for the World Wide Web Consortium (W3) and Semantic Web theory and standards (which also flirt with the universal library ideal).

COMPUTER CATALOGUING AND STANDARDS CHANGE

As Brisson (1999) said, with the Internet and the explosion of Web information, the world has discovered cataloguing. When libraries began to use MARC format for their library catalogues in the late '60s, they converted the existing records on cards into electronic form for storage and retrieval. Moreover, since the beginning of the computer era, it has been clear that computers were useful for any task based on looking up information in tables, from cracking military codes to tracking student records or the legendary genealogy projects of the Church of the Latter-Day Saints (the "Mormons"). Computer catalogues can do cross-indexing by themselves, looking up any of several fields over thousands or millions of records at lightning speeds. For a large library this is a wonderful thing–in the time it takes to find the first card that has the author you wanted, the computer found all of them.

But this comes with a drawback. For example, the correct way to write one of the authors' names is "McCathieNevile," but other people could (and do) write it McCathie-Nevile, MacCathyneville, MacCarthy-Nevile, or even MacKazinevil if you ask to write it to a Spaniard. A person can readily match all of those with a modicum of intelligence, the thing that comes naturally to people. But computers are notoriously not intelligent. It is possible to write rules they can follow which will match all things almost the same, but again they don't manage to reject the right things, so you are left reading through a large number of records that are close, according to the rules, but obviously not right.

Moreover, with the growth of electronic catalogues, it was no longer possible to write notes on the card, like "Tim usually hides this book in the opposite shelf" easily. In order to add more useful information, cataloguing systems became extremely complex–a complete MARC record is something that most catalogue systems hide from real users, and with good reason–it is a scary thing to behold.

Similarly, computers need standard ways of cataloguing and classifying in ways that people do not, because they cannot make the leap to connect "rabbits" with "bunnies" except where the brand "Playboy" is involved, and they just don't learn the word "coney" because it is too rare for programmers to run across it. (Or perhaps was until *The Lord of the Rings* taught it to a new geeky audience.) Subject schemes have become extremely complex, in order to describe them in the hierarchies that traditional database and catalogue systems rely on.

Library cards and library records are possibly the most distributed rights management artefacts in the world, and there is a great amount of content that doesn't get examined enough because of licensing restrictions. Attribute-based authentication systems can now open the door to bringing more of the world's recorded knowledge into a common setting without impinging identity or privacy. There is potential for a great improvement in both libraries and Web search systems if we could identify some ways for them to easily talk to each other.

Representing and organizing information in a digital form has a long tradition in libraries, using various rules and standards. The now-venerable MARC format is joined by a large variety of new formats and metadata schemas based on SGML, XML, or even HTML. Standards in libraries are changing, even in the highly structured world of AACR and MARC[5] both in terms of encoding standards like MARC21 and content standards, defined now as RDA (Resource Description and Access) (JSC, 2005-06).

The global information society, where the universal character of the Web claims to offer democratic access to the information, needs more than ever the ideas of internationalisation and interoperability behind the BUC (Bibliographic Universal Control), now as a *Universal Web Control*.

TRADING FREEDOM FOR POWER

Traditional databases have to be constructed in advance, describing the information that you want to add to it before you ever start. If you learn, later, of a better way to classify something, it is a very complex job to add this, and in a distributed system it is likely to be done in different places by different people. The Dewey system, while it provided some common order to libraries everywhere, provides a good example of how hierarchies can become unmanageable, with different people classifying the same resource in slightly different ways leading to it existing in radically different parts of the library. Unfortunately, when you are looking for information on the relationship of Tancred of Antioch to his Uncle Bohemond (or Boamund . . .) of Taranto it is not very interesting to realise that most other people making more general enquiries find the things they are looking for. It is simply a frustration that you have to look in two different places for the same book because two slightly different librarians classified it slightly differently. We are exaggerating at this point, because the catalogue usually makes it fairly fast to find out where the book is in this library. The point is that some people are being inconvenienced and there is no easy remedy. We are thinking of the "new user" that never saw a card catalogue, and has been using Web search engines for 5 or 6 years.

We gave up some of our freedom, the ability to easily scribble on the card and add notes, for the power of a fast search. It is not impossible to add a new field to a database, but it is traditionally very expensive. Making a database understand a new format for a few books is simply not worth the effort, so it does not happen. (Making it work across different catalogues is an enormous amount of work–it is not clear that it can be done except in rare cases.) Is there a way we can get the best of both worlds, without having to run from the computer to the cards and back? . . . Spoiler: YES.

A SEMANTIC WEB: A MORE LIBRARIAN WEB

Let's begin with a description of our suggested solution, and then have a look at how it works. (That way when it gets technical we have already understood the punch line, and we can skip the rest.)

The Semantic Web is built on machine-understandable data, not just machine-readable data (MARC). As Tim Berners Lee (2000) said in his book *Weaving the Web*[6]: If HTML and the Web made all online documents seem to be an enormous single (but multilingual and somewhat schizophrenic) book, the Semantic Web would make all the information seem to be in one enormous data base. The Web needed some structure to constrain mark up in order to achieve standardization and interoperability between metadata schemas, and RDF is a language which allows both machines and human beings to process, organize, and retrieve digital information. The Semantic Web pursues the idea of a *Web Universal Control* (although not formally stated) from mark up structures that can represent ontological knowledge representation.

We want a way of describing things. It should work to quickly look up common things (in the library case, an author, or a title, or a subject), but it should also be reasonable to use it for a small handful of special cases. And in the ideal world we normally only dare visit late at night in our dreams, it should be possible to make our little solution for a handful of things we have locally work everywhere, and work easily with someone else's solution for a similar problem that they developed without talking to us. Just because the Gupapuyngu-speaking folks at the school in Yirrkala and the biological researchers at the Mongolian academy of sciences have no language in common, and have only once ever wanted to mention the same subject, doesn't mean that it should be difficult to discover what that subject was.

So we want to be able to describe things in a way that allows other people to re-use our descriptions when they discover them, adding them at that point to their system. Actually, we want a way for third parties (who have a language in common with the people at each end of this discussion) to describe these descriptions. And of course we want to be able to automatically process the descriptions themselves. This gives us the power of a computer search, the ability to scribble on the virtual library cards, and as an added bonus a way to transfer things across different communities after they are built, without needing direct coordination, and without rebuilding the cataloguing system itself.

We have some pieces in place. We can put anything on the Web, with a URI (Uniform Resource Identifier, a Web address, like http://www. example.com/some/magic/address or similar) and we know people can get to it. That takes care of the "how are we going to share this with people we don't know." We even have engines that crawl around the Web looking at the things there, and letting other people find them. What we need is a way of making descriptions that does what we are looking for. And lo and behold, this is one of the ideas behind the design of the Semantic Web.

Before the Web, discussion about cataloguing was mainly limited to librarians talking about rules, standards, and authority control. In the mid-1990s every Internet community started to develop their own perceptions and their own ways to describe and retrieve electronic resources, through metadata schemas and standards. And it started the different tensions between metadata and cataloguing, between machine understandable data and human understandable data, between MARC and mark up, and so on, generating ink rivers and a lot of bytes of information in the specialised bibliography.[7] Dovey (1999) already talked seven years ago about different schools: the bibliographic control school compared to the structuralist school and the school of structured data. Campbell (2004) recognized that different communities require different granularities of description and he talks about communities of electronic information and a bibliographic organization systems community. The Semantic Web community shared with the "school of bibliographic control" the desire for interoperability and "universal control" of Web resources. In that community, such interoperability and the control it gives are based on formal languages and metadata schemas, both machine and human understandable data.

A question here is why there is such a big gap between library-oriented and other information "worlds" in the perception of universal access to information? Assuming that these essential gaps can be filled, there remain legitimate reasons why a standards-in-common solution poses its own enduring problems, even within the compelling context of interoperability (Howarth, 2005). Lynne Howarth used Stu Weibel's words to point out the need for convergence and cooperation of all these schools, groups, YAMS (*Yet Another Metadata Standard*) and Internet communities: *"The Internet can be thought of as a World-Wide Commons in which many previously-distinct resource description communities are mixed together."*

Several authors (Tillet, 2003; Gradmann, 2005) have envisioned FRBR (Functional Requirements of Bibliographic Records) as the approach to make catalogues more visible and easier to use for any Internet community. Semantic Web technologies and the conceptual framework of FRBR are two promising areas for making librarian and generic WWW information services converge or even prepare some sort of integration scenario (Gradmann, 2005).

In the Semantic Web, universal information retrieval approach is as different as it was in the traditional school of bibliographic control and UNIMARC approach. Tim Berners-Lee and other Semantic Web promoters in and out W3C (such as, James Hendler, Ora Lassila, Eric Miller, Dieter Fensel, or Ivan Herman) are hoping to create a meaningful Web of data. So the computer could learn both about the data and about the information needed to process such data. But the main objective is the same: the global and interoperable Web information processing, which in this case will be founded on RDF, Metadata schemas, and content vocabularies (schemes). Who is guiding the Semantic Web is not the library World, but rather the W3C. The Semantic Web approach needs librarians, because the Semantic Web is, as we said before (Méndez, 2004), a "more librarian Web." Likewise, librarians need the Semantic Web to make their metadata interoperate, not only in MARC-standards domain, but in the entirety of the Web, redefining the traditional strengths and skills of library information organization for the Semantic Web and/or Universal Access era.

WHAT THE SEMANTIC WEB LOOKS LIKE: AN EASY WAY TO SHOW RDF

The Semantic Web is an idea that it is possible to extract information from the Web at large. The language used most often by the inventors of the Web to do this is called the Resource Description Framework (RDF, 2006), which even sounds like the boxes of cards, or like "Resource Description and Access," the newest version of Anglo-American Cataloguing Rules.[8]

The RDF suite of specifications[9] consist of six W3C recommendations (RDF, 2006), and they are perhaps the most powerful and most important standard if the Web is to achieve its full potential (Ahmed et al., 2001), that grew out of a requirement to apply descriptions to information resources. It is intended to allow the computer processing of distributed information on the Web. We will devote this part of the paper to explain the RDF model and syntax and RDF schema from the perspective of library cataloguing or "resource description."

In a simplest level RDF is an XML-based language to describe resources, which underpins the Semantic Web paradigm. A resource in RDF stands for either electronic resources, like files (an (X)HTML Web site, for example) or concepts (like RDF/OWL representations of concepts in a thesaurus or Knowledge Organization System) or even a person who has an URI (for example, an e-mail in a FOAF–Friend Of A Friend–description). An RDF resource is basically "anything that has identity." Another easy way to explain it is Jul's (2003) definition: *A resource is any item we wish to describe–one can think of it as what you get when you click on a URL.*

Writing RDF (RDF Model and Syntax)

RDF is based on three-part statements of the form "**something** has **some relation** to **some other thing**." People who like formal language call these three parts respectively: subject, predicate, and object of "the triple," or statement. And it (normally) uses a URI (such as a Web address) to identify each member of the triple (although the object can also be "plain text," a so-called *Literal*).

Subject-Predicate-Object, the three elements that compound a statement or RDF triple, could be also understood as Entity-Relation-Entity in a relational database paradigm or Class-Property-Value in the object-oriented landscape. Let's explain what these elements of an RDF statement means:

- A Subject [in our example (Figure 1): http://www.bartleby.com/ 173] is the resource that is being described by the ensuing predicate and object, and the URI (URL) stands for a unique concept.

- Predicate [in our example (Figure 1): dc:title; dc:language and dc:creator] is a relation between the subject and the object or a property type referred to the resource which will have a value or object. In RDF, as we will explain below (Table 2), we would define a unique URI for any predicate.
- An Object is either the resource referred to by the predicate or a literal value [in our example (Figure 1), the values: Albert Einstein, en, and Relativity: The Special and General Theory].

See the code below to identify all these elements → Understanding the following code isn't necessary for understanding this article–all the actual RDF examples here are for completeness, and are accompanied by English explanations of the relevant bits.

```
<rdf:RDF xmlns:rdf='http://www.w3.org/1999/02/22-rdf-syntax-ns#'
xmlns:dc='http://purl.org/dc/elements/1.1/'>
<rdf:Description rdf:about='http://www.bartleby.com/173'>
 <dc:creator>Albert Einstein</dc:creator>
 <dc:language>en</dc:language>
 <dc:title>Relativity: The Special and General Theory</dc:title>
</rdf:Description>
</rdf:RDF>
```

This code means: There is a thing which we identify with the URI http://www.bartleby.com/173, and which has some properties and values: The creator is "Albert Einstein," the language is "en" (English, from an ISO standard vocabulary for langauges), and the title is "Relativity: The Special and General Theory." So far, there is nothing in this that doesn't seem like a normal library record. The terms we have used to describe our resource are all pretty common, and they come from a standard vocabulary meant for library-like cataloguing called Dublin Core.

One of the useful things about information is that the more of it you have (so long as it is consistent–but we'll ignore that problem for the minute), the more you can do with it. RDF has a simpler approach to information than most systems. If you give an RDF processor two sets of statements about the same thing (a thing identified by the same URI), it just treats them as one collection of statements. Unlike many of its predecessors, the idea behind RDF is not cataloguing according to a predefined scheme in quite the way we are used to. In order to provide useful descriptions, we do indeed need to have some common terms. But in-

FIGURE 1. Graphical Representation of a Basic RDF Statement (RDF Model)

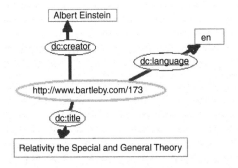

In this and following figures in this paper, the oval (○) represents an URI, a resource; The square (□) represents a value or literal, and the circle in the arrow (-○→) a property or association (a predicate).

stead of building a database, and then finding out afterwards what fits into the database, the Semantic Web is a collection of descriptions, not very different from a library catalogue except in the scope of material. Computers can understand such a collection, present it so humans can also read the information, and by following simple well-defined rules computers can infer further semantic information.

A practical upshot of the way this is done is that we can use any kind of description we like. Let's start, like any decent library card did, with a bit more about the creator, since names can be shared by so many people:

```
<rdf:RDF xmlns:rdf='http://www.w3.org/1999/02/22-rdf-syntax-ns#'
  xmlns:dc='http://purl.org/dc/elements/1.1/'
  xmlns:foaf='http://xmlns.com/foaf/0.1/'>
<rdf:Description rdf:about='http://www.bartleby.com/173'>
<dc:creator>
<foaf:Person>
<foaf:name>Albert Einstein</foaf:name>
<foaf:birthday>14 March 1879</foaf:birthday>
</foaf:Person>
</dc:creator>
<dc:language>en</dc:language>
<dc:title>Relativity
The Special and General Theory</dc:title>
<dc:date>1920</dc:date>
<dc:identifier>http://www.bartleby.com/173</dc:identifier>
</rdf:Description>
</rdf:RDF>
```

Here, we have used some terms that were created for describing actual people. We may not know how many people called Albert Einstein wrote something called "Relativity: The Special and General Theory" in 1920, but in case there are a few at least we know that the one we mean was born in 1879.

Importantly, we have here just one random example of annotating the card with something new and different. We could have used any defined term, from vocabularies about describing books, or the kind of words used in text, or detailed taxonomies of literary style or subjects. We could have mixed all of these and other things together. That's what real RDF does in the wild: enabling us to put metadata from multiple vocabularies (and even from multiple sources) in the same record (Figure 2).

Just as any collection of information in RDF can be merged, it can also be decomposed into the three-part statements we mentioned. The technical way of encoding information described according to different "cataloguing schemes" (or vocabularies, or ontologies) is with XML namespace. In the example above, we are merging three vocabularies

FIGURE 2. RDF Statements with Different Vocabularies (Dublin Core and Friend Of A Friend)

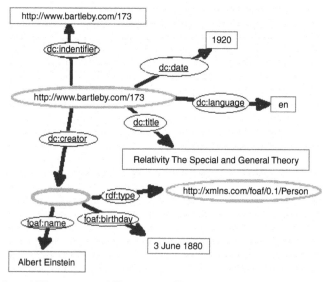

In this figure, the oval (○) represents an URI, a resource; The square (□) represents a value or literal, and the circle in the arrow (-○→) a property or association (a predicate).

(RDF's own basic vocabulary, Dublin Core, and FOAF), using three namespace declarations to define which terms in the description are associated with which vocabulary:

```
xmlns:rdf='http://www.w3.org/1999/02/22-rdf-syntax-ns#'
xmlns:dc='http://purl.org/dc/elements/1.1/'
xmlns:foaf='http://xmlns.com/foaf/0.1/'
```

As an alternative to looking at pictures trying to represent the code for human consumption, we can list the statements that the code makes in a table. Thus, the individual statements represented in Figure 2 are shown in Table 2.

Those who have been following the code and the pictures in detail might have already noticed that we managed to have an **object** in the collection (a circle in the pictures) that is not labelled with a URI. That is a little modelling trick to be able to stack up lots of statements–similar to the way we use "which" or "that" in English, to avoid repeating the

TABLE 2. Definition of the Statements in Our Example (Properties in Triples)

Subject	Predicate	Object
http://www.bartleby.com/173	http://purl.org/dc/elements/1.1/title	"Relativity The Special and General Theory"
http://www.bartleby.com/173	http://purl.org/dc/elements/1.1/creator	"Albert Einstein"
http://www.bartleby.com/173	http://purl.org/dc/elements/1.1/language	"en"
http://www.bartleby.com/173	http://purl.org/dc/elements/1.1/date	"1920"
http://www.bartleby.com/173	http://purl.org/dc/elements/1.1/identifier	"http://www.bartleby.com/173"
http://www.bartleby.com/173	http://purl.org/dc/elements/1.1/creator	Something (let's call it X here)
The thing called X	http://www.w3.org/1999/02/22-rdf-syntax-ns#type	http://xmlns.com/foaf/0.1/Person
The same X	http://xmlns.com/foaf/0.1/name	"Albert Einstein"
The same X	http://xmlns.com/foaf/0.1/birthdate	"14 March 1879"

name of something. Except here we can also use it to completely avoid naming something.

"The person whose name is Albert Einstein, and whose birthday is 14 March 1879" seems to be pretty clearly identifying something. But it has no URI of its own (in the picture, one oval shape–in green–is unlabelled to reflect this). On the other hand, we could compare a couple of structures and decide whether they mean the same thing or not. With the FOAF[10] vocabulary that we have used in this example, it is not assumed that having the same name and birthday are enough to say that two people are the same. But it does have a term for a mailbox (a personal e-mail address). In its definition the vocabulary does say, using some Semantic Web glue, that any two people who have the same mailbox are considered to be the same person. This gives us a simple rule for inferring more information. Any two sets of statements about people, where each person has the same e-mail address, are all about the same person.

So we know that we can gather up descriptions to build a collection of information. And we can use any kind of description that has been defined for the Semantic Web. So how are these terms defined? What is the process for getting new terms or whole new vocabularies?

Defining New Vocabulary (RDF Schema)

The Semantic Web uses URIs to identify terms, and to build descriptions. Moreover, several of the vocabularies built in the Semantic Web are about describing terms. So a complete definition of a term is usually made using the basic RDF vocabulary (sometimes people might use OWL, which is a vocabulary that provides for more detailed descriptions).[11] In our cards metaphor, if you want to define a new term, you make a new card for it and put it in the catalogue. Then, when you are looking through the catalogue and do not recognise a term, you simply look it up in the same catalogue. With RDF you can add new properties, new elements, or even new vocabularies as easily as it was done in the card catalogue era, but much easier to use, since the lookup is almost instantaneous.

When you name your elements, they will have to be unique within the schema but they do not have to be globally unique. This is the job of the namespaces we mentioned in the section before. With RDF Vocabulary Language (RDF/S) we could create properties, subsets of properties and classes, and even "seeAlso" additional information like cross-references in the card boxes (Figure 3).

```
<rdf:RDF xmlns:rdf="http://www.w3.org/1999/02/22-rdf-syntax-ns#"
 xmlns:rdfs="http://www.w3.org/2000/01/rdf-schema#">
<rdf:Description
rdf:about="http://myuri.example.org/terms#term0001">
 <rdf:type rdf:resource="http://www.w3.org/1999/02/22-rdf-syntax-
ns#Property"/>
 <rdfs:label xml:lang="fr">Traducteur</rdfs:label>
 <rdfs:label xml:lang="en">Translator</rdfs:label>
 <rdfs:label xml:lang="es">Traductor</rdfs:lbel>
 <rdfs:comment xml:lang="fr">Une personne, organisation, ou autre
agent qui a traduit le sujet de cette propriete</rdfs:comment>
 <rdfs:comment xml:lang="en">A person, organisation, or other
agent who translated the subject of this property</rdfs:comment>
 <rdfs:comment xml:lang="es">Una persona, organización, u otro
agente que tradujo el sujeto de esta propiedad</rdfs:comment>
 <rdfs:subProperty
rdf:resource="http://purl.org/dc/elements/1.1/contributor"/>
 <rdfs:range rdf:resource="http://xmlns.com/foaf/0.1/Agent" />
</rdf:Description>
</rdf:RDF>
```

Here we have a resource, identified by the URI http://myUri.example.
org/terms#term0001. We have said that it has the type of an RDF Property. Using the RDF Vocabulary Description Language (RDF/S, 2004) *label* and *comment* terms we have provided human-readable explanations of our property in three languages (Spanish, English, and French). This is important. In general discussion of tags we have often give them names based on the text inside the pointy brackets–the actual element name we use for the computer. But that is really just the last bit of a URI, a Web address, and may or may not be meaningful to a human reader.

In principle, it seems to make sense that we choose names we can remember, and it is not a bad idea. However, it is fairly clear that the names that are easy to remember in Arabic are not as easy to remember in Japanese, and vice versa. So these informal "tag names" are formally defined with real, per-language labels that people can read. At the same time, there is a URI that doesn't change, because computers don't speak human languages anyway and don't make a stylistic difference between "real" words and random strings of text. In this way, we can share a URI across languages, and allow people to search for it in a real language.

FIGURE 3. Creating New Properties with RDF/S (*Translator* in Spanish, English and French)

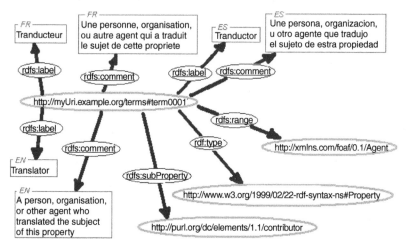

In this figure, the oval (○) represents an URI, a resource; The square (□) represents a value or literal, and the circle in the arrow (-○→) a property or association (a predicate).

We have also declared that it is an RDF subProperty of the Dublin Core contributor property. That is, if something has a translator X, then it has a Dublin Core contributor X. While not all contributors are translators, all translators are contributors. We will see below a concrete example of what this means. Finally, we declared a range for the property. This is a claim that all objects of declarations that use the property have a given type–in this case they are FOAF Agents.

In other words, we have related the URI defined to some English, Spanish, and French text that can be used to present the information to people. We have also related it to other terms in other vocabularies. It allows us to go to the catalogue with some basic rules, and find not just the information we want, but the definitions of new things added to the cards, which we can relate in various ways to definitions that are already known.

RDF/S can be used to make statements defining and describing in a formal (machine-understandable) way, application-specific and existing vocabularies (for example, DCMES, Dublin Core Metadata Element Set)[12] or for creating new vocabularies or new elements of an existing one. Jul (2003) also recognizes this advantage of RDF from

MARC. Several different namespaces would be needed for a standard library bibliographic record or for a resource description that uses library rules and tools. This author also points out that things that may take several years to change in cataloguing rules or in MARC format (like introduce a new element, code, or rule), in RDF could take seconds, where the owner of the namespace might introduce pretty quickly as we did in our example.

Scribbling on the Cards

In library cards we could scribble any kind of information, about a book or a library material quickly. We can do the same in RDF, enriching more and more our description capabilities and more precise resources description. Let's include now a new term in our example. We can use our new term (my:term0001), just like any other:

```
<rdf:RDF xmlns:rdf='http://www.w3.org/1999/02/22-rdf-syntax-ns#'
 xmlns:dc='http://purl.org/dc/elements/1.1/'
 xmlns:foaf='http://xmlns.com/foaf/0.1/'
 xmlns:my='http://myuri.example.org/terms#'>
<rdf:Description rdf:about='http://www.bartleby.com/173'>
<dc:creator>
<foaf:Person>
<foaf:name>Albert Einstein</foaf:name>
<foaf:birtdate>14 March 1879</foaf:birthdate>
</foaf:Person>
</dc:creator>
<my:term0001>
<foaf:Person>
<foaf:name>Robert W Lawson</foaf:name>
</foaf:Person>
</my:term0001>
<dc:language>en</dc:language>
<dc:title>Relativity
The Special and General Theory</dc:title>
<dc:date
rdf:datatype="http://www.w3.org/2001/XMLSchema#gYear">1920</dc:dat
e>
<dc:identifier>http://www.bartleby.com/173</dc:identifier>
</rdf:Description>
</rdf:RDF>
```

In library cards we could scribble any kind of information, about a book or a library material quickly. We can do the same in RDF, enriching more and more our description capabilities and more precise resources description. Let's include now a new term in our example. We can use our new term (my:term0001), just like any other (Figure 4).

As we noted above, our translator property is defined as a sub-Property of the Dublin Core contributor property. This means that if we give this example to an RDF/S (Vocabulary Description Language) aware processor, it will make the inference that the thing we are describing has a Dublin Core contributor property whose value is a FOAF Person with the FOAF name "Robert W Lawson." This is useful when we want to search a large collection of records, especially if they have been encoded at different times, for different purposes, but with vocabularies that are related to others. In fact it is often possible to take several collections of RDF, describe some relations between properties, and do useful searching across the collections.

FIGURE 4. Graphic Representation of a New Term (my:term0001) in Our Example

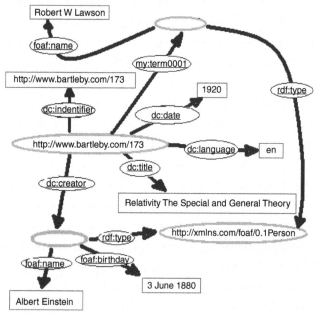

In this figure, the oval (O) represents an URI, a resource; The square (□) represents a value or literal, and the circle in the arrow (-O→) a property or association (a predicate).

CONCLUSION

There are a number of additional RDF components that we have not addressed in this article, but which can be used to make it easier to tie the various vocabularies to each other. OWL[12] also allows for various constraints to be specified, such as the fact that a person should only have one birthday. In our definition of a translator above, we could have declared a domain for the property–that is, specified a type that all subjects have, if we could think of a suitable definition of that type (should it be a person? or an organisation? or some combination of those?). Or we can wait for someone else to make the relevant RDF (for example, if Dublin Core proposed a translator term that would be a subProperty of contributor in its RDF/S for Metadata Terms). When that property is described, they, we, or anyone, can declare the two as equivalent by using a term from OWL.

We have not discussed some of the deeper mechanics of how to use RDF in this work for practical reasons, but there is a wealth of literature and tools available already (RDF, 2006). The power of RDF comes in part from its simplicity, but it is quite easy to make nonsensical statements because the original definition of a term did not consider the size of the catalogue that is available.

W3C has developed a series of RDF standards over the last three years (RDF, 2006). RDF has been integrated into a variety of applications from library catalogues and directories to syndication of news and content to personal collections of music, photos, and events, using existing schemas (like DC)[13] or creating new ones. When plans of Universal Bibliographic Control (UBC) were first presented, the standards were not there to support full implementation. Despite the Paris Principles (1961) there was no international standard which could ensure the UBC, and later MARC format would get it. Today, RDF has the potential to be the backbone for the Semantic Web, and help us achieve "Universal Web Control."

It is important to remember that RDF is just a technology, and it is the Semantic Web that is a way of making the Web more useful. We have seen that we can all scribble on the cards in the RDF catalogue, but the main challenge remains the same–how do we ensure that as much useful information as possible gets on there, and as little unreliable or incorrect information is added? On the global scale of the Web, this is in fact a complex problem, but not just a technological one.

Librarianship, including cataloguing and classification, have evolved over the centuries, and continue to demonstrate innovative. This new dimension is based on information architecture, structured knowledge representation, and on the Semantic Web, where standards (old and new) are in continuous evolution. This continuous development means, on a technical level, standards will keep changing and librarians and cataloguers will keep adapting to this evolution. Against Mark Twain's idea: *I'm all for progress; it's change I don't like*, librarians have learned to adapt their professional competencies and their attitude to the Web and the Semantic Web requirements to achieve metadata interoperability and perhaps the UWC too.

NOTES

1. Some examples of this are:

- The European project in the late twentieth century called *Bibliotheca Universalis*. One of the pilot projects of the GIS (Global Information Society) arose from the 1995's G7 Activities about Information Society. In some way, *Bibliotheca Universalis* could be considered the basis for the current TEL (The European Library) project: http://www.theeuropeanlibrary.org.
- Traditional examples of digital global libraries, born with the vocation of being "universal." We are thinking on projects such us: Project Gutenberg <http://www.gutenberg.org> or Cervantes Virtual Library in Spain <http://www.cervantesvirtual.com>.
- The Universal Library from the University of Carnegie Mellon <http://tera-3.ul.cs.cmu.edu/>. The last news appeared in *Library Journal* in April 2006, which considers the OCA (Open Content Alliance) plan against Google's books digitisation project "The Birth of the Universal Library" (Bengtson 2006).

2. Wikipedia: http://www.wikipedia.org.
3. Flickr: http://www.flickr.com.
4. Del.icio.us: http://del.icio.us.
5. See MARC 21 XML Schema: http://www.loc.gov/standards/marcxml.
6. We must point out that we are using the Spanish version of the book and these Berners-Lee's remarks and reflections are in p. 171 in the cited version (Berners-Lee, 2000) and we made a free translation from it, which might not coincide with his original words.
7. We only need to check the last 4-5 years of *Cataloging & Classification Quarterly* <http://catalogingandclassificationquarterly.com/ccqissue.html> (ISSN: 0163-9374) and *Journal of Internet Cataloging* <http://www.haworthpressinc.com/store/product.asp?sku=J141> (ISSN: 1091-1367) to show several examples of all these tensions and scientific discussion.
8. For more information about RDA, please see JSC (2005-06), or http://www.rdaonline.org.

9. The W3C Public Access Specifications for W3C are understood as *de facto* standards. When they achieved the level of Recommendation they are ready to be applied for industry and software. RDF specifications are Recommendations since February 2004 (See: RDF, 2006).

10. FOAF (Friend Of A Friend), See FOAF Project site at: http://www.foaf-project.org.

11. OWL stands for Web Ontology Language and it is the formal language created by W3C Semantic Web activity for representing and encoding ontologies. OWL builds on RDF and RDF Schema and adds more vocabulary for describing properties and classes: among others, relations between classes (e.g., disjointness), cardinality (e.g., "exactly one"), equality, richer typing of properties, characteristics of properties (e.g., symmetry), and enumerated classes. To explain OWL goes further the objectives of this article. For more information about OWL, please see the official W3C site at: http://www.w3.org/2004/OWL.

12. DCMES (Dublin Core Metadata Element Set), i.e., the fifteen elements which are recognised as an ISO standard (ISO 15836), has its own RDF Schema defined in: http://dublincore.org/2003/03/24/dces# where all the elements and its semantics values are described as RDF properties. For example, the element "title" in RDF/S looks like this:

```
<rdf:Property rdf:about="http://purl.org/dc/elements/1.1/title">

<rdfs:label xml:lang="en-US">Title</rdfs:label>

<rdfs:comment xml:lang="en-US">A name given to the
resource.</rdfs:comment>

<dc:description xml:lang="en-US">Typically, a Title will be a name
by which the resource is formally known.</dc:description>

<rdfs:isDefinedBy rdf:resource="http://purl.org/dc/elements/1.1/" />

<dcterms:issued>1999-07-02</dcterms:issued>

<dcterms:modified>2002-10-04</dcterms:modified>

<dc:type
rdf:resource="http://dublincore.org/usage/documents/principles/#el
ement" />

<dcterms:hasVersion
rdf:resource="http://dublincore.org/usage/terms/history/#title-
004" />

</rdf:Property>
```

13. To check some of these (more or less) well know schemas, see SchemaWeb at: http://www.schemaweb.info.

REFERENCES

Ahmed, Kal et al. (2001). *Professional XML Meta Data*. Birmingham: Wrox Press, 2001.

Bengtson, Jonathan B. (2006). The Birth of the Universal Library. *Library Journal*, April 15, 2006. Available online at: http://www.libraryjournal.com/article/CA6322017.html.

Berners Lee, Tim, James Hendler, Ora Lassila (2001). The Semantic Web. *Scientific American*, vol. 284, n. 5, p. 34-43. Available online at: http://www.sciahttp://www.haworthpress.com/Store/E-Text/ViewLibraryEText.asp?s=J104&m=0v=39m. com/article.cfm?articleID=00048144-10D2-1C70-84A9809EC588EF21.

Berners-Lee, Tim (2000). *Tejiendo la red: el inventor del World Wide Web nos descubre su origen.* Madrid: Siglo veintiuno, 2000. [Spanish version of Berners-Lee's book: *Weaving the Web.* San Francisco: Harper, 1999].

Brisson, Roger (1999). The World Discovers Cataloging: A Conceptual Introduction to Digital Libraries, Metadata and the Implications for Library Administrations. *Journal of Internet Cataloging*, vol. 1, n. 4, p. 3-30.

Campbell, Grant D. (2004). The metadata-bibliographic organization nexus. In *International Yearbook of Library and Information Management 2003-2004: Metadata applications and Management.* Maryland: Scarecrow, 2004, p. 185-203.

Daconta, Michael C., Leo J. Obrst, Kevin T. Smith (eds.) (2003). *The Semantic Web: A Guide to the Future of XML, Web Services, and Knowledge Management.* Indianapolis: Wiley, 2003.

Dovey, Matthew J. (1999) "Stuff" about "Stuff"–the Differing Meanings of "Metadata." *Vine (Theme issue: Metadata. Part 1)*, 1999, n. 116, p. 6-13.

Gradmann, Stefan (2005). rdfs:frbr–Towards an Implementation Model for Library Catalogs Using Semantic Web Technology. *Cataloging & Classification Quarterly*, 2005, vol. 39, n. 3/4, p. 63-75.

Hjelm, Johan (2001). *Creating the Semantic Web with RDF: Professional Developer's Guide.* New York, etc.: Wiley Computer Publishing, John Wiley & Sons.

Howarth, Lynne C. (2005). Metadata and Bibliographic Control: Soul-Mates or Two Solitudes? *Cataloging & Classification Quarterly*, 2005, vol. 40, n. 3/4, p. 37-55.

Jones, Wayne, Judith R. Ahronheim, and Josephine Crawford (eds.) (2002). *Cataloging the Web: Metadata, AACR, and MARC 21.* Lanham: Scarecrow Press, 2002.

JSC (2005-06). Joint Steering Committee for Revision of Anglo-American Cataloguing Rules. *RDA: Resource Description and Access.* Library and Archives Canada, Firs issued July 2005, rev. 3 august 2006. Available online at: http://www.collectionscanada.ca/jsc/docs/5rda-prospectusrev2.pdf.

Jul, Erik (2003). MARC and Mark up. *Cataloging & Classification Quarterly*, vol. 36, n. 3/4, p.141-153.

McCathieNevile, Charles (2005). RDF for XMLers. *Upgrade: The European Journal for Informatics Professional*, February 2005, vol. VI, n. 1, p. 39-44.

Méndez, Eva (2004). La Web semántica, una web 'más bibliotecaria.' *Boletín de la SEDIC*, 2004, n. 4. Available online at: http://www.sedic.es/p_boletinclip41_confirma.htm.

Méndez Rodríguez, Eva Mª (2005). Libraries and Information Systems Need XML/RDF . . . but Do They Know It? *Upgrade: The European Journal for Informatics Professional*, February 2005, vol. VI, n. 1, p. 51-56.

RDF (2004). World Wide Web Consortium. RDF/XML Syntax Specification (Revised): W3C Recommendation 10 February 2004. Dave Beckett, ed. W3C, 2004. Available online at: http://www.w3.org/TR/rdf-syntax-grammar.

RDF/S (2004). World Wide Web Consortium. RDF Vocabulary Description Language 1.0: RDF Schema: W3C Recommendation 10 February 2004. Dan Brickley and R. V. Guha, eds. W3C, 2004. Available online at: http://www.w3.org/TR/rdf-schema.

RDF (2006). Ivan Herman, Ralph Swick and Dan Brickley, (eds.). World Wide Web Consortium, rev. 19 July 1006. Available online at: http://www.w3.org/RDF.

Tillett, Barbara B. (2003). AACR2 and Metadata: Library Opportunities in the Global Semantic Web. *Cataloging & Classification Quarterly*, vol. 36, n. 3/4, p.101-119.

doi:10.1300/J104v43n03_03

Library of Congress Controlled Vocabularies and Their Application to the Semantic Web

Corey A. Harper
Barbara B. Tillett

SUMMARY. This article discusses how various controlled vocabularies, classification schemes, and thesauri can serve as some of the building blocks of the Semantic Web. These vocabularies have been developed over the course of decades, and can be put to great use in the development of robust Web services and Semantic Web technologies. The article covers how initial collaboration between the Semantic Web, Library and Metadata communities are creating partnerships to complete work in this area. It then discusses some core principles of authority control before talking more specifically about subject and genre vocabularies and name authority. It is hoped that future systems for internationally shared authority data will link the world's authority data from trusted sources to benefit users worldwide. Finally, the article looks at how encoding and markup of vocabularies can help ensure compatibility with the current and future state of Semantic Web development and provides examples of how this work can help improve the findability and navigation of information on the World Wide Web. doi:10.1300/J104v43n03_04 *[Article copies available for a fee from The Haworth Document Delivery Service: 1-800-HAWORTH. E-mail address: <docdelivery@haworthpress.com> Website: <http://www.HaworthPress.com> © 2007 by The Haworth Press, Inc. All rights reserved.]*

[Haworth co-indexing entry note]: "Library of Congress Controlled Vocabularies and Their Application to the Semantic Web." Harper, Corey A., and Barbara B. Tillett. Co-published simultaneously in *Cataloging & Classification Quarterly* (The Haworth Information Press, an imprint of The Haworth Press, Inc.) Vol. 43, No. 3/4, 2007, pp. 47-68; and: *Knitting the Semantic Web* (ed: Jane Greenberg, and Eva Méndez) The Haworth Information Press, an imprint of The Haworth Press, Inc., 2007, pp. 47-68. Single or multiple copies of this article are available for a fee from The Haworth Document Delivery Service [1-800-HAWORTH, 9:00 a.m. - 5:00 p.m. (EST). E-mail address: docdelivery@haworthpress.com].

Available online at http://ccq.haworthpress.com
© 2007 by The Haworth Press, Inc. All rights reserved.
doi:10.1300/J104v43n03_04

KEYWORDS. Controlled vocabularies, Semantic Web building blocks, authority control

INTRODUCTION:
LIBRARY OF CONGRESS TOOLS
AND LAUNCHING THE SEMANTIC WEB

An essential process is the joining together of subcultures when a wider common language is needed. Often two groups independently develop very similar concepts, and describing the relation between them brings great benefits . . . The Semantic Web, in naming every concept simply by a URI, lets anyone express new concepts that they invent with minimal effort. Its unifying logical language will enable these concepts to be progressively linked into a universal Web.

Thus concludes Tim Berners-Lee's seminal 2001 *Scientific American* article on the Semantic Web (Berners-Lee, Hendler, & Lasilla, 2001). The concepts established here are strong ones, and the vision of a thoroughly interconnected Web of data that these concepts suggest, could prove a catalyst for the way we research, develop, interact with, and build upon ideas, culture, and knowledge. The idea presented here, of independent groups working with similar concepts, is applicable to the very technologies that can serve as the Semantic Web's underpinnings. The Semantic Web communities and library communities have both been working toward the same set of goals: naming concepts, naming entities, and bringing different forms of those names together. Semantic Web efforts toward this end are relatively new, whereas libraries have been doing work in this area for hundreds of years. The tools and vocabularies developed in libraries, particularly those developed by the Library of Congress, are sophisticated and advanced. When translated into Semantic Web technologies they will help to realize Berners-Lee's vision.

Semantic Web technologies are now, in their own right, starting to reach a state of maturity. Berners-Lee, the director of the World Wide Web Consortium (W3C) and Eric Miller, W3C Semantic Web Activity Lead, frequently describe these technologies in terms of the Semantic Web Stack (see Figure 1). Many of the components depicted as layers in the Semantic Web Stack are already in place, although not nearly as widely implemented as most Semantic Web proselytizers would like.

FIGURE 1. W3C Semantic Web Stack

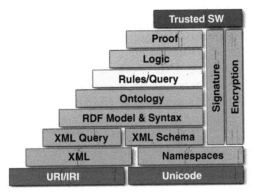

Development on the various levels depicted in this graphic has been a long time in the making. In a recent interview with Andrew Updegrove (2005) in the *Consortium Standards Bulletin*, Berners-Lee identifies one cause of the slow rate of development, implying that each layer is dependant on the layers below it. "We were asked to hold up the query and rules work because people didn't want to start on it until the ontology work had finished, so for some we were in danger of going too fast."

As the technologies represented by the Semantic Web Stack continue to mature, there is a tremendous potential for the library community to play a significant role in realizing Berners-Lee's vision. In a presentation at Dublin Core 2004 (Miller, 2004, Slide 26), as well as in a number of other presentations over the years, Eric Miller implored the library community to become active in Semantic Web development. Miller outlines the role of libraries in the Semantic Web as follows:

- Exposing collections–use Semantic Web technologies to make content available
- Web'ifying Thesaurus/Mappings/Services
- Sharing lessons learned
- Persistence

While all of these roles are significant, the idea of moving thesauri, controlled vocabularies, and related services into formats that are better able to work with other Web services and software applications is particularly significant. Converting these tools and vocabularies to Semantic Web standards, such as the Web Ontology Language (OWL), will provide limitless potential for putting them to use in myriad new ways. This will enable the integration of research functionality–such as searching and browsing diverse resources, verifying the identity of a particular resource's author, or browsing sets of topics related to a particular concept–into all sorts of tools, from online reference sources and library catalogs to authoring tools like those found in Microsoft's Office Suite.

Miller (2004, Slide 27) also emphasizes the role that libraries can play in helping to realize the trust layer in the Semantic Web Stack, stating, "Libraries have long standing trusted position that is applicable on the Web." The Semantic Web has a lot to gain by recruiting libraries and librarians and involving them in the development process. The W3C's stated mission is "to lead the World Wide Web to its full potential by developing protocols and guidelines that ensure long-term growth for the Web." This focus on protocols and guidelines helps explain why the Semantic Web Stack includes little to no mention of content. For example, it includes an ontology layer, which is primarily represented by OWL–a Web Ontology Language–a specification for adding Semantic Web enabling functionality to existing ontologies. More recently, another Semantic Web technology–Simple Knowledge Organization System (SKOS) Core–has been designed for the encoding of the contents of thesauri. The W3C's emphasis has been on how to encode ontologies, which fits with their stated mission. The source of ontologies and vocabularies is outside the scope of the W3C's concerns, although the usefulness of such ontologies is certainly dependant on their validity and trustworthiness. This is where Miller's thoughts on the role of libraries seem most relevant. Libraries have a long-standing history of developing, implementing, and providing tools and services that make use of numerous controlled vocabularies. Presumably, part of the process of "web'ifying thesaurus, mappings and services" involves converting existing tools into Semantic Web standards, such as OWL and SKOS. Miller and other vocabulary experts recognize that this would be of tremendous value to Semantic Web initiatives. Taking these steps would reduce the need for Semantic Web development to revisit decisions made over the centuries that libraries have been organizing and describing content, which ties into the related idea of "sharing lessons learned."

INCREMENTAL PROGRESS–INITIAL DEVELOPMENTS

Progress on bridging the gap between the Semantic Web community and the library community has been underway for some time. A variety of projects are in progress, or completed, that will help to bring more of the tools that libraries develop into the Semantic Web and more general Web Services spheres. Many of these projects are being developed within the Dublin Core Metadata Initiative (DCMI), which draws heavily on both the Semantic Web and library communities, as well as a variety of other information architecture and metadata communities.

One example of such collaboration is the expression of a sub-set of MARC Relator Terms (Network Development and MARC Standards Office–Library of Congress, 2006) in RDF for use as refinements of the DC contributor element. Relator terms allow a cataloger to specify the role that an individual played in the creation of a resource, such as illustrator, calligrapher, or editor. Allowing some of these terms to be used as refinements of contributor allows the expression of much more specific relationships between individuals and the resources they create. An example of the use of MARC Relator Terms, both in a MARC record and in Dublin Core, can be seen in Figure 2. Figure 2a depicts a mnemonic MARC record with personal name added entries for correspondents. The 700 tags at the end of this record each include a subfield e, which contains a MARC Relator term identifying the role of these individuals. The corresponding Dublin Core Record in Figure 2b represents this same information using the 'marcrel' namespace with the Relator code 'CRP,' which corresponds to the term 'correspondent.' The concept of author added entry, represented by MARC tag 700 in Figure 2a, is implicit in the Dublin Core example because the Relator terms are all element refinements of dc:contributor.

Another example of collaboration can be seen in the ongoing work to bind the Metadata Object Description Schema (MODS) metadata element set (Library of Congress, 2006, June 13) to RDF and to the DC Abstract Model so that MODS terms, or alternately new DC properties derived from or related to these MODS terms, could be available to Dublin Core Application Profiles (Heery & Patel, 2000). Similar collaborations between the Institute of Electrical and Electronics Engineers Learning Object Metadata group (IEEE-LOM) (IEEE Learning Technology Standards Committee, 2002) and DCMI resulted in an RDF binding of IEEE-LOM, which essentially serves to make IEEE-LOM metadata statements and records useable within the context of the Semantic Web. A summary of this process was reported at the Ariadne

FIGURE 2a. Relator Terms in a MARC record (Shown in MARC tag 700, subfield e)

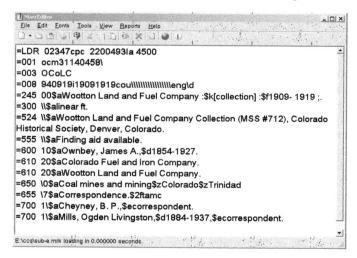

MARC Record Shown in MarcEdit, freely distributed MARC Record editing software. Available online at: http://oregonstate.edu/~reeset/marcedit/html/.

FIGURE 2b. MARC Relator Terms in a DC record (Shown in <marcrel:CRP> tag)

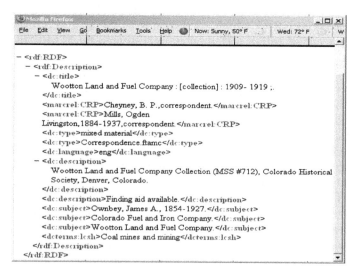

Conference in 2003 (Nilsson, Palmer, & Brace, 2003, November). This presentation resulted in a joint-task force between the IEEE and DCMI communities to formally map the IEEE-LOM Schema to the DCMI Abstract Model as well. Progress on this process can be tracked on the DC Education Working Group's Wiki (Joint DCMI/IEEE LTSC Taskforce, 2006, March). However, both of these examples apply to metadata elements and resource descriptions themselves. The progress that has been made on bringing tools from the library world into the Semantic Web has, thus far, been entirely focused on the idea of exposing library collections. Incorporating elements used in library resource descriptions into the sets of resource properties that are used to enable the Semantic Web is a large step, and enables library metadata to interoperate with Dublin Core and other RDF encoded metadata. Authority records, library thesauri, and library controlled vocabularies, if converted into formats that support Semantic Web technologies, have an even greater potential for revolutionizing the way users–and machines–interact with information on the Internet.

AUTHORITY CONTROL–CORE PRINCIPLES

The benefits and virtues of authority control have been debated and restated for decades. When we apply authority control, we are reminded how it brings precision to searches, how the syndetic structure of references enables navigation and provides explanations for variations and inconsistencies, how the controlled forms of names, titles, and subjects help collocate works in displays, how we can actually link to the authorized forms of names, titles, and subjects that are used in various tools, like directories, biographies, abstracting and indexing services, and so on. We can use the linking capability to include library catalogs in the mix of various tools that are available on the Web. In order to enable these capabilities in a Web-based environment, it will be necessary to move the records that facilitate linking and aggregating in the library into more universal and generalized encoding. The Library of Congress is taking steps in this direction, particularly through work on MARCXML for Authority Records (Library of Congress, 2005, April 22) and the Metadata Authority Description Schema (MADS) (Library of Congress, 2005, December 14), along with crosswalks to go between them. A next logical step is to begin work on translating this data into the Resource Description Framework (RDF), which is not a trivial task.

SUBJECT AND GENRE VOCABULARIES
FOR THE SEMANTIC WEB

There are a vast number of controlled vocabularies for various forms of subject access to library materials. Some of these vocabularies are classification schemes, such as *Dewey Decimal Classification* (DDC) and *Library of Congress Classification* (LCC). Others are controlled lists of subject headings or terms, which adhere to national and international guidelines for thesaurus construction, like the *Library of Congress Subject Headings* (LCSH), the two *Thesauri for Graphic Materials: Subject Terms* (TGM I) and *Genre & Physical Characteristic Terms* (TGM II), *Guidelines on Subject Access to Individual Works of Fiction, Drama, Etc.* (GSAFD), and the *Ethnographic Thesaurus*. Some of the subject thesauri published by The Getty, such as *The Getty Thesaurus of Geographic Names* (TGN) and *The Art and Architecture Thesaurus* (AAT) are truly hierarchical thesauri.

Many of these controlled vocabularies are registered as DCMI Encoding Schemes in the DCMI Terms namespace. Registered Encoding Schemes qualifying the DC Subject element include (DCMI Usage Board, 2005, January 10):

- Dewey Decimal Classification (DDC),
- Library of Congress Classification (LCC),
- Library of Congress Subject Headings (LCSH),
- Medical Subject Headings (MeSH),
- National Library of Medicine Classification (NLM),
- The Getty Thesaurus of Geographic Names (TGN),
- Universal Decimal Classification (UDC).

However, when these vocabularies are used as values of DC Subject in metadata records outside of the library context, the syndetic structure of the source vocabulary is all but lost. There is no way for search tools or other applications to make use of information about related terms and variant forms as part of the entry vocabulary. In some cases, item metadata for Dublin Core records is included within a larger system that relies heavily on MARC data, such as OCLC WorldCat. When this is true, many of the Library of Congress controlled vocabularies are indirectly linked to these Dublin Core records by virtue of the availability of MARC authority records for the controlled vocabularies in those systems. Systems outside of these application environments need to be able to retrieve and translate or otherwise make use of MARC authority record data to make effective use of the hierarchies, equivalency relationships, and structures in the content of controlled vocabularies.

These vocabularies present tremendous potential for improving access to Web resources and Semantic Web data, as well as enhancing networked applications. Search engine results could be dramatically improved, both in terms of precision and recall. Different subject vocabularies covering the same concept space could be merged together or associated, providing an environment where differences in terminology between different communities would provide less of a barrier to effective browsing of resources. Front-end interfaces could be built for a variety of online reference tools that take advantage of the rich structure of relationships between topics that is provided by controlled vocabularies. In some regards, libraries are only now realizing the full potential of catalog records to provide innovative and new browsing interfaces. An example can be seen in North Carolina State Library's new, Endeca powered, catalog interface (North Carolina State University [NCSU] Libraries, 2006), which is presently built entirely on the structure of bibliographic records. This new catalog interface allows users to refine a search by navigating through record clusters that share a particular property. Drawing on the idea of faceted classification, clusters can be grouped by subtopic, genre, language, time-period, geographic region, and in a variety of other ways. These facets are derived from information in various access points, subject headings and subdivisions in a particular bibliographic result set. It is easy to envision a similar technique being used to broaden searches and even to present initial browse interfaces to specific collections of information resources. When interfaces start to leverage the power of authority control in new and interesting ways, the benefit to users will be immense.

Another example of initiatives to leverage authority control is OCLC Research's Terminology Services project to "offer accessible, modular, Web-based terminology services" (OCLC Research, 2006). The Terminologies Pilot Project in October 2005 explored techniques for encoding sample vocabularies, means of mapping between them to help users identify relationships, and methods for incorporating the resulting services into other applications and tools. These services are the beginning of a rich tapestry of semantics that can be delivered within a user's current context, whatever that context is. In some cases, the services may be entirely carried out by server-side applications. Almost any application that serves content dynamically could include a navigation system that draws on the hierarchies and relationships between terms in LCSH, and could provide search interfaces that draw on term equivalencies to retrieve a broader set of resources when doing keyword searches.

Additionally, there could be services that exist within client side applications, pulling vocabulary structures from the network and integrating them into authoring tools. One such service component prototyped for the OCLC pilot uses the Microsoft Office 2003 Research Services Pane to access genre terms. " . . . if a college student wishes to categorize a reading list of fiction titles based on genre, he could copy the titles into a Microsoft Excel 2003 workbook, open the Research services pane, send a search to the OCLC Research GSAFD vocabulary service, and then place the results into his document" (Vizine-Goetz, 2004). This provides the user with the ability to browse and search genre categorizations without having to leave the application in which the search results will be used. Additionally, the more sources of data are made available in this way, the more automated the process can be. If the Research Services Pane had access to bibliographic records, genre or subject categorization could be fully automated and available at the touch of a button. A cataloger could use a similar tool to suggest appropriate terms from a controlled vocabulary, which will lead to lots of cost saving opportunities.

Similar applications could be developed as browser plug-ins or extensions. A sidebar application could be built for FireFox that could harness the power of controlled vocabularies when browsing Web resource that provide some degree of keyword tagging or folksonomy support. Imagine browsing a resource like Flickr (Flickr, 2006), and being able to query LCSH for relationships that may be defined between subject terms through the tags labeling the subject of a particular photographic image and tags for various related concepts. The sidebar could include hyper-linked broader, narrower, equivalent, and associative terms that would pull together additional photographs tagged with those related terms. In a different context, such an application could attempt to scan html source code for word frequency and try to guess the primary topics, returning related terms from a controlled vocabulary, and perhaps linking to search engine results for the concepts represented. Additionally, a similar service could be provided using a word highlighted by the user. The possibilities are endless.

NAME AUTHORITY FOR THE SEMANTIC WEB

The benefits of authority control described above–search precision, more powerful navigation, collocation, and linking between various tools and resources–apply to metadata about the creators of resources as well as to subject access. The library community is well positioned to play a significant role in these developments. Libraries have been dealing with identification, disambiguation, and collocation of names of content creators since the beginning of cataloging. The different forms of name used by the same creator in various print publications and other types of resources have always led to some degree of difficulty in grouping works together. The syndetic structure of name authority files has proven itself a very useful tool to help collocate works by an author regardless of the form of name on a particular item. The proliferation of resources on the Web extends the scope of the collocation problem.

Initiatives are appearing in the Web community to help provide better mechanisms for identifying persons, families, and corporate entities that have a role with respect to information resources. InterParty is a European Commission funded project exploring the interoperation of "party identifiers," which would provide standard identification numbers to serve the same purpose that authorized forms of names serve in library applications: to help collocate and disambiguate individual content creators (Information Society Technologies, 2003). More recently, some of the InterParty members and others submitted a similar proposal for International Standard Party Identifiers (ISPI) as an ISO standard (Lloret & Piat, 2006). More directly related to Semantic Web Development is the Friend Of A Friend (FOAF) project. FOAF is about "creating a Web of machine-readable homepages describing people, the links between them and the things they create and do" (The Friend Of A Friend [foaf] Project, n.d.). Finding ways to integrate these initiatives with existing mechanisms for name authority control in libraries can help to bring library catalogues into the mix of tools available on the Web. Additionally, the availability of library authority data in a more Web-friendly format has the potential to positively influence the organization of the broad spectrum of Web content already available. The development of a virtual international authority file (VIAF) has been a key idea moving forward this initiative.

A Virtual International Authority File (VIAF)

Presently, authority files are maintained and developed by a large range of national bibliographic agencies. To make the most of this potential, it is useful to first integrate the somewhat disparate sources of authority data that exist even within the library community. These agencies develop files that are generally focused on the creators of content relevant to a particular national and cultural identity. As geographic boundaries become more and more porous, and culture becomes much more international, there is increasingly overlap between the authority files maintained by these agencies. The concept of a Virtual International Authority File (VIAF) has been discussed since the 1970s within the International Federation of Library Associations and Institutions (IFLA). Initially, IFLA envisioned a single shared file; more recently the concept has evolved into one of linking existing national and regional authority files. The primary objective of this vision is to facilitate sharing the workload and reducing cataloging costs within the library community. The community is expanding, especially in Europe, where libraries are viewed as one of many "memory institutions," along with archives, museums, and rights management agencies. Ideally, authority files can be freely shared among all of these communities. A shared file would reduce the cost of doing authority work by avoiding repetition of effort while combining various forms of names that are particular to resource published within the context of a particular region, culture, or nation. Combining or clustering the forms of name will result in a much richer set of authority information, enabling users to access information in the language, scripts, and form they prefer. Additionally, a single international authority file system will be far more useful when integrated into various Web retrieval tools and Web content descriptions. Such a tool could be used by a wide range of Web systems to improve the precision of user's searches and to provide the user's preferred display of the language and script of names.

Authority records are used to collocate resources that utilize varying forms of name, but collocation does not need to dictate the script or language used by the end user display. Figure 3 shows how a single entity–whether it is a concept, person, place, or thing–has a variety of labels that identify it in different languages and scripts. Traditionally, library systems have relied on a preferred label for all entities, although the preference would vary depending on the geographic context of the system. Merging or linking records that utilize different languages and scripts allows the end-user to select the language and script used to display information about entities irrespective of system's default preference. This is appropriate in a truly global Web, where geographic and national boundaries are considerably less significant.

A variety of projects have sought to address this language challenge in recent years, exploring mechanisms to combine individual authority files. One such project, the European Commission funded AUTHOR project, converted a sample of authority records from five European bib-

FIGURE 3. One Entity–Many Labels

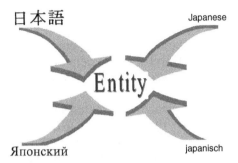

Figure from Tillett, Barbara B. "Authority Control: State of the Art and New Perspectives," co-published simultaneously in *Cataloging & Classification Quarterly*, v. 38, no. 3/4, 2004, p. 23-41; and *Authority Control in Organizing and Accessing Information: Definition and International Experience* (ed.: Arlene G. Taylor and Barbara B. Tillett). The Haworth Press, Inc., 2004, p. 23-41.

liographic agencies in France, England, Belgium, Spain, and Portugal into the UNIMARC format and made them available as a searchable file. "The challenge was that each library has its own language, cataloging rules, bibliographic record format and local system for its online authority file" (Tillett, 2001). Combining these records into a single UNIMARC file required a large amount of record normalization. No attempt was made to link the records for the same entity.

More recently, OCLC Online Computer Library Center Inc., the Library of Congress, and Die Deutsche Biblioteck (DDB) began a joint project to test the idea of a VIAF. OCLC used matching algorithms to link name authority records of these two national bibliographic agencies and built a server to store the combined records. Additional phases of the project will involve ongoing maintenance to update the central file when either source is updated and possibly the development of a multilingual end user interface (Morris, 2003). Following the evaluation of the project, the addition of new partners will be explored, particularly those potential partners with non-roman authority records.

LEVERAGING A VIAF ON THE SEMANTIC WEB

When combined with developments in the broader metadata, Web-design, and Semantic Web communities, the power and utility of VIAF outside of libraries becomes clear. Authority record data can be associated more easily with a variety of Web resources, allowing users and potentially machines to immediately start to evaluate the information they are looking at. A quick search of bibliographic data related to a given resource author allows the retrieval of her dissertation, which could be mined for data about the degree granting institution. Other bibliographic records could be retrieved to help evaluate the original Web resource and related works could offer pathways to additional relevant resources.

As other resources start including metadata that uses identifiers or headings to link to a VIAF, the opportunity to connect more interesting bits of information can add significant value to any Web-based information resource. Wikipedia entries, journal articles, Who's Who biographical info, an individual's blog, their homepage, or the homepage of their place of work can all be interconnected, as well as linked to journal articles, bibliographic records in catalogs and in e-commerce sites, and a variety of other scholarly resources. These interconnections have extensive implications for research. Once there is a corpus of biographical information combined into a data store that is connected to authority data (as well as associated bibliographic data), the information can be used to make inferences about any document, article, Web page, or blog entry that turns up when searching for information. For example, imagine a blog post that includes information about its author's identity. This information could be referenced against available biographical data and used to make inferences about the veracity and objectivity of the post's content. If the author were affiliated with the Recording Industry Association of America (RIAA), a trade group representing the U.S. recording industry, or the Electronic Frontier Foundation (EFF), a non-profit legal organization focused on defending "digital rights," heavily involved in fighting bad uses of Digital Rights Management technology, and opposing limitations on fair use, the statement is likely to be much less objective than content posted by a Harvard law professor. While an agent or search tool couldn't necessarily flag such resources as potentially biased without additional information about the affiliate organization, it would still be very useful to present these additional facts to the user when returning search results.

The metadata community has a number of initiatives underway for describing people, both as agents of resource creation and for the utility of describing relationships between people, describing connections between people and organizations, and for capturing other contact information and other descriptive information about individuals and groups.

Examples of such initiatives include the Dublin Core Agents Working Group's work on defining a metadata standard for agent description and identification. Ultimately, this work should result in the development of an Application Profile for agent description. Also, work has been completed on "Reference Models for Digital Libraries: Actors and Roles" within the DELOS/NSF Working Group. This work culminated in Final Report, issued in July 2003. Interestingly, this work goes well beyond the scope of authors and content creators; instead the DELOS/NSF model categorizes Actors as Users, Professionals, and Agents. In this context, agents are the traditional content creators that help populate a digital library and professionals are the developers of the digital library itself and the providers of digital library services. The scope of their work may be much deeper than is necessarily relevant to discussions of authority control on the Semantic Web, although the models used and conclusions drawn may prove to play an important role in future discussions about authority control for names.

Another initiative, the Friend Of A Friend (FOAF) project described earlier, is of particular use to the Semantic Web community, because it was conceived with the Semantic Web in mind and is built upon the RDF data model. FOAF expresses identity through any property value pair, allowing you to aggregate data about individuals using any unique property, such as an e-mail address or the URL for a home page. FOAF is primarily designed for community building, but when the possible privacy issues of sharing personal data are resolved there is much potential for FOAF to help aggregate public information about individuals.

FOAF could be used to aggregate all sorts of resources, both by and about individuals–again, resources such as, Wikipedia entries, journal articles, Who's Who biographical info, the individual's homepage, their blog, or their place of work. This information could be glommed into a program like Piggy Bank (Simile, 2006)–a FireFox extension for viewing, collecting, and merging RDF encoded data, developed by the Simile (Semantic Interoperability of Metadata and Information in unLike Environments) project–or any other Semantic Web enabled tool, and processed along with other local or remote data stores. For example, a local data store of vcards and/or FOAF data might include private data, such as phone number, calendaring system, and e-mail address. The very presence of that particular identifier in a local store of RDF data about people might change the context of any information interaction with a Wikipedia or Who's Who entry.

Using any "unique" property to identify entities will certainly help to aggregate most of them, but it would miss entities that are not described using a particular piece of identifying information. Inferences about which descriptions represent the same entity will only go so far in establishing a positive match. The ability to completely aggregate such data becomes even more powerful when the identifying properties can be referenced against the VIAF to determine alternate forms of name and representations in alternate scripts. This allows a query of available RDF data to be much more comprehensive when deciding what pieces of data should be aggregated.

MARKUP AND ENCODING OF AUTHORITY DATA

One of the most valuable activities that libraries and librarians can engage in, both to help realize the Semantic Web and to generally increase the findability of electronic resources in general, is the process of creating versions of vocabularies in machine-readable format. Thesauri, authority files, classifications schemes, and subject heading lists–collectively referred to as Knowledge Organization Systems–have enormous potential for enhancing the discoverability and organization of resources in a networked environment. The potential only increases when such systems are provided in formats designed for emerging Web technology, such as OWL and SKOS–two of the ontology schema of the Semantic Web.

> Knowledge organization systems can enhance the digital library in a number of ways. They can be used to connect a digital library resource to a related resource. The related information may reside within the KOS itself or the KOS may be used as an intermediary file to retrieve the key needed to access it in another resource. A KOS can make digital library materials accessible to disparate communities. This may be done by providing alternate subject access, by adding access by different modes, by providing multilingual access, and by using the KOS to support free text searching. (Hodge, 2000)

The perceived benefits of knowledge organization systems listed above are of particular importance, and apply to networked resources beyond the scope of digital library materials. The availability of machine-readable representations of various thesauri and other controlled vocabulary enables more effective search and retrieval, better browse functionality and general organization of materials online, and the automatic creation of context sensitive linkages between available resources and data sets. Additionally, and most importantly for Semantic Web development, providing controlled vocabularies outside of traditional library systems enables a variety of applications to more effectively merge and manipulate data and information from disparate sources.

There are many steps that need to be taken to realize this set of goals. Firstly, the library and Semantic Web communities must agree on how best to encode these vocabularies. Many of the subject schemes listed above already exist in one or more machine-readable representations. Much of LCSH exists in MARC records in library catalogs and the databases of cataloging services such as OCLC's WorldCat and RLIN 21. All of the LC controlled vocabularies (LC classification, LCSH subject authority, and the name authority records) are available as complete files of MARC 21 or MARCXML formatted authority records through the Cataloging Distribution Service of the Library of Congress (2005) (free test files are also available). The Getty (2003) provides licensed access to its vocabularies in three formats: XML, relational tables, and MARC, and provides sample data from each vocabulary for free. At first glance, these formats do not appear to be of much use in the context of RDF, but the standardization and global use of MARC makes it possible to convert these into RDF-friendly data. One approach is the creation of URIs to identify each terminal node on the source XML structure as a unique concept that can be used as a property in the RDF and DC Abstract Model sense. This prospect has the potential to retain as much of the detail available in the source format as possible, but may prove unnecessary and undesirable due to the complexity of the resultant sets of properties. On the other hand, the information from MARC records may in fact be useful for automatic processes and machine activities. The richness of MARC authority data, and the time and effort invested in developing, encoding, and sharing this data, provides a unique and powerful set of vocabularies. However, it remains to be seen whether the complexity of the resulting XML records would be an impediment to interoperability.

An alternative approach involves simply cross-walking the XML data into an already defined RDF-friendly form. Along the way, detail about relationships between terms will likely be lost, but the end product will probably be much simpler to work with. One possible target RDF vocabulary, the Simple Knowledge Organization System (SKOS) Core (W3C Semantic Web Activity, 2004, February), has much potential in this context. SKOS Core provides a model for expressing the structure of what they refer to as a 'Concept Scheme.' "Thesauri, classification schemes, subject heading lists, taxonomies, terminologies, glossaries and other types of controlled vocabulary are all examples of concept schemes" (Miles, Mathews, Wilson, & Brickley, 2005, September). SKOS Core provides a means of expressing most of the semantic relationships included in most library subject vocabularies. For example, "prefLabel" and "altLabel" represent "use" and "use for" references, while "broader" and "narrower" are used to identify hierarchical relationships. SKOS allows for the creation of new labels and the encoding of more specific types of relationships as well. Additionally, SKOS provides mechanisms for various types of notes–scopeNote, definition, example, and note. The SKOS Core community has drafted documentation on "Publishing a Thesaurus on the Semantic Web" (Miles, 2005, May), which provides a guide for using SKOS to both describe and encode vocabularies in RDF.

Converting large controlled vocabularies into RDF data is certainly a good way to get sample data sets to use to build prototype services. However, the long-term maintenance of such data stores may be problematic. As changes are made to the source vocabulary, those changes need to be propagated through to all the various formats that the vocabulary is made available in. In the context of SKOS, this is a manageable task. SKOS extensions have been proposed to allow for versioning and the tracking of changes made to controlled vocabularies over time (Tennis, 2005). However, in cases where vocabularies are likely to be managed in a variety of different formats, the SKOS extensions are less helpful. Another approach is to harvest the source data in its native format and translate it into a variety of output formats either as nightly batch processes or on-the-fly as data is requested. Progress is being made in this area, such as OCLC's work on exposing vocabularies in a variety of delivery formats, including MARCXML and SKOS (Dempsey et al., 2005).

It doesn't matter whether the data store is MADS, MARC, RDF, or some arbitrary flavor of XML, it can be transformed into another format either on-the-fly or as a batch process. A centralized name authority database could be created from the national authority files available in various library communities and stored as normalized MARC 21. If this data store is deemed useful to the Friend Of A Friend (FOAF) community, the data can be turned into RDF. Similarly, Web services like Flickr could convert and makes use of Library of Congress Subject headings to augment both the searching and development of their folksonomies.

CONCLUSION

Berners-Lee suggested that, "The vast bulk of data to be on the Semantic Web is already sitting in databases . . . all that is needed [is] to write an adapter to convert a particular format into RDF and all the content in that format is available" (Updegrove, 2005). The data, metadata, and thesauri available in various library databases and systems present a unique opportunity to take a large step forward in the development of the Semantic Web.

The realization of the Semantic Web vision, which isn't too far from Berners-Lee's original vision for the World Wide Web itself, involves a remarkably broad set of goals. Part of the Semantic Web vision is about aiding resource discovery by creating tools to help searcher's refine and develop their searches, and to aid in the navigation of search results. These improvements will be augmented by the improved metadata that will result from making these same tools and vocabularies available to resource authors. Information professionals are too few in numbers to describe and catalog all of the Web's resources. Resource authors will have to play an active role in describing the materials they publish, perhaps having their descriptions refined and further developed by automated processes and by information professionals. Research in this area has been taking place in a variety of author communities, including scientific, government, and educational institutions (Greenberg & Robertson, 2002). Such collaborative efforts need not be limited to authors and metadata professionals. Other domain experts can add further descriptive information through the process of tagging and reviewing materials. This marriage of the folksonomy and controlled vocabularies would serve as a step towards what Peter Morville has elegantly referred to as "the Sociosemantic Web" (Morville, 2005).

Another large part of the Semantic Web vision is about enabling "agents" or systems to insert a searcher's/user's individual context or perspective into a search for information. This necessarily involves interacting with the elements that make up that context, such as schedules, contacts, group membership, profession, role, interests, hobbies, location, etc. Systems can then be developed that "understand" the searcher's needs, based on who the searcher is and the searcher's "context" or demographics. Developing this kind of machine understanding involves encoding the vast wealth of information available electronically in such a way that it can be negotiated according to a searcher's individual "context." Even if privacy issues hinder our ability to automate the incorporation of personal information into the "context" of a specific information interaction, there is still a tremendous amount of value in making external information sources more readily accessible for machine processing, and making the information more interoperable, easier to interpret and ultimately combined and used in novel and interesting ways. More importantly, even if it is possible to automate the user side of this process, there will undoubtedly be a user base that chooses not to trust these context-dependant decisions to Semantic Web "agents" described in Berners-Lee's writings. In the case of either of these two scenarios, the tools that support Semantic Web technology will still make most searchers' experiences more pleasant and much less frustrating.

ACKNOWLEDGEMENTS

The authors are indebted to the sound boarding, feedback, and editorial input of many people, and would particularly like to thank Lori Robare and Jane Greenberg for their input.

REFERENCES

Berners-Lee, T., Hendler, J., & Lassila, O. (2001). The Semantic Web [Electronic version]. *Scientific American*, 284 (5), 34-43. Retrieved April 15, 2002, from: http://www.sciam.com/article.cfm?articleID=00048144-10D2-1C70-84A9809EC588EF21.

Cataloging Distribution Service–Library of Congress. (2005). *MARC Distribution Services: Your Source for Machine Readable Cataloging Records via FTP*. Retrieved March 22, 2006, from: http://www.loc.gov/cds/mds.html.

DCMI Usage Board. (2005, January 10). *DCMI Metadata Terms*. Retrieved March 22, 2006, from: http://dublincore.org/documents/dcmi-terms/.

Dempsey, L., Childress, E., Godby, C. J., Hickey, T. B., Houghton, A., Vizine-Goetz, D., & Young, J. (2005). Metadata switch: thinking about some metadata management and knowledge organization issues in the changing research and learning landscape. Forthcoming in LITA guide to e-scholarship (working title), ed. Debra Shapiro. Retrieved April 15, 2006, from: http://www.oclc.org/research/publications/archive/2004/dempsey-mslitaguide.pdf.

Flickr. (2006). *Popular Tags on Flickr Photo Sharing*. Retrieved April 1, 2006, from: http://www.flickr.com/photos/tags/.

The Friend Of A Friend (FOAF) Project. (n.d.). Retrieved April 12, 2006, from: http://www.foaf-project.org/.

The Getty. (n.d.). Obtain the Getty Vocabularies. Retrieved March 22, 2006, from: http://www.getty.edu/research/conducting_research/vocabularies/license.html.

Greenberg, J. & Robertson, D. W. (2002) Semantic Web Construction: An Inquiry of Authors' Views on Collaborative Metadata Generation. In: *Metadata for e-Communities: Supporting Diversity and Convergence. Proceedings of the International*

Conference on Dublin Core and Metadata for e-Communities, 2002, Florence, Italy. October 13-17. Retrieved April 15, 2006, from: http://www.bncf.net/dc2002/program/ft/paper5.pdf.

Heery, R. & Patel, M. (2000). Application profiles: mixing and matching metadata schemas. *Ariadne*, 25 Retrieved April 24, 2006, from: http://www.ariadne.ac.uk/issue25/app-profiles/.

Hodge, G. (2000). *Systems of Knowledge Organization for Digital Libraries*. The Digital Library Federation. Retrieved April 12, 2006, from: http://www.clir.org/pubs/reports/pub91/contents.html.

IEEE Learning Technology Standards Committee. (2002, July). *Draft Standard for Learning Object Metadata*. Retrieved March 22, 2006, from: http://ltsc.ieee.org/wg12/files/LOM_1484_12_1_v1_Final_Draft.pdf.

Information Society Technologies. (2003). *InterParty*. Retrieved April 12, 2006, from: http://www.interparty.org/.

Joint DCMI/IEEE LTSC Taskforce. (2006, March). *DCMI Education Working Group Wiki*. Retrieved March 22, 2006, from: http://dublincore.org/educationwiki/DCMIIEEELTSCTaskforce.

Library of Congress. (2005, April 22). *MARCXML–MARC 21 XML Schema: Official Web Site*. Retrieved April 15, 2006, from: http://www.loc.gov/standards/marcxml/ (includes Test authority data for Classification, Names, and Subjects).

Library of Congress. (2005, December 14). *MADS–Metadata Authority Description Schema: Official Web Site*. Retrieved April 15, 2006, from: http://www.loc.gov/standards/mads/ (includes MARCXML Authorities to MADS crosswalk).

Library of Congress. (2006, June 13). *MODS: Metadata Object Description Schema*. Retrieved June 30, 2006, from: http://www.loc.gov/standards/mods/.

Lloret, R., & Piat, S. (2006). *Outline for ISO Standard ISPSI (International Standard Party Identifier)*. Retrieved April 12, 2006, from: http://www.collectionscanada.ca/iso/tc46sc9/docs/sc9n429.pdf.

Miles, A. (2005, May). *Quick Guide to Publishing a Thesaurus on the Semantic Web: W3C Working Draft* 17 May 2005. Retrieved April 15, 2006, from: http://www.w3.org/TR/2005/WD-swbp-thesaurus-pubguide-20050517/.

Miles, A., Mathews, B., Wilson, M., & Brickley, D. (2005, September) SKOS Core: Simple Knowledge Organisation for the Web In: *Proceedings of the International Conference on Dublin Core and Metadata Applications*, Madrid, Spain, 12-15 September 2005. p. 5-13. Retrieved April 15, 2006, from: http://www.slais.ubc.ca/PEOPLE/faculty/tennis-p/dcpapers/paper01.pdf.

Miller, E. (2004, October). The Semantic Web and Digital Libraries (Keynote presentation). In *International Conference on Dublin Core and Metadata Applications*, 2004. Shanghai, China, 11-14 October 2006. PowerPoint presentation retrieved April 1, 2006 from: http://dc2004.library.sh.cn/english/prog/ppt/talk.ppt.

Morris, S. (2003, September). *Virtual International Authority* [press release]. Retrieved April 15, 2006, from: http://www.loc.gov/loc/lcib/0309/authority.html.

Morville, P. (2005). *Ambient Findability. Sebastopol*, CA: O'Reilly.

Network Development and MARC Standards Office–Library of Congress. (2006, June 23). *MARC Code Lists for Relators, Sources, Description Conventions*. Retrieved June 30, 2006, from: http://www.loc.gov/marc/relators/.

Nilsson, M., Palmer, M., & Brase, J. (2003, November). The LOM RDF binding–principles and implementation. Paper presented at *The 3rd Annual Ariadne Conference*, Leuven, Belgium. Retrieved March 22, 2006, from: http://rubens.cs.kuleuven. ac.be/ariadne/CONF2003/papers/MIK2003.pdf.

North Carolina State University (NCSU) Libraries. (2006). *Endeca at the NCSU Libraries*. Retrieved March 6, 2006, from: http://www.lib.ncsu.edu/endeca/.

OCLC Research. (2006). *Terminology Services*. Retrieved March 22, 2006, from: http://www.oclc.org/research/projects/termservices/.

Tennis, J. (2005). SKOS and the Ontogenesis of Vocabularies. In *Proceedings of the International Conference on Dublin Core and Metadata Applications*, Madrid, Spain, 12-15 September 2005. Retrieved April 15, 2006, from: http://purl.org/dcpapers/2005/Paper33.

Tillett, B. (2001). Authority control on the Web. In *Proceedings of the Bicentennial Conference on Bibliographic Control for the New Millennium: Confronting the Challenges of Networked Resources and the Web*, Washington, D.C., November 15-17, 2000. Sponsored by the Library of Congress Cataloging Directorate. Edited by Ann M. Sandberg-Fox. Washington, D.C.: Library of Congress, Cataloging Distribution Service, p. 207-220. Retrieved April 15, 2006, from: http://www.loc.gov/catdir/bibcontrol/tillet_paper.html.

Simile. (2006). *Piggy Bank*. Retrieved March 22, 2006, from: http://simile.mit.edu/piggy-bank/.

Updegrove, A. (2005, June). The Semantic Web: An Interview with Tim Berners-Lee. *Consortium Standards Bulletin*, 5 (6), Retrieved February 9, 2006, from: http://www.consortiuminfo.org/bulletins/semanticweb.php.

Vizine-Goetz, D. (2004). Terminology services: Making knowledge organization schemes more accessible to people and computers. *OCLC Newsletter*, 266. Retrieved March 22, 2006, from http://www.oclc.org/news/publications/newsletters/oclc/2004/266/.

W3C Semantic Web Activity. (2004, February) *Simple Knowledge Organisation System (SKOS)*. Retrieved March 22, 2006, from: http://www.w3.org/2004/02/skos/.

doi:10.1300/J104v43n03_04

SKOS:
Simple Knowledge Organisation
for the Web

Alistair Miles
José R. Pérez-Agüera

SUMMARY. This article introduces the Simple Knowledge Organisation System (SKOS), a Semantic Web language for representing controlled structured vocabularies, including thesauri, classification schemes, subject heading systems, and taxonomies. SKOS provides a framework for publishing thesauri, classification schemes, and subject indexes on the Web, and for applying these systems to resource collections that are part of the Semantic Web. Semantic Web applications may harvest and merge SKOS data, to integrate and enhance retrieval service across multiple collections (e.g., libraries). This article also describes some alternatives for integrating Semantic Web services based on the Resource Description Framework (RDF) and SKOS into a distributed enterprise architecture. doi:10.1300/J104v43n03_05 *[Article copies available for a fee from The Haworth Document Delivery Service: 1-800-HAWORTH. E-mail address: <docdelivery@haworthpress.com> Website: <http://www.HaworthPress.com> © 2007 by The Haworth Press, Inc. All rights reserved.]*

The contributions of the members of the Semantic Web Interest Group mailing list public-esw-thes@w3.org are gratefully acknowledged.

[Haworth co-indexing entry note]: "SKOS: Simple Knowledge Organisation for the Web." Miles, Alistair, and José R. Pérez-Agüera. Co-published simultaneously in *Cataloging & Classification Quarterly* (The Haworth Information Press, an imprint of The Haworth Press, Inc.) Vol. 43, No. 3/4, 2007, pp. 69-83; and: *Knitting the Semantic Web* (ed: Jane Greenberg, and Eva Méndez) The Haworth Information Press, an imprint of The Haworth Press, Inc., 2007, pp. 69-83. Single or multiple copies of this article are available for a fee from The Haworth Document Delivery Service [1-800-HAWORTH, 9:00 a.m. - 5:00 p.m. (EST). E-mail address: docdelivery@haworthpress.com].

KEYWORDS. Knowledge Organization Systems, KOS, taxonomies, thesauri, classification schemes, glossaries, RDF, OWL, Semantic Web, Web services, software agents

INTRODUCTION

SKOS, Simple Knowledge Organization System, is a formal language for representing a controlled structured vocabulary. By "controlled structured vocabulary" we mean to include:

- **Thesauri** broadly conforming to the ISO 2788:1986 guidelines such as the UK Archival Thesaurus (UKAT, 2004), the General Multilingual Environmental Thesaurus (GEMET), and the Art and Architecture Thesaurus (AAT) (ISO 5964:1985).
- **Classification schemes** such as the Dewey Decimal Classification (DDC), the Universal Decimal Classification (UDC), and the Bliss Classification (BC2).
- **Subject heading systems** such as the Library of Congress Subject Headings (LCSH) and the Medical Subject Headings (MeSH).

A key feature of these vocabularies is that they are intended for use within information retrieval applications, i.e., they are used to describe items in a collection in a controlled way, allowing semantically precise and unambiguous retrieval.

SKOS is an application of the Resource Description Framework (RDF). Because RDF is a formal language that has well defined logical properties, any controlled structured vocabulary represented using SKOS is machine-understandable, i.e., a computer application can read it, "make sense" of it, and use it to provide functionalities such as rich visual search and browse user interfaces.

RDF is also the language of the Semantic Web. By design, RDF supports the distributed publication of data. This means that a controlled structured vocabulary (BS8723, 2004) published using SKOS can be linked to and/or merged with other data sources, such as subject indexes or other vocabularies. This enables, for example, the typical situation where a retrieval service is required across a number of separately maintained collections, to be implemented without complex database integration.

SKOS is under active development at the time of writing, within the scope of the W3C's Semantic Web Best Practices and Deployment

Working Group. The SKOS Core Guide (Miles and Brickley, 2005a) and the SKOS Core Vocabulary Specification (Miles and Brickley, 2005b), the two primary documents describing the usage of SKOS, are published as W3C Working Drafts.

This article gives three examples of the use of SKOS: a category taxonomy, a thesaurus, and a classification scheme. The examples are given in the RDF/XML serialization syntax (Beckett, 2004), although note that RDF may be serialized according to other syntaxes such as Turtle/N3. In prose, prefixes such as "skos:" are used to abbreviate URIs. The following table gives the prefix conventions used.

Prefix	URI
skos:	http://www.w3.org/2004/02/skos/core#
dc:	http://purl.org/dc/elements/1.1/
dct:	http://purl.org/dc/terms/
rdf:	http://www.w3.org/1999/02/22-rdf-syntax-ns#
rdfs:	http://www.w3.org/2000/01/rdf-schema#
owl:	http://www.w3.org/2002/07/owl#

Abbreviated URIs are underlined, for example, <u>skos:prefLabel</u> stands for the URI "http://www.w3.org/2004/02/skos/core#prefLabel." Note also that the xml:base attribute provides a URI base for relative URIs within an RDF/XML document.

A WEBLOG TAXONOMY IN RDF

```
<rdf:RDF
    xmlns:skos="http://www.w3.org/2004/02/skos/core#"
    xmlns:rdf="http://www.w3.org/1999/02/22-rdf-syntax-ns#"
  xmlns:dc="http://purl.org/dc/elements/1.1/"
    xml:base="http://www.wasab.dk/morten/blog/archives/author/mortenf/skos.rdf">

<skos:ConceptScheme rdf:about="#scheme">
<dc:title>Morten Frederiksen's Categories</dc:title>
<dc:description>Concepts from the weblog "Binary Relations" based on category
usage by Morten Frederiksen.</dc:description>
<dc:creator>Morten Frederiksen</dc:creator>
</skos:ConceptScheme>

<skos:Concept rdf:about="#c1">
<skos:prefLabel xml:lang="en">General</skos:prefLabel>
<skos:narrower rdf:resource="#c23"/>
<skos:narrower rdf:resource="#c30"/>
<skos:inScheme rdf:resource="#scheme"/>
</skos:Concept>

<skos:Concept rdf:about="#c23">
<skos:prefLabel xml:lang="en">Travelling</skos:prefLabel>
<skos:broader rdf:resource="#c1"/>
<skos:inScheme rdf:resource="#scheme"/>
</skos:Concept>
```

```
<skos:Concept rdf:about="#c30">
<skos:prefLabel xml:lang="en">Politics</skos:prefLabel>
<skos:broader rdf:resource="#c1"/>
<skos:inScheme rdf:resource="#scheme"/>
</skos:Concept>

</rdf:RDF>
```

The example above is adapted from Morten Frederiksen's Web log categories. Morten's categories are arranged in a category hierarchy, and include the following (Frederiksen, 2006):

General

   Travelling

   Politics

Morten uses these categories to organise the entries in his Web log–each entry can belong to one or more categories.

The SKOS representation of these categories is shown above. Each category is represented as a resource of type skos:Concept–this class is the basic building block of all SKOS descriptions. Each concept has a preferred label, given by the skos:prefLabel property. Note that the language ("en") has been given for the preferred labels–a concept may be given labels and annotations in multiple languages. Concepts are linked to other concepts via "semantic relation" properties, in this case the skos:broader and skos:narrower properties indicating a generalization/ specialization relationship. Finally, the concepts are all part of a "concept scheme," represented as a resource of type skos:ConceptScheme. The concepts are linked to the concept scheme in which they participate by the skos:inScheme property. Some descriptive metadata is also given using the Dublin Core Metadata Terms (DCMI Usage Board, 2003-2005).

A THESAURUS IN RDF

```
<rdf:RDF
 xmlns:rdf="http://www.w3.org/1999/02/22-rdf-syntax-ns#"
 xmlns:skos="http://www.w3.org/2004/02/skos/core#"
 xmlns:dc="http://purl.org/dc/elements/1.1/"
 xml:base="http://www.ukat.org.uk/thesaurus/concept/">

<skos:ConceptScheme rdf:about="http://www.ukat.org.uk/thesaurus">
<dc:title>The UK Archival Thesaurus</dc:title>
</skos:ConceptScheme>
```

```
<skos:Concept rdf:about="1750">
<skos:prefLabel xml:lang="en">Economic cooperation</skos:prefLabel>
<skos:altLabel xml:lang="en">Economic co-operation</skos:altLabel>
<skos:scopeNote>Includes cooperative measures in banking, trade, industry etc.,
between and among countries.</skos:scopeNote>
<skos:broader rdf:resource="4382"/>
<skos:narrower rdf:resource="2108"/>
<skos:narrower rdf:resource="9505"/>
<skos:narrower rdf:resource="15053"/>
<skos:narrower rdf:resource="18987"/>
<skos:related rdf:resource="3250"/>
<skos:inScheme rdf:resource="http://www.ukat.org.uk/thesaurus"/>
</skos:Concept>

</rdf:RDF>
```

The example above is adapted from an extract of the UK Archival Thesaurus (UKAT, 2004). The extract would typically be presented in the traditional thesaurus style as follows:

Economic cooperation

UF	Economic co-operation
BT	Economic policy
NT	Economic integration
NT	European economic cooperation
NT	European industrial cooperation
NT	Industrial cooperation
RT	Interdependence
SN	Includes cooperative measures in banking, trade, industry, etc., between and among countries.

The UKAT (2004) broadly conforms to the ISO 2788:1986 guidelines for the development and construction of thesauri. When representing such a thesaurus using SKOS, a URI must first be allocated to each of the *conceptual units* of the thesaurus, that is, to each unit of the thesaurus that has a distinct meaning. In this example, the URI "http://www.ukat.org.uk/thesaurus/concept/1750" has been allocated to the conceptual unit established by the descriptor "Economic cooperation." The use of URIs to uniquely and unambiguously refer to precise meanings is of course essential in a Semantic Web context, where data is being aggregated and merged from multiple sources.

The lexical value of a descriptor (i.e., the character string) is mapped to the literal value of the <u>skos:prefLabel</u> property in the appropriate language (in this case "en"). The lexical values of any non-descriptors are mapped to literal values of the skos:altLabel ("alternative label") property. Any annotations such as scope notes are mapped to the appropriate documentation property, in this case the skos:scopeNote property is used. Other documentation properties available include skos:definition, skos:historyNote, and skos:editorialNote. It is also possible to define custom documentation properties via the extensibility mechanisms used in SKOS (see below).

As in the previous example, the skos:narrower and skos:broader semantic relation properties have been used to indicate generalization/ specialization relationships. Also, the skos:related semantic relation property has been used–this property indicates an associative relationship between two concepts. Again, it is possible to define custom semantic relation properties via extensibility.

The example above only shows the RDF description of the single "Economic cooperation" concept. Of course, each of the narrower, broader, and related concepts linked from this concept would have its own RDF description, and these would all form part of the RDF description of the thesaurus as a whole.

A thesaurus such as the UKAT is typically used to construct a subject index over a collection of items. That is, the thesaurus is used to describe the subject matter of the items in a consistent, precise, and unambiguous way, which then enables precise and unambiguous searching. SKOS includes the properties skos:subject and skos:primarySubject for describing the subject matter of resources in a controlled way. The skos:subject property is very similar to the dc:subject property (in fact it is a sub-property of the latter), however, whereas the range of the dc:subject property is unconstrained, only resources of type skos:Concept may act as values to the skos:subject property. For example, the RDF/XML snippet below uses the "Economic cooperation" concept from the UKAT to describe the subject matter of a Web page.

```
<rdf:RDF
  xmlns:rdf="http://www.w3.org/1999/02/22-rdf-syntax-ns#"
  xmlns:skos="http://www.w3.org/2004/02/skos/core#">

  <rdf:Description rdf:about="http://www.example.com/money.html">
    <skos:subject rdf:resource="http://www.ukat.org.uk/thesaurus/concept/1750"/>
  </rdf:Description>

</rdf:RDF>
```

The skos:primarySubject property is a sub-property of skos:subject, and allows you to distinguish one concept as the primary or principal subject, where the subject matter of an item covers several concepts.

A CLASSIFICATION SCHEME IN RDF

The example below is adapted from an extract of the Physics and Astronomy Classification Scheme (PACS) (AIP, 2003).

```
<rdf:RDF
 xmlns:rdf="http://www.w3.org/1999/02/22-rdf-syntax-ns#"
 xmlns:skos="http://www.w3.org/2004/02/skos/core#"
 xmlns:dc="http://purl.org/dc/elements/1.1/"
 xml:base="http://www.w3.org/2001/sw/Europe/reports/thes/ns/pacs/" >

<skos:ConceptScheme rdf:about="http://www.w3.org/2001/sw/Europe/reports/thes/ns/pacs">
<dc:title>Physics and Astronomy Classification Scheme</dc:title>
<dc:creator>American Institute of Physics</dc:creator>
<skos:hasTopConcept rdf:resource="90."/>
</skos:ConceptScheme>

<skos:Concept rdf:about="90.">
<skos:prefLabel>GEOPHYSICS, ASTRONOMY, AND ASTROPHYSICS</skos:prefLabel>
<skos:narrower rdf:resource="91."/>
<skos:inScheme rdf:resource="http://www.w3.org/2001/sw/Europe/reports/thes/
ns/pacs"/>
</skos:Concept>

<skos:Concept rdf:about="91.">
<skos:prefLabel>Solid Earth physics</skos:prefLabel>
<skos:broader rdf:resource="90."/>
<skos:narrower rdf:resource="91.10.-v"/>
<skos:inScheme rdf:resource="http://www.w3.org/2001/sw/Europe/reports/thes/
ns/pacs"/>
</skos:Concept>

<skos:Concept rdf:about="91.10.-v">
<skos:prefLabel>Geodesy and gravity</skos:prefLabel>
<skos:broader rdf:resource="91."/>
<skos:narrower rdf:resource="91.10.Pp"/>
<skos:inScheme rdf:resource="http://www.w3.org/2001/sw/Europe/reports/thes/
ns/pacs"/>
</skos:Concept>

<skos:Concept rdf:about="91.10.Pp">
<skos:prefLabel>Gravimetric measurements and instruments</skos:prefLabel>
<skos:broader rdf:resource="91.10.-v"/>
<skos:inScheme rdf:resource="http://www.w3.org/2001/sw/Europe/reports/thes/
ns/pacs"/>
</skos:Concept>

</rdf:RDF>
```

This extract would normally be presented as follows:

90. GEOPHYSICS, ASTRONOMY, AND ASTROPHYSICS

91. Solid Earth physics

91.10.-v Geodesy and gravity

91.10.Pp Gravimetric measurements and instruments

Because each "class" or "category" in a classification scheme estab-
lishes a distinct meaning, a URI must be allocated for each. For example, in the above the URI "http://www.w3.org/2001/sw/Europe/reports/
thes/ns/pacs/91.10.-v" has been allocated to the "Geodesy and gravity"
category.

Although the conceptual units of a classification scheme are sometimes referred to as "classes" they are usually not "classes" in the
stricter logical sense, although they are used to "classify" documents by
their subject matter. Also, the hierarchical relationships between them
are usually not strict class subsumption relationships. Hence, it is inappropriate to model a classification scheme as a subsumption hierarchy
of RDFS or OWL classes (Dean and Schreiber, 2004). The SKOS notions of a "concept" and of a "broader/narrower" generalization hierarchy are a better fit, and help to avoid unexpected or inappropriate
inferences being drawn by RDFS or OWL reasoners.

The example above uses the same features previously described in
other examples. Namely the skos:Concept and skos:ConceptScheme
classes as the basic building blocks, the skos:prefLabel labelling property, and the skos:broader and skos:narrower semantic relation properties. This example also introduces the skos:hasTopConcept property,
which is used to explicitly indicate which concepts are the topmost in
the generalization hierarchy.

As with thesauri, the typical use of a classification scheme is to describe the subject matter of some items in a controlled and unambiguous
way. However, whereas a thesaurus is typically used to describe one or
more subjects of an item, a classification scheme is used to classify
items by their *primary subject*. Hence, when representing a subject classification in RDF (Miles, 2004), use the skos:primarySubject property.
Additional subjects can then be added using the skos:subject property,
without losing the unique classification by primary subject.

The snippet below illustrates the use of the skos:primarySubject
property to represent a subject classification of an item.

```
<rdf:RDF
 xmlns:rdf="http://www.w3.org/1999/02/22-rdf-syntax-ns#"
 xmlns:skos="http://www.w3.org/2004/02/skos/core#">

 <rdf:Description rdf:about="http://www.example.com/all-about-gravity.html">
 <skos:primarySubject
 rdf:resource=" http://www.w3.org/2001/sw/Europe/reports/thes/ns/pacs/91.10.-v"/>
 </rdf:Description>

</rdf:RDF>
```

EXTENDING SKOS

SKOS can be extended by refinement. This means that third parties can declare and use classes and/or properties that *refine* (i.e., are sub-classes or sub-properties of) SKOS classes or properties. The valid RDFS inferences can then be applied by anyone to *infer* a pure SKOS representation of a controlled structured vocabulary from a representation that uses custom refinement extensions. This strategy guarantees backwards compatibility for refinement extensions.

```
@prefix skos: <http://www.w3.org/2004/02/skos/core#>.
@prefix rdf: <http://www.w3.org/1999/02/22-rdf-syntax-ns#>.
@prefix rdfs: <http://www.w3.org/2000/01/rdf-schema#>.
@prefix x: <http://www.example.com/skos-extension#>.

x:prefScientificLabel a rdf:Property;
 rdfs:label 'preferred scientific label';
 rdfs:comment 'The preferred lexical label for scientists.'@en;
 rdfs:subPropertyOf skos:prefLabel;

 .

x:altScientificLabel a rdf:Property;
 rdfs:label 'alternative scientific label';
 rdfs:comment 'An alternative lexical label for scientists.'@en;
 rdfs:subPropertyOf skos:altLabel;

 .

x:prefNonScientificLabel a rdf:Property;
 rdfs:label 'preferred non-scientific label';
 rdfs:comment 'The preferred lexical label for non-scientists.'@en;
 rdfs:subPropertyOf skos:altLabel;

 .

x:altNonScientificLabel a rdf:Property;
 rdfs:label 'alternative non-scientific label';
 rdfs:comment 'An alternative lexical label for non-scientists.'@en;
 rdfs:subPropertyOf skos:altLabel;

 .
```

Any of the classes or properties in the SKOS Core Vocabulary can be extended in this way. For example, a controlled vocabulary might require different labels for different audiences, e.g., scientific and non-scientific users. In this case we can declare refinement extensions to the SKOS labelling properties skos:prefLabel and skos:altLabel, as shown above (N.B. the examples in this section use the Turtle syntax for RDF).

Once declared, the extensions can be used, as shown in the following box. In the example given, the custom labelling properties are used to attach scientific and non-scientific labels to the concept of "aspirin."

```
@prefix skos: <http://www.w3.org/2004/02/skos/core#>.
@prefix x: <http://www.example.com/skos-extension#>.
@prefix eg: <http://www.example.com/thesaurus#>.


eg:concept002 a skos:Concept;
  x:prefScientificLabel 'acetylsalicylic acid'@en;
  x:altScientificLabel '2-acetoxybenzoic acid'@en;
  x:prefNonScientificLabel 'aspirin'@en;

.
```

By drawing valid RDFS conclusions, we can then derive a pure
SKOS representation of the same concept, as shown below. Note that
only one of the four extension properties was declared as a sub-property
of skos:prefLabel–this ensured that, after all valid inferences are made,
there is still only one preferred lexical label in any given language (it
wouldn't make sense for something to have more than one "preferred"
label). When declaring refinement extensions, some care is required to
ensure that the conclusions they entail are all sensible.

```
@prefix skos: <http://www.w3.org/2004/02/skos/core#>.
@prefix eg: <http://www.example.com/thesaurus#>.

eg:concept002 a skos:Concept;
  skos:prefLabel 'acetylsalicylic acid'@en;
  skos:altLabel '2-acetoxybenzoic acid'@en;
  skos:altLabel 'aspirin'@en;

.
```

The same basic extension mechanism can also be used to construct
hybrid SKOS/OWL ontologies–that is, structured vocabularies that
have some features of an ontology and some features of a thesaurus or
classification scheme. Such hybrid ontologies are a compromise between the cost of creating and maintaining more precise semantics and
the benefits of richer search and browse applications. The example on
the following page is adapted from the Semantic Web Environmental
Directory (SWED).

INTEGRATION WITHIN AN ENTERPRISE ARCHITECTURE

How can SKOS support the use of controlled structured vocabularies
within a distributed enterprise software architecture?
    The simplest way to make a controlled vocabulary available within a
distributed environment is to publish the SKOS representation of the

entire vocabulary as a single RDF/XML document on an HTTP server. Any other component within the enterprise can then simply retrieve the vocabulary by issuing an HTTP GET request. However, if the vocabulary is large, this may not be a practical solution, because it forces every component to retrieve the entire vocabulary, even if it only needs a small part of it.

To solve this problem, the SKOS representation of the vocabulary can be made available via a SPARQL service. SPARQL Query is an RDF query language (W3C Candidate Recommendation at the time of writing), and allows data from one or more RDF graphs to be queried and selected, in a similar way to the relational query language SQL. The SPARQL Protocol gives network protocol bindings for a SPARQL service, i.e., it describes the network interactions that can be used to query a data source and obtain results. RDF toolkits can be expected to support SPARQL Query and Protocol off the shelf, which greatly simplifies the task of deploying a query service for a controlled vocabulary.

```
@prefix skos: <http://www.w3.org/2004/02/skos/core#>.
@prefix rdf: <http://www.w3.org/1999/02/22-rdf-syntax-ns#>.
@prefix rdfs: <http://www.w3.org/2000/01/rdf-schema#>.
@prefix owl: <http://www.w3.org/2002/07/owl#>.
@prefix foaf: <http://xmlns.com/foaf/0.1/>.
@prefix x: <http://www.example.com/ontology#>.

## Set up the framework

x:EnvironmentalOrganisation a owl:Class;
 rdfs:label 'Environmental Organisation';
 rdfs:comment 'The class of organisations whose core business has something to do
 with the natural environment.'.

x:topicOfInterest a owl:ObjectProperty;
 rdfs:label 'topic of interest';
 rdfs:comment 'The main topic of interest of an organisation.';
 rdfs:domain x:EnvironmentalOrganisation;
 rdfs:range x:TopicOfInterestConcept.

x:TopicOfInterestConcept a owl:Class;
 rdfs:label 'Topic of Interest Concept';
 rdfs:comment 'The class of concepts used to describe the topic of interest of an
 organisation.';
 rdfs:subClassOf skos:Concept.

x:activity a owl:ObjectProperty;
 rdfs:label 'activity';
 rdfs:comment 'The primary activity of an organisation.';
 rdfs:domain x:EnvironmentalOrganisation;
 rdfs:range x:ActivityConcept.

x:ActivityConcept a owl:Class;
 rdfs:label 'Activity Concept';
 rdfs:comment 'The class of concepts used to describe the activity of an
 organisation.';
 rdfs:subClassOf skos:Concept.
```

```
# Declare some activity and topic-of-interest concepts

x:topicConcept001 a x:TopicOfInterestConcept;
 skos:prefLabel 'Sustainable development';
 skos:narrower x:topicConcept010.

x:topicConcept010 a x:TopicOfInterestConcept;
 skos:prefLabel 'Ecotourism';
 skos:broader x:topicConcept001.

x:activityConcept002 a x:ActivityConcept;
 skos:prefLabel 'Education and training';
 skos:narrower x:activityConcept012.

x:activityConcept012 a x:ActivityConcept;
 skos:prefLabel 'Awareness raising';
 skos:broader x:activityConcept002.

# Now use all the above to describe an environmental organisation

x:org1 a x:EnvironmentalOrganisation;
 rdfs:label 'Society for Environmental Exploration (SEE)';
 x:topicOfInterest x:topicConcept001;
 x:activity x:activityConcept012;
 foaf:homepage <http://www.frontier.ac.uk/>.
```

A potential drawback to using a SPARQL service may be that, because SPARQL is a very general RDF query language, the query processor may not be optimized for tasks specific to a particular type of data and application. Controlled structured vocabularies are typically used within information retrieval applications, and therefore a similar set of operations is likely to be repeated. Also, for information retrieval applications, response time is an important factor in system acceptance, and therefore some form of optimization may be necessary.

An optimized data service for controlled vocabularies might use a number of techniques to provide fast and efficient access to the data. For example, hash tables could be used to map string values of lexical labels to programmatic objects representing concepts, hence providing a very efficient "entry" into a vocabulary structure. Because the functionalities are specialized, they are typically encapsulated within a custom programmatic interface, which could then be bound to concrete network and interaction protocols such HTTP and SOAP. Notably, it is quite reasonable to use an RDF encoding with, e.g., SOAP messages, and therefore SKOS and RDF can be used as a basis for data encoding at the interface level (Ogbuji, 2002). This type of solution provides a compromise between the need to provide specialized functionality and the use of standard data encodings and interaction protocols.

CONCLUSIONS

This article has introduced the Simple Knowledge Organisation System (SKOS), with examples of its use for the RDF representation of three types of controlled structured vocabulary: a taxonomy, a thesaurus, and a classification scheme. Controlled vocabularies are typically used to describe the subject matter of information resources in a consistent and unambiguous way, to enable semantically precise retrieval, and SKOS also provides basic support for representing a subject index or subject classification over a collection of items.

SKOS is, at the time of writing, a work in progress, and a number of outstanding issues remain. Although SKOS may become a W3C Recommendation, development is likely to continue until December 2007 before this may be achieved. Therefore, all comments, suggestions and feedback relating to practical experience and/or theoretical considerations are warmly welcomed, and should be sent to the public-esw-thes@w3.org mailing list.

REFERENCES

AIP (2003). American Institute of Physics. Physics and Astronomy Classification Scheme. American Institute of Physics.

Beckett, D., ed. (2004). RDF/XML Syntax Specification (Revised), W3C Recommendation 10 February 2004. World Wide Web Consortium. See <http://www.w3.org/TR/rdf-syntax-grammar/>.

Brickley and Guha R. V., eds. (2004). RDF Vocabulary Description Language 1.0: RDF Schema, W3C Recommendation 10 February 2004. World Wide Web Consortium. See <http://www.w3.org/TR/rdf-schema/>.

Brickley, D., Miller, L. (2005). FOAF Vocabulary Specification, Namespace Document 3 April 2005–(Back In Business Edition).

BS8723 (2004). Structured Vocabularies for Information Retrieval. BSI Public Draft.

Cross, P., Brickley, D., Koch, T. (2001). RDF Thesaurus Specification (draft). ILRT Technical Report Number 1011. Intitute for Learning Research Technology.

DCMI Usage Board. (2003). DCMI Grammatical Principles 2003-11-18. Dublin Core Metadata Initiative. See <http://dublincore.org/usage/documents/principles/>.

DCMI Usage Board. (2005). DCMI Metadata Terms 2005-06-13. DCMI Recommendation, Dublin Core Metadata Initiative. See <http://dublincore.org/documents/dcmi-terms/>.

Dean, M. and Schreiber, G., eds. (2004). OWL Web Ontology Language Reference, W3C Recommendation 10 February 2004. World Wide Web Consortium. See <http://www.w3.org/TR/owl-ref/>.

Frederiksen, M. (2006). SKOS Output from Binary Relations Weblog. See <http://www.wasab.dk/morten/blog/archives/author/mortenf/skos.rdf>.

Hayes, P. ed. (2004). RDF Semantics, W3C Recommendation 10 February 2004. World Wide Web Consortium. See <http://www.w3.org/TR/rdf-mt/>.

ISO 2788:1986. Documentation–Guidelines for the Establishment and Development of Monolingual Thesauri, 2nd ed.

ISO 5964:1985. Documentation–Guidelines for the Establishment and Development of Multilingual Thesauri, 2nd ed.

Jacobs, I. ed. (2005). World Wide Web Consortium Process Document, 14 October 2005. World Wide Web Consortium. See <http://www.w3.org/Consortium/Process/>.

Klyne, G. and Carroll, J. J. eds. (2004). Resource Description Framework (RDF): Concepts and Abstract Syntax, W3C Recommendation 10 February 2004. World Wide Web Consortium. See <http://www.w3.org/TR/rdf-concepts/>.

Kokkelink, S. and Schwanzl, R. (2002). Expressing Qualified Dublin Core in RDF/XML 2002-05-15. DCMI Proposed Recommendation, Dublin Core Metadata Initiative. See <http://dublincore.org/documents/dcq-rdf-xml/>.

Mail Archives for public-esw-thes@w3.org see <http://lists.w3.org/Archives/Public/public-esw-thes/>.

Manola, F. and Miller, E. eds. (2004). RDF Primer, W3C Recommendation 10 February 2004. World Wide Web Consortium. See <http://www.w3.org/TR/rdf-primer/>.

Matthews, B. M. and Miles, A. J. (2003). Review of RDF Thesaurus Work, A review and discussion of RDF schemas for thesauri, SWAD-Europe Deliverable 8.2. World Wide Web Consortium. See <http://www.w3.org/2001/sw/Europe/reports/thes/8.2/>.

Matthews, B. M., Wilson, M. D., Miller, K., and Ryssevik, J. (2001). Internationalising Data Access Through LIMBER. Proc. third international workshop on internationalisation of products and systems. See <http://epubs.cclrc.ac.uk/bitstream/401/Limber_IWIPS.pdf>.

McGuiness, D. L. and Van Harmelen, F. eds. (2004). OWL Web Ontology Language Overview, W3C Recommendation 10 February 2004. World Wide Web Consortium. See <http://www.w3.org/TR/owl-features/>.

Miles, A. J. (2004). RDF Encoding of Classification Schemes, SWAD-Europe Deliverable 8.5. World Wide Web Consortium. See <http://www.w3.org/2001/sw/Europe/reports/thes/8.5/>.

Miles, A. J. and Brickley, D. eds. (2005a). SKOS Core Guide, W3C Editor's Working Draft 15 February 2005. World Wide Web Consortium. See <http://www.w3.org/TR/swbp-skos-core-guide/>.

Miles, A. J. and Brickley, D. eds. (2005b). SKOS Core Vocabulary Specification, W3C Editor's Working Draft 2005-04-27. World Wide Web Consortium. See <http://www.w3.org/TR/swbp-skos-core-spec/>.

Ogbuji, U. (2002). Using RDF with SOAP: beyond remote procedure calls. See <http://www-106.ibm.com/developerworks/webservices/library/ws-soaprdf/>.

Powell, A. et al., eds. (2001). Namespace Policy for the Dublin Core Metadata Initiative (DCMI) 2001-10-26. DCMI Recommendation, Dublin Core Metadata Initiative. See <http://dublincore.org/documents/dcmi-namespace/>.

Smith, M. K., Welty, C., and McGuiness, D. L. eds. (2004). OWL Web Ontology Language Guide, W3C Recommendation 10 February 2004. World Wide Web Consortium. See <http://www.w3.org/TR/owl-guide/>.

SW Best Practice. (2001). Semantic Web Best Practices and Deployment Working Group homepage, see <http://www.w3.org/2001/sw/BestPractices/>.

SWAD-E. (2001). The SEMANTIC Web Advanced Development for Europe project homepage. See <http://www.w3.org/2001/sw/Europe/>.

UKAT, (2004). The UK Archival Thesaurus, 2004. See <http://www.ukat.org.uk/>.

W3C-Glosary. (2004). Glossary from World Wide Web Consortium Process Document in RDF. See <http://www.w3.org/2003/03/glossary-project/data/glossaries/Process.rdf>. W3C Glossary and Dictionary Project. World Wide Web Consortium.

doi:10.1300/J104v43n03_05

Scheme Versioning in the Semantic Web

Joseph T. Tennis

SUMMARY. This paper describes a conceptual framework and methodology for managing scheme versioning for the Semantic Web. The first part of the paper introduces the concept of vocabulary encoding schemes, distinguished from metadata schemas, and discusses the characteristics of changes in schemes. The paper then presents a proposal to use a value record–similar to a term record in thesaurus management techniques–to manage scheme versioning challenges for the Semantic Web. The conclusion identifies future research directions. doi:10.1300/J104v43n03_06 *[Article copies available for a fee from The Haworth Document Delivery Service: 1-800-HAWORTH. E-mail address: <docdelivery@haworthpress.com> Website: <http://www.HaworthPress.com> © 2007 by The Haworth Press, Inc. All rights reserved.]*

KEYWORDS. Indexing, classification, versioning, controlled vocabulary management, indexing language management

STRUCTURES IN THE SEMANTIC WEB

The Semantic Web is a collection of structures that work together (or interoperate). These structures constrain the range of possible interpretations in order to enable the transfer of meaning across the Web.

[Haworth co-indexing entry note]: "Scheme Versioning in the Semantic Web." Tennis, Joseph T. Co-published simultaneously in *Cataloging & Classification Quarterly* (The Haworth Information Press, an imprint of The Haworth Press, Inc.) Vol. 43, No. 3/4, 2007, pp. 85-104; and: *Knitting the Semantic Web* (ed: Jane Greenberg, and Eva Méndez) The Haworth Information Press, an imprint of The Haworth Press, Inc., 2007, pp. 85-104. Single or multiple copies of this article are available for a fee from The Haworth Document Delivery Service [1-800-HAWORTH, 9:00 a.m. - 5:00 p.m. (EST). E-mail address: docdelivery@haworthpress. com].

Schemas and schemes work together to constrain meaning. Schemas are the total set of assertions that can be made about a resource. A resource is anything that is addressable on the Web. For example, a surrogate for a person is a resource as much as a Web page is a resource. Both of these are addressable by URIs–Uniform Resource Identifiers (Connolly, 2006). The Dublin Core Element Set Version 1.1 (ISO Standard 15836-2003) is a particular type of schema. See Table 1.

1. Title
2. Creator
3. Subject
4. Description
5. Publisher
6. Contributor
7. Date
8. Type
9. Format
10. Identifier
11. Source
12. Language
13. Relation
14. Coverage
15. Rights

TABLE 1. Fifteen Elements Dublin Core Element Set–An Example of a Schema

Schemas work with schemes. Schemes are the range of values that can be provided for an assertion about a resource (date-time format, authority list, controlled vocabulary, etc.). There are two types of schemes: Vocabulary encoding schemes and Syntax encoding schemes. Vocabulary encoding schemes indicate that the value is a term from an indexing language, such as the value "China–History" from the Library of Congress Subject Headings. Syntax encoding schemes indicate that the value is a string formatted in accordance with a formal notation, such as the ISO 8601 date-time format, "2000-01-01" as the standard expression of a date. An example of the value taken from Vocabulary encoding scheme is given in Table 2 below.

3. Subject	Eugenics

TABLE 2. Value Provided for the Subject Elements in the DCES

This value, *eugenics*, came from a vocabulary encoding scheme. It came from the Library of Congress Subject Headings (LCSH). We could have taken the same subject from a different vocabulary encoding scheme, the Dewey Decimal Classification, for example. That might look like this, in Table 3 below:

3. Subject	176

TABLE 3. Value Provided for the Subjet Element of the DCES

As we can see from these examples, schemas allow us to say that a resource has an attribute (a subject), and a scheme allows us to make explicit what that subject is (the value of that attribute). However, we can also see another level of complexity that arises from this act of metadata creation.

We must now say where this value comes from. Furthermore, it is not enough to say that the value in Table 3 came from the Dewy Decimal Classification (DDC), but we also have to say what edition of the DDC. In so doing, we cite a place that one can reference this value. Furthermore, by declaring one edition instead of another, we also call into question the potential and demonstrable change in meaning from edition to edition, such that notation 176 (hereafter all occurrences of three digits together, or three digits followed by a decimal are DDC notations) in DDC means something different in different editions. The same can be said of terms in the relative index, and their position in the schedules. Table 4 provides an example how eugenics has changed in discipline and other characteristics in DDC.

Eugenics		100	300	500	600
Year	Edition and relative index entry				
1911	7th			575.6	
1942	14th rev. enl.				
	Eugenic method crimol.		364.3018		
	crime prevention		364.42		
	evolution			575.1	
	hygiene				613.94
	mental psychology	136.3			

Eugenics		100	300	500	600
Year	*Edition and relative index entry*				
1958	**16th**			613.94	
	Eugenic practices crime prevention		364.42		
	Hygiene				613.94
		[301.323 officially killed]	[575.1 officially killed]		
2003	**22nd**	363.92			
	crime prevention		363.4		
	ethics	176			
	health				613.94
	social services		363.92		
	sterilization services		363.97		

TABLE 4. Eugenics in Four DDC Schedules

In this table we see eugenics contextualized in disciplines, and refined with additional words. We can speculate on the many reasons why eugenics has changed over the years. DDC does provide us with some general reasons for change (OCLC, 2006). We can interpret, in this case, that different aspects of eugenics have surfaced over the years, the term has been used in different ways in the literature (and DDC wants to reflect that change both in scholarship and in viewpoint), and they want to reduce bias. To reflect these differences, the entry for eugenics in the relative index points to many different places in schedules–and in some cases, no longer points to places it once did.

In Semantic Web applications using DCES, we might use many versions of a scheme. For example, in a hundred years of creating metadata for resources we are likely to go through as many versions of DDC as we have in the past hundred years. We would then see instances of metadata from DDC 22 through DDC 37, and it is also possible, with digitization projects, to see resources with metadata back to DDC 7 online. Further, DDC is not the only scheme that goes through revisions. Every vocabulary encoding scheme that is kept up to date is revised. They are revised so they can maintain their purpose: to retrieve documents; or to couch it in terms of bibliographic control: to find, collocate, and identify resources.

If schemes are used to find, collocate, and identify items in the Semantic Web applications, like they are in catalogues, then we must be sensitive to the versioning of these schemes, and the changes affecting the values from these schemes. In some domains, schemes change even more rapidly than DDC, and in a distributed networked environment, managing the semantics of these changes is vital to the functioning and utility of these schemes. To that end, scheme versioning is a management activity that requires a conceptual framework and a methodology. It is important that this conceptual framework and methodology are in place before more metadata is created. As we have learned for electronic records systems, the conceptual models must be built into the metadata for the system to fulfill its purpose (Duranti, Eastwood, and MacNeil, 2002).

This paper looks at the conceptual framework and one consequent methodology in order to aid interoperability on the Semantic Web synchronically and diachronically–at one point in time, but also through time.

METHODOLOGIES AND CONCEPTUAL FRAMEWORKS FOR SCHEME CHANGE

The methodologies for scheme versioning management might be simple or they might need to be more robust. It is possible that noting a change is enough in some contexts. This depends on the purpose of the scheme, the system that employs the scheme, and the professionals and users engaged with the system. For example, if the purpose of the scheme were to represent the subject matter of a resource coextensively (completely and expressing every aspect of the subject), then professionals and users alike would benefit from a robust scheme version management methodology–one where differences and similarities between the old and the new scheme were made explicit. If the scheme were not semantically rich (not used to represent many aspects of the resources, for example), then a less robust scheme version management methodology might be all that was required.

Regardless of methodology, scheme version management requires a conceptual framework in order to understand (1) the phenomenon of change in schemes, (2) what characteristics of change need to be made explicit in a methodology to manage this change, (3) to serve the purpose of scheme viability through versioning. Scheme viability is an important consideration here. Schemes are built for particular purposes, and versioning should not change those purposes. If anything, the purposes of schemes should be strengthened through change. Managing that change will ensure constant and consistent improvement. The follow section outlines the conceptual framework of scheme change.

CONCEPTUAL FRAMEWORK FOR SCHEME CHANGE

This section outlines the characteristics of scheme change in order to better represent the phenomenon of scheme change. We address change in relation to scheme viability at the end of this section.

Characteristics of Scheme Change

Scheme change occurs in three general categories: structural change, word-use change, and textual change. Structural change deals with the relationship structures in schemes and how editors alter them. Word-use change affects definitions, word forms, lead-in terms, etc. Though both structural changes and word-use changes are semantic, the latter do not explicitly affect relationship structures. Textual changes can affect both structural and word-use changes. Textual changes are changes in the interpretation and assignment of values to types of resources. The first two fall into the purview of the editors, while the third falls to both the editor and indexers. The following characteristics of scheme changes are adapted from Soergel (1974), Aitchison, Gilchrist, and Bawden (2000), Ranganathan (1967), and Beghtol (1986).

Structural Change

Structural changes affect a user's navigation through the scheme. Structural changes affect the semantics of a scheme because they change the relationships that obtain between values in that scheme. Structural change falls into five basic changes.[1] The five basic changes are:

- Addition of a new value
- Change in synonym structure (use eugenics to lead to both genetics and psychology)
- Change in equivalence structures (e.g., USE and/or USED FOR)
- Assignment of value to another group in the hierarchy
- Addition or elimination of associative relationship (e.g., RT).

The degree to which these changes affect indexing or classification is dependent on the purpose and structure of the scheme before the change.

That is, if a scheme is a thesaurus built on principles of mutual exclusivity (only one place for each concept–no overlap) then these changes are dramatic. If the scheme is not built on principles of mutual exclusivity, then navigation is hindered, but not confounded through these changes. In either case, it is desirable in a digital environment–in a Semantic Web–to track these characteristics of change in order to mange the meaning communicated through indexing and retrieval process.

Word-Use Change

The second type of change is word-use change. Word-use changes do not affect navigation through the structure. They are changes that preserve the structure of a scheme, while adding or replacing words. This may affect indexing practice, but it does not affect the scheme structurally. Word-use changes are:

- New word used as lead-in
- New synonyms added (replaced one for one, for example, *genetics* for *eugenics*)
- New preferred value added
- Change in definition of value

Like structural changes, combinations of these changes can occur. The effect of word-use on scheme versioning is powerful. In our example of eugenics, the lead-in terms, the synonyms, and the definition all affect the use of the value. Eugenics has been a concept that has affected a number of areas of science, social science, and philosophy. How words are used to present this concept affect the way it will be used by the indexer. One can also imagine a scenario where a value may be present in the scheme, but not used because of the definition. If this remains a constant in the use of the scheme, then this has ramifications for the structure. The value may disappear for example if its not used. So it is not structure alone that affects structural changes. Textual changes also affect structural changes, as well as word-use changes.

Textual Changes

Textual changes are changes in the relationships between texts and a version of the scheme. There are two primary types of textual changes. The first is textual warrant change and the second is the document-set change. Textual warrant is a term that is close to literary warrant–but does not mean the same thing. Textual warrant is the combination of all texts (literature of the field, user studies, search logs, checklists, etc.) that would be used to create a value or relationship in a scheme. Soergel calls these sources and authorities (Soergel, 1974). Any change in this collection of texts results in a change of the evidence considered when managing the scheme, and hence managing changes to the scheme.

The second kind of textual change is the document-set change. In this case a set of documents has been indexed and given a value (for example, 575.6). This set will change as the scheme changes, and therefore shifting the representation power of the scheme. So the texts once classed under 575.6 are not the same kind of texts, because the relationship between the document set and the value has changed.[2]

Scheme Viability

Schemes are built for the purpose of information retrieval–to find, collocate, and identify resources. They do this by establishing a set of values and relationships between values. Changes to a scheme must strengthen this purpose, yet in the context of multiple versions of schemes, it is not always clear what values mean, and what relationships obtain between values. A clear methodology of tracking changes made to values in schemes enables a scheme to carry out its mission across various versions.

Methodology

How does one track these changes? In order to track changes, each value must be identified as an entity in relation to other values at a point in time. Also, each characteristic of change must be accounted for–so that structural, word-use, and textual changes can be made explicit. To create an explicit statement about values in this way is to create a value record, like a term record used in thesaurus construction and maintenance. The next section identifies the components of a value record for the purpose of tracking changes in schemes.

VALUE RECORDS

Scheme versioning, tracked through changes in values, can be managed with value records, an expansion on term records. Thesaurus management manuals and standards suggest the use of a term record to manage values (Soergel, 1974; Aitchison, Gilchrist, and Bawden, 2000;

ANSI/NISO, 2005; Anderson and Perez-Carballo, 2005a). An edited example of Soergel's term record is provided in Table 5 below.

01. Hierarchical Level	01. When terms are later sorted into hierarchies, based on BT and NT descriptors, each term will fall at a particular hierarchical level.
02. Type: DS, OP, NP, EL, CH	02. These codes indicate the current status of the main term in field 10: DS = descriptor (authorized term); OP = other preferred term (but not adopted as an authorized descriptor); NP = non-preferred term; EL = eliminate term; CH = change term information.
03. Subject Field	03. In order to find different terms indicating the same, or essentially the same concept, terms must be sorted conceptually. The subject field is the first large category for conceptual sorting. For faceted thesauri, these first level categories will be the main facets.
05. Notation	05. Later, when cards are sorted into final conceptual order, a notation can be assigned to maintain this order.
10. MT	10. This is the main term for this card. All the information on the card will relate to this term.
12. Standard Abbreviation	12. A standard abbreviation for a term is often helpful to indexers, who can use it to save time. Later, before an index is prepared for users, most abbreviations would be expanded to the full standard form. (Abbreviations can be the standard form when they are better known, as with acronyms such as "radar" and "Unesco.")
20. Variant Spellings	20. Variant spellings go here (as well as variant abbreviations).
30. Synonymous Terms (ST), including Equivalent Terms (ET)	30. Synonymous and equivalent terms go here.
40. Classification	
42. Category (CA)	40./42. This field can be used for finer categorization within the broad subject field, noted in field 03.
44. Broader Terms (BT)	44. Broader terms go here.
45. Narrower Terms	45. Narrower terms go here.
46. Related Terms	46. Related terms go here.
50. Translations	50. If the thesaurus is to be multilingual, than the equivalent terms in others languages go here.
60. Definition, Scope Note	60. A definition of the term, if needed, or a scope note explaining the usage of the term in the indexing language, goes here.
65. Sources/Authorities	65. Here is recorded the source of the term, or the authority for the definition/scope note.
70. Unspecified Relation (UN)	70. Any terms whose relationship to the main term has not yet been determined can go here.
81. Editor/Date	81. The name or initials of the thesaurus editor, plus the date, go here.

TABLE 5. Soergel's Term Record from Anderson and Perez-Carballo (2005b)

In this term record Soergel has given each area its own numerical notation. The 0x area uses numerical codes to place this term record in relation to others. 1x area identifies the main term. 2x variant spellings, 3x identifies types of equivalence relationships, 4x syndectic relationships (broader, narrower, and related terms), 5x translations if needed, 6x definition, scope note, and sources/authorities that give the term meaning,

7x provides a space for terms with unspecified relationships to the main term, and 8x, identifies the author and date of creation for this thesaurus. As can be seen from the comments on the right side of the table, this term record is used primarily for the creation of thesauri. Yet we could easily transfer these areas to other types of schemes besides thesauri, and identify values instead of terms. These features could be used as starting points for creating a value record that would account for characteristics of scheme change. We would make some additions. For example, Aitchison, Gilchrist, and Bawden (2000, 148-149) suggest an additional field: Frequency of Occurrence. This would identify how many times the value has been used. Another aid to creating a value record is the SKOS specification.

SKOS–Simple Knowledge Organisation System is a w3c area of work that develops specifications and standards to support the use of schemes in the Semantic Web (Miles, n.d.). SKOS creates these specifications in line with RDF (Miller, Swick, and Brickely, 2006) and OWL, two other w3c metadata recommendations. SKOS provides a set of assertions that can be interpreted as a value record. Table 6 outlines a selection of the SKOS assertions.

Types of Labels	
skos:prefLabel,	Preferred label for a concept
skos:altLabel,	Alternative label of a concept
skos:hiddenLabel,	Hidden label accessible to applications only for search
Types of Notes	
skos:definition	A complete explanation of the intended meaning of a concept
skos:scopeNote	Some, possibly partial, information about the intended meaning and/or use of a concept, which can be phrased as information about what is or isn't included within the meaning ('scope') of the concept.
skos:example	An example of the use of a concept
skos:historyNote	Instructions or useful information for users of the scheme, specifically relating to significant changes to the meaning/form/state of a concept.
skos:editorialNote	Information that is an aid to administrative housekeeping, such as reminders of editorial work still to be done, or warnings in the event that future editorial changes might be made.
skos:changeNote	Fine-grained changes to a concept, for the purposes of administration and maintenance.
Types of Relationships	
skos:semanticRelation	
skos:broader	Broader relationship
skos:narrower	Narrower relationship
skos:related	Associative relationship

TABLE 6. SKOS Assertions

SKOS provides some of the same assertions as Soergel, for example, the Types of Labels mimic his term record. Yet, in Table 6 we see more fields designed to manage change in a scheme. The Types of Notes assertions provide history notes, editorial notes, and change notes. These structures provide us with information on versioning. Thus the Soergel term record provides us information on relationships and definitions, the Types of Notes in SKOS provide us with the ability to create evidence of change. The combination of these two sets of assertion, these records, will allow us to make explicit relationship between values in different versions of schemes. These are the first steps in managing scheme versioning.

The next step for the effective use of a value record is to create explicit statement of these characteristics. The next section combines the Soergel and SKOS term records, with suggestions from Aitchison, Gilchrist, and Bawden to create a value record–a record that can account for scheme change.

Scheme Change Value Record

If we were to combine elements from the value records above, and make explicit in these records how to handle the characteristics of scheme change, we would be one step close to managing semantic change on the Semantic Web. Table 7 outlines what a value record would look like if it accounted for the characteristics of scheme change. The major changes are shown in italics.

01. Hierarchical Level	01. When values are later sorted into hierarchies, based on BT and NT descriptors, each value will fall at a particular hierarchical level.
02. Type: DS, OP, NP, EL, CH	02. These codes indicate the current status of the main value in field 10. For example in a thesaurus we might have: DS = descriptor (authorized term); OP = other preferred term (but not adopted as an authorized descriptor); NP = non-preferred term; EL = eliminate term; CH = change term information (which can be subdivided by versioning or not versioning)
03. Subject Field	03. In order to find different values indicating the same, or essentially the same concept, terms must be sorted conceptually. The subject field is the first large category for conceptual sorting. For faceted thesauri, these first level categories will be the main facets.
04. Classification	04 This field can be used for finer categorization within the broad subject field, noted in field 03.
05. Conceptual Notation	05. Later, when cards are sorted into final conceptual order, a notation can be assigned to maintain this order.

06. Scheme	06. Scheme name and identifier (citation to the scheme or a URI).
07. Version of the Scheme	07. Version of the scheme. For example Edition 22 of the DDC.
08. Date of Version of Scheme	08. Date of Version of Scheme
09. Accession Number	09. A unique number given to the value record when it is created.
10. Main Value	10. This is the main value (term) for this card. All the information on the card will relate to this value (term).
11. Version Number	11. Version of the value (corresponding to the scheme, but attached here to each term). For example, 22 for edition 22 of DDC.
12. Standard Abbreviation	12. A standard abbreviation for a value is often helpful to indexers, who can use it to save time. Later, before an index is prepared for users, most abbreviations would be expanded to the full standard form. (Abbreviations can be the standard form when they are better known, as with acronyms such as "radar" and "Unesco.")
15. First Addition Version Number	15. Version number of value when term was added. (May be redundant to 11 until changes occur)
16. Deletion Version Number	16. Version number of value when it was deleted.
18. Addition of Main Value	18. Main value and version number of value (May be redundant with 10, until changes occur).
19. Deletion of Main Value	19. Main value and version number of value.
20. Variant Spellings	20. Variant spellings go here (as well as variant abbreviations).
30. Synonymous Values	30. Synonymous and equivalent values go here.
31. Equivalent Values	31. Equivalent Values go here.
32. Addition of Synonyms	32. Synonyms and version number of value.
33. Deletion of Synonyms	33. Synonyms and version number of value.
34. Addition of Equivalence Structure	34. Equivalent value and version number of the value.
35. Deletion of Equivalence Structure	35. Equivalent value and version number of the value
36. Addition of Lead-in Values	
37. Deletion of Lead-in Values	
40. Broader Values	40. Broader values go here.
41. Narrower Values	41. Narrower values go here.
42. Related Values	42. Related values go here.
43. Addition of Broader Values	43. Broader value and version number the value.
44. Deletion of Broader Values	44. Broader value and version number the value.
45. Addition of Narrow Values	45. Narrower value and version number of the value.
46. Deletion of Narrow Values	46. Narrower value and version number of the value.
47. Addition of Related Values	47. Related Value and version number of the value.
48. Deletion of Related Values	48. Related Value and version number of the value.
50. Translations	50. If the scheme is to be multilingual, than the equivalent values in others languages go here.
60. Definition	60. A definition of the value
61. Scope Note	61. Scope note explaining the usage of the value in the indexing language, goes here.

62. History Note	62. Instructions or useful information for users of the scheme, specifically relating to significant changes to the meaning/form/state of a value.
63. Change Note	63. Narrative of changes to a value, for the purposes of administration and maintenance.
64. Editorial Note	64. Information that is an aid to administrative housekeeping, such as reminders of editorial work still to be done, or warnings in the event that future editorial changes might be made.
65. Sources/Authorities	65. Here is recorded the source of the term, or the authority for the definition/scope note.
66. Addition of Sources/Authorities	66. Sources/Authorities for the value and its version
67. Deletion of Sources/Authorities	67. Source/Authorities for the value and its version.
68. Addition of Definition	68. Definition and version number of the definition (from main value record)
69. Deletion of Definition	69. Definition and version number of the definition (from main value record)
70. Unspecified Relation (UN)	70. Any terms whose relationship to the main term has not yet been determined.
80. Editor	80. The name of the scheme editor
81. Record Creator	81. The name of the value record creator
86. Contact Information	86. Contact information for the scheme editor
87. Date Record Created	87. Date the record was created.
90. Information System(s)	90. Information system(s) that use this value (and its URI)
91. Frequency of Use	91. Number of times value has been used
92. Document-Set Date	92. Date Document-Set was created
93. Document-Set Resources	93. Set of documents indexed by the value. Provide the citations and if possible locators for these resources

TABLE 7. A Value Record

The Soergel term record has been rearranged slightly to bring the areas of the value record into a more meaningful sequence. As can be seen from Table 7 above, changes in schemes are operationalized as simple additions and deletions. In order to track the changes a scheme goes through, a value record should track the additions and deletions of values in relation to other values, word-use attached to the value, and its link to texts (both texts indexed and sources for values). The following section describes how structural, word-use, and textual change can be reflected in an example value record modeled off of Table 7 above.

The Value Record and Characteristics of Scheme Change

In order to make the term record meaningful to scheme version management, we first have to add a version number to each value in a scheme.

This appears as assertion 11 in the value record–Table 7. This allows us to track each value as a separate entity, but still tied with all other entities in the same version of the scheme (assertion 06 and 07 Scheme and Version of Scheme respectively).

Structural Change Reflected in the Value Record

All five types of structural changes are represented in the value record. These assertions should be repeatable as often as needed. To reflect the addition of a new value to a scheme, the editor can use assertion 15 Addition of Value and signify the version number, placing it in a sequence with other values. To change synonym structure addition and deletion happens in assertions 32 and 33 (Addition and Deletion of Synonyms). The same goes for equivalence structures in assertion 34 and 35, and associative relationships in assertion 47 and 48. In order to show a change in hierarchical grouping the value must be deleted from one set of broader and narrower relationships to a new set. This requires four types of assertions: addition and deletion from broader values, and addition and deletion of narrower values (assertions 43-46).

Word-Use Change

Changes in word-use are similar, in that they follow the addition/deletion format. So that new lead-in values, new synonyms, new preferred values, and changes in definitions. These additions and deletions are above in assertions 36-37, 32-33, 18-19, and 68-69 respectively.

Textual Change

Textual changes are reflected through sources and authorities and in document sets created at a particular point in time. For Textual Warrant change, assertions 66 and 67 (Addition and Deletion of Sources/Authorities) make explicit which sources and authorities were used for which version of the value. For Document-Set Changes, once the frequency of use is added (assertion 91), then it is possible to compare this number with set of documents (or resources) that are and have been indexed with this particular value. The set of documents is represented in assertion 93, Document-Set Resources, and it is dated in assertion 92, Document-Set Date.

Example: Value Record of Eugenics in DDC

In order to illustrate the addition and deletion aspects of the value record, we present examples using the value 613.94, from the DDC. The first, in Table 8, points to a hypothetical record for a value created for the 1942 14th revised and enlarged edition of the DDC. Table 9 that follows is a value record created for the 22nd edition.

01. Hierarchical Level	
02. Type: DS, OP, NP, EL, CH	DS
03. Subject Field	Medical Sciences
04. Classification	613.94
05. Conceptual Notation	613.94
06. Scheme	Decimal Classification
07. Version of the Scheme	14th Revised Enlarged Edition
08. Date of Version of Scheme	1942
09. Accession Number	
10. Main Value	613.94
11. Version Number	14 rev. enl.
12. Standard Abbreviation	N/A
15. First Addition Version Number	14 rev. enl.
16. Deletion Version Number	
18. Addition of Main Value	613.94
19. Deletion of Main Value	
20. Variant Spellings	
30. Synonymous Values	Stirpiculture. Eugenics.
31. Equivalent Values	
32. Addition of Synonyms	
33. Deletion of Synonyms	
34. Addition of Equivalence Structure	
35. Deletion of Equivalence Structure	
36. Addition of Lead-in Values	Eugenics (from Relativ Index 14th rev enl edition)
37. Deletion of Lead-in Values	
40. Broader Values	613.9 Hygiene of Offspring. Heredity.
41. Narrower Values	
42. Related Values	613.91 Congenital Defects of the Body
42. Related Values	613.92 Inherited Mental Disability
42. Related Values	613.93 Transmitted Disease
42. Related Values	Heredity in 575.1

43. Addition of Broader Values	
44. Deletion of Broader Values	
45. Addition of Narrow Values	
46. Deletion of Narrow Values	
47. Addition of Related Values	
48. Deletion of Related Values	
50. Translations	
60. Definition	
61. Scope Note	Stirpiculture. Eugenics. [editors might see more than what is in the schedule]
62. History Note	
63. Change Note	
64. Editorial Note	
65. Sources/Authorities	
66. Addition of Sources/Authorities	
67. Deletion of Sources/Authorities	
68. Addition of Definition	
69. Deletion of Definition	
70. Unspecified Relation (UN)	
80. Editor	Constantin J. Mazney, editor; Myron Warren Getchell. associate editor.
81. Record Creator	Joseph T. Tennis
86. Contact Information	
87. Date Record Created	2006-04-01
90. Information System(s)	
91. Frequency of Use	
92. Document-Set Date	
93. Document-Set Resources	

TABLE 8. Value Record for a Class14th Revised and Enlarged Edition of DDC

01. Hierarchical Level	
02. Type: DS, OP, NP, EL, CH	DS
03. Subject Field	Technology–Medicine and Health–Personal Health and Safety
04. Classification	613.94
05. Conceptual Notation	613.94
06. Scheme	Dewey Decimal Classification
07. Version of the Scheme	22nd Edition
08. Date of Version of Scheme	2003

09. Accession Number	
10. Main Value	613.94
11. Version Number	22
12. Standard Abbreviation	
15. First Addition Version Number	14 rev. enl.
16. Deletion Version Number	N/A
18. Addition of Main Value	613.94
19. Deletion of Main Value	
20. Variant Spellings	
30. Synonymous Values	Birth control and reproductive technology
31. Equivalent Values	363.96 22nd
32. Addition of Synonyms	
33. Deletion of Synonyms	Stirpiculture. Eugenics. 14th revised and enlarged edition
34. Addition of Equivalence Structure	
35. Deletion of Equivalence Structure	
36. Addition of Lead-in Values	Eugenics–heath (from Relative Index 22nd edition)
37. Deletion of Lead-in Values	Eugenics (from Relativ Index 14th rev enl edition)
40. Broader Values	Birth control, reproductive technology, sex hygiene
41. Narrower Values	613.942 Surgical. . .
41. Narrower Values	613.943 Chemical. . .
42. Related Values	
42. Related Values	
42. Related Values	
42. Related Values	
43. Addition of Broader Values	
44. Deletion of Broader Values	613.9 Hygiene of Offspring. Heredity.
45. Addition of Narrow Values	
46. Deletion of Narrow Values	613.91 Congenital Defects of the Body
46. Deletion of Narrow Values	613.92 Inherited Mental Disability
46. Deletion of Narrow Values	613.93 Transmitted Disease
47. Addition of Related Values	
48. Deletion of Related Values	Heredity in 575.1
50. Translations	
60. Definition	
61. Scope Note	Stirpiculture. Eugenics. [editors might see more than what is in the schedule]
62. History Note	
63. Change Note	
64. Editorial Note	
65. Sources/Authorities	

66. Addition of Sources/Authorities	
67. Deletion of Sources/Authorities	
68. Addition of Definition	
69. Deletion of Definition	
70. Unspecified Relation (UN)	
80. Editor	Mitchell, Joan S., Beall, Julianne, Martin, Giles., Matthews, Winton E., New, Gregory R.
81. Record Creator	Joseph T. Tennis
86. Contact Information	
87. Date Record Created	2006-04-01
90. Information System(s)	
91. Frequency of Use	
92. Document-Set Date	
93. Document-Set Resources	

TABLE 9. Value Record for 22nd Edition of DDC

In Table 9 we see how the value is changed, but retains its links back to the value and relationships in the earlier version (Edition 14 rev. enl.). We see what was deleted, and what was added. This is the first step in aiding semantics of the Semantic Web across versions of schemes. By making these changes explicit–both in this value record, and in conceptualizing the categories of change we put ourselves in a better position to manage the dynamic and quickly evolving world of the Semantic Web.

Future Work

The next stages of research and development in the Semantic Web will test these conceptualizations and methodologies, and then move them into machine-readable assertions about resources. Allowing editors to manipulate different versions of schemes for management and retrieval purposes.

CONCLUSION

The National Science Digital Library has embarked on a Registry project where they aim to store schemes for reuse and interoperability (Sutton and Hillmann, 2006). As more schemes are added to this registry, and as different versions of those schemes are added to the registry, researchers and developers at NSDL will have to wrestle with scheme versioning. This registry must account for the structural, word-use, and textual changes schemes go through. This scheme registry will be a proof of concept application for scheme versioning in a Semantic Web environment. They are building metadata for schemes that move beyond SKOS–pushing the edge of what we know about contemporary scheme management. It is hoped that the value record, conceptual framework, and methodology developed in this paper will be an aid in their work, and others, toward developing a more robust and meaningful Semantic Web.

Schemes change, and if the Semantic Web is going to be a Web of meaning, then it must be a web of meaning that is dynamic, not static. If schemes form a major part of Semantic Web metadata, then we have to account for scheme versioning in ways that are both human and machine-readable. The value record presented above is a step toward making the elements of scheme versioning explicit so that we might construct management tools to aid in a dynamic and meaningful development of the next web, the Semantic Web.

NOTES

1. Other structural changes beyond these seven are combinations of two or more changes. For example, splitting one value into many is an act of adding new values, adding new preferred terms, or perhaps changing lead-in terms to preferred terms.

2. In bringing up this concept of a document-set and its shifting representation, I am invoking an analytical device similar to Melanie Feinberg's (2005), though not identical in use; they are similar in composition.

REFERENCES

Aitchison, J. Gilchrist, A, and Bawden, D. (2000). *Thesaurus construction and use: a practical manual*. London: Aslib.

Anderson, J. D. and Perez-Carballo, J. (2005a). *Information retrieval design*. DRAFT. http://www.scils.rutgers.edu/~carballo/ird2005.html.

Anderson, J. D. and Perez-Carballo, J. (2005b). Chapter 13: Vocabulary Management. In *Information retrieval design*. DRAFT. http://www.scils.rutgers.edu/~carballo/chapters/chapter13.htm.

ANSI/NISO. (2005). *Guidelines for the construction, format, and management of monolingual controlled vocabularies*. Bethesda, MA: National Information Standards Organization.

Connolly, D. 2006. *Uniform resource identifier (URI) activity statement.* http://www.
w3.org/Addressing/Activity.

Beghtol, C. (1986). Bibliographic classification theory and text linguistics: aboutness
analysis, intertextuality and the cognitive act of classifying documents. *Journal of
Documentation* 42(2):84-113.

Duranti, L., Eastwood, T., and MacNeil, H. (2002). *Preservation of the integrity of
electronic records.* Dordrecht: Kluwer.

Feinberg, M. (forthcoming). Expression of feminism in three classifications. In *Advances in classification research.* Information Today Inc.: Medford, New Jersey.

Miles, A. (2006). *Simple Knowledge Organisation System (SKOS).* http://www.w3.
org/2004/02/skos/.

Herman, I. E. and Hendler, J. (eds.) (2006). *Web ontology language (OWL).* http://
www.w3.org/2004/OWL/.

Herman, I. Swick, R., and Brickley, D. (eds.) (2006). *Resource description framework.*
http://www.w3.org/RDF/.

OCLC. (2006). Dewey Decimal Classification: New Features in Edition 22. http://
www.oclc.org/dewey/versions/ddc22print/new_features.pdf.

Ranganathan, S. R. (1967). *Prolegomena to library classification.* 3rd edition. Bombay: Asia Publishing.

Soergel, D. (1974). *Indexing languages and thesauri: construction and maintenance.*
Los Angeles: Melvile.

Sutton, S. and Hillmann, D. (2006). *NSDL Metadata Registry.* http://eg2.ischool.
washington.edu/registry.

doi:10.1300/J104v43n03_06

Roles for Semantic Technologies and Tools in Libraries

G. Philip Rogers

SUMMARY. Interest is growing in Semantic technologies such as XML, XML Schema, ontologies, and ontology languages, as well as in the tools that facilitate working with such technologies. This paper examines the current library automation environment and identifies semantic tools and technologies that might be suitable for use in some libraries and other knowledge-intensive organizations. doi:10.1300/J104v43n03_07 *[Article copies available for a fee from The Haworth Document Delivery Service: 1-800-HAWORTH. E-mail address: <docdelivery@haworthpress.com> Website: <http://www.HaworthPress.com> © 2007 by The Haworth Press, Inc. All rights reserved.]*

KEYWORDS. Applications, software, Semantic Web, semantic tools, XML, ontologies

INTRODUCTION

. . . Internet resources tend to break the mold. They cause problems. They challenge our notions of the form and function of the catalog. The rules for cataloging them are in a nascent state. Our present exacting cataloging methods are too slow to handle their

[Haworth co-indexing entry note]: "Roles for Semantic Technologies and Tools in Libraries." Rogers, G. Philip. Co-published simultaneously in *Cataloging & Classification Quarterly* (The Haworth Information Press, an imprint of The Haworth Press, Inc.) Vol. 43, No. 3/4, 2007, pp. 105-125; and: *Knitting the Semantic Web* (ed: Jane Greenberg, and Eva Méndez) The Haworth Information Press, an imprint of The Haworth Press, Inc., 2007, pp. 105-125. Single or multiple copies of this article are available for a fee from The Haworth Document Delivery Service [1-800-HAWORTH, 9:00 a.m. - 5:00 p.m. (EST). E-mail address: docdelivery@haworthpress.com].

Available online at http://ccq.haworthpress.com
© 2007 by The Haworth Press, Inc. All rights reserved.
doi:10.1300/J104v43n03_07

volume and complexity in reasonable turnaround times. They change so often that they overwhelm our capacity to maintain them. They force us to question conventional assumptions and workflows . . . I suggest that Internet resources are driving fundamental changes that demand new operational and organizational assumptions about bibliographic control. (Calhoun, 2000, pp. 3-4)

The next several years hold both promise and peril for libraries, library patrons, and those who work in libraries. As more people turn to the Web to meet their information needs, they find that they have easy and immediate access to information. Given the traditional central role of the library in providing custody of and access to trusted information resources, many members of the library community justifiably question the quality and the completeness of the information that people typically find on the Web. However, due to dramatic changes in information-seeking behaviors, libraries are faced with numerous challenges, not least of which is the need to make information about their collections readily available not only to their patrons, but also to other institutions.

As the popularity of the Web has grown, it has become increasingly difficult to provide people with immediate access to dynamic and fresh content, and in most cases it is not because the content does not exist–it is because people do not know how or where to find such content. Giving people the ability to locate information resources more easily is one of the reasons that researchers are calling for a more "Semantic Web." According to Marshall and Shipman (2003), there are a number of different expectations in regard to the Semantic Web, based on the following three perspectives: (1) the Semantic Web as a universal library that can meet the needs of people in many different information-seeking contexts; (2) the Semantic Web as an interconnected series of Web Services (or "agents") that perform work at the behest of their human taskmasters; or, (3) the Semantic Web as a federated database and knowledge base that can meet the needs of both humans and their software agents. This paper focuses on the first perspective–the Semantic Web as a universal library.

As expressed by Tim Berners-Lee, James Hendler, and Ora Lassila (2001), and further elaborated upon by numerous organizations and individuals over the last several years, the core elements of the Semantic Web that are reasonably well-defined include the following standards and tools: (1) XML, a markup language that provides a syntax for structured documents without imposing semantic constraints on the meaning of such structured documents; (2) XML Schema, a language that precisely defines the structure of XML documents; (3) Resource Description Framework (RDF), a data model that defines "resources" (objects) and the relations among them, as well as providing semantics for this data model; (4) RDF Schema, a vocabulary that describes properties and classes of RDF resources, including semantics for expressing hierarchical relationships among such properties and classes; and (5) Web Ontology Language (OWL), a language that describes properties and classes, relations among classes, and numerous other characteristics. Figure 1 depicts a layered structure[1] that shows the nature of the relationships among these standards and tools.

This paper begins by exploring the nature of the challenges currently facing libraries, including a brief overview of selected library automation software and the extent to which it addresses such challenges. The discussion then shifts to the extent to which semantic technologies and tools can address library challenges. For instance, the need for interoperability among library systems through shared meaning, vocabulary, and syntax is greater than ever. The paper concludes with suggestions for future research.

OVERVIEW OF CHALLENGES FACING LIBRARIES

Challenges facing libraries can be examined from a number of perspectives. Two perspectives that best facilitate the level of analysis for

FIGURE 1. Semantic Web Layers

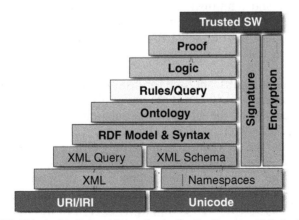

this paper are challenges facing the information practitioner, and challenges facing the information consumer. Information practitioners include people who work in libraries and other institutions that manage information, while information consumers include those who seek to locate information resources in any form.

Library Challenges from an Information Practitioner Perspective

In a climate characterized by shrinking budgets and growing expectations, many administrators, particularly those in larger institutions, turn to automated systems in the hope that such systems will improve efficiency and reduce operating costs. As noted by Cibbarelli in the January 2003 ILS Marketplace column, the users of Integrated Library Systems (ILSs) tend to rate some ILS functions more highly than others. Even among the five ILSs with the highest overall user satisfaction scores (8.0 or higher), areas where the user satisfaction scores tended to trend lower than the total user satisfaction score included acquisitions, authority control, cataloging, prepackaged reports, and report creation.

Significant as their shortcomings might be in more traditional areas such as acquisitions, authority control, and cataloging, library automation systems leave considerably more to be desired in what might best be referred to as "transitional" areas. Transitional functionality, which vendors are seeking to address primarily with Electronic Resource Management (ERM) modules or systems, includes features such as Web interfaces for users of databases and e-journals, as well as interfaces for managing information about licensing costs and various other management and administrative tasks associated with electronic resources. As Breeding points out in his May 2005 "Systems Librarian" column, vendors tend to sell ERM offerings as add-on modules. He goes on to say that such offerings

> . . . require significant time for installation, configuration, and ongoing operation . . . [and] are not easily integrated with the other components of the library's automation environment. In many cases, even when the product has been developed by the same vendor as the ILS, it's based on an entirely different database architecture, or even a completely different database product. In an era where the general trend is to consolidate all of an organization's business systems into a single database environment, the tendency for library automation components to rely on different ones goes against the grain. (Breeding, 2005, p. 40)

The compelling need for ERM functionality is clearly demonstrated by the steps many academic libraries have taken to catalog electronic resources. Perhaps the most obvious sign of the trend toward greater investment in electronic resources is the allocation of personnel. Boydston and Leysen (2002) note a rapid increase in the number of librarians who catalog Web resources, from 1.2 percent in 1987 to 31.4 percent in 1997. Furthermore, they observe that the nature of the work that catalogers perform continues to change as well, with a corresponding increase in tasks such as managing networks and workflows and maintaining databases.

Yet another sign of the changes taking place in libraries can be seen in their organizational structure. Calhoun (2000) explains how the traditional library organizational structure is based on a workflow designed for the processing of print resources. Such a workflow follows a linear process in that print resources go from one person or group to the next, in an ordered sequence. By way of contrast, the workflow for processing electronic resources is often an iterative, collaborative, non-linear process.[2] Figure 2[3] provides a high-level comparison of the workflows for physical (printed) resources, shown on the left side, and electronic resources, shown on the right. Among the most significant differences are the licensing issues associated with electronic resources, as well as numerous technical challenges that affect the acquisition and management of electronic resources.[4]

Given the significant differences in the management of printed resources vis-à-vis electronic resources, there will continue to be a need for systems and tools that enable libraries to adapt to the burgeoning digital environment. Breeding (January 2005) speculates that two factors, in particular, impact the frequency of and extent to which library automation vendors introduce new features and functions. One factor is that the Request for Proposal (RFP) process that libraries typically follow, which is characterized by detailed checklists that tend to be similar from one institution to the next, can result in stifling innovation among library automation vendors. That is, because library automation vendors are for-profit enterprises, if they find that the vast majority of institutions are asking for essentially the same features, the vendors have little incentive to offer features that a relatively small number of institutions request, particularly when the requesting institutions are not among the largest customers. A second factor is that if library automation vendors were to switch to a model where add-on modules were instead embedded into their core ILS offerings, the likely result might well be that

FIGURE 2. Comparison of Physical and Electronic Resource Acquisition and Management Processes

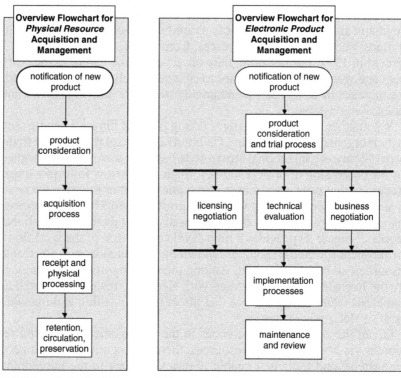

such ILS offerings would become prohibitively expensive for all but the best-funded institutions.

In response to a very fluid and dynamic environment, library automation vendors are still in the early stages of introducing and enhancing their ERM offerings. Libraries, for their part, have to choose from among several alternatives, such as getting by with little to no automation, developing a customized solution (often in collaboration with other institutions, to reduce cost), or buying an ERM from a library automation vendor, either as a stand-alone system, as an add-on module for to an existing ILS, or as part of the purchase of some other comprehensive third party software solution. Meyer summarizes some of the unique functionality associated with ERM offerings as follows:

> . . . ERM is all about administrative metadata. Early library systems captured the bibliographic metadata for library materials. Later systems incorporated financial data when the acquisitions module was added to the ILS. Now we are at a stage in which we are trying to manage new kinds of information about our library resources, including URLs, usernames and passwords for access or statistics, and authentication methods. The ILS is simply not the best place to capture these types of data elements . . . There is no uniform way for recording methods for remote database access, such as IP authentication or password-based login, in a MARC record. ERM systems address these kinds of data elements and also enable actions like efficiently tracking the relationship between a particular resource and the various vendors who may provide access to it. (Meyer, 2005, p. 22)

Library Challenges from an Information Consumer Perspective

Even as libraries struggle to acquire or maintain information systems that meet their needs, they must at the same time adapt to the rapidly changing needs of their patrons. Due primarily to the ubiquitous nature of the Web and the abundance of resources that it provides, the formation seeking and information retrieval habits of the general population have changed dramatically over the span of a generation. For instance, as the population ages, with each passing year there will be fewer people who have any memory of using a traditional library catalogue as the primary means of locating information.

The changing role of the library among the younger generation is perhaps best observed in academic libraries. During the 2005 ACRL National Conference, Hisle remarked that a trend that is likely to continue among academic libraries is a move toward an information commons service model, such that libraries provide more open areas that encourage collaboration and multitasking by providing a mixture of traditional library services, technical and multimedia services, and other services that encourage meeting and collaboration, such as a cafe.

Chad and Miller (2005) are among those calling for a Library 2.0, where libraries democratize access to information and thereby "bring down the walls around our own systems and our own information" (p. 9). Indeed, as noted by Warren and Alsmeyer (2005), over ten years ago, the U.S. National Science Foundation (NSF) identified numerous research challenges that face libraries, and chief among them was the need to deliver greater interoperability, which could facilitate the exchange of documents, queries, and services by providing a common view across different library components. Other key research challenges cited by the NSF included improved collection management to enable the storage, indexing, and retrieval of unstructured and semistructured data, and more intuitive interfaces to enable users to more readily locate and retrieve information objects.

Beacom (2000) offers additional insight on the ways that the information-seeking behaviors of information consumers are changing and how these changes affect the packaging and delivery of information resources. Beacom observes that although catalog records and the resources that they describe have traditionally been treated as distinct objects, the content that the information resources contain, as well as the metadata that describes the information resources, are inextricably linked. He goes on to say that the catalog has been undergoing a gradual transformation such that it is becoming a multimedia delivery system, in addition to its traditional role of acting as a finding aid. And Beacom further calls for tight integration between the catalog and a user's workspace, providing a seamless user experience.

RECENT PROJECTS THAT ADDRESS GAPS IN COVERAGE IN LIBRARY AUTOMATION SYSTEMS

A review of recent projects can provide insight into library processing areas where needs are not completely addressed by existing library automation systems. Two of the most obvious areas are closely interrelated and constitute the beginning of a typical library workflow–acquisitions and cataloging. At the University of Maryland Libraries, for instance, a review of Cataloging First Time In (2000) noted the following areas where problems were observed in processes and tools: (1) lack of automated authority control; (2) lack of automation and organization of standard cataloging functions; (3) lack of consistency in the sorting and priority flagging of materials; (4) lack of consistency in processing instructions from one collection to another; (5) lack of automation in the tracking of record collection and activity statistics; (6) labor-intensive retrieval of items from an uncataloged materials queue; (7) cataloging of bulk-collected gift materials before a proper determination is made on the suitability of the materials for an academic collection; and (8) cataloging of materials requiring preservation treatment before the administration of preservation treatment.

As already noted, cataloging the rapidly growing number of electronic resources continues to place great demands on libraries of all sizes. Reliance on the Online Computer Library Center (OCLC) and the Research Libraries Information Network (RLIN) seems likely to continue to increase, and certainly meets the need where cooperative approaches are beneficial, but systems such as OCLC and RLIN can provide only limited support for projects focusing on the cataloging of locally produced electronic resources.[5] To be sure, as noted by Boydston and Leysen (2002), the decision on whether to catalog a particular electronic resource will continue to be based on criteria such as the extent to which the resource supports an institution's research goals or curriculum (much like print resources), as well as whether the resource is a serial subscription or a purchased monograph. Depending on numerous factors that vary from one institution to another, a decision is made in regard to whether full-level cataloging, less-than-full-level cataloging, local cataloging, or no cataloging at all is appropriate. Many libraries continue to report that they do not catalog free Web-based resources, due to factors such as instability and lack of control over the content of such resources.

Even for Web resources that are included in catalogs, it is often the case that an efficient means of running queries to locate items in some collections is lacking. Finding solutions to challenges such as a lack of ability to locate a particular resource might best be seen in the context of approaches that are more typically associated with the for-profit sector, such as Business Intelligence (BI) or Knowledge Management (KM). To name one example, Kelly (2005) describes the Museum Informatics Project (MIP) at the University of California Berkeley, where the project team took a BI approach as a means of improving collection tracking, making it possible to run ad hoc queries against collection databases, and facilitating the generation of reports without the assistance of Information Technology (IT) personnel. Three Berkeley collections are benefiting from the MIP approach, with key outcomes such as a time savings for staff members, improved access to the resources in the collections, and a high level of user satisfaction with the new system.

Mimno, Jones, and Crane (2005) report the results from a digitization project at the Perseus Digital Library (PDL). After investing several years in the digitization of a 55-million-word collection of American Civil War documents, these authors found that after tagging the electronic versions of these resources in conformance with Text Encoding

Initiative (TEI) guidelines, it was then possible to automatically generate 60,000 catalog records that provided coverage to the sub-section
level of each resource. That is, they were able to efficiently apply component (analytical) cataloging to a very large collection.[6]

For an example of a project that is broader in scope, one of the best recent examples is the development of the Evergreen open source ILS for
system-wide use by the Georgia Public Libraries Service (GPLS). The
GPLS initiative is intriguing not only because of the open source ILS
that it developed, which includes modules and tools for circulation, cataloging, and inventory control,[7] but also because the project was designed to encourage the involvement of as many libraries as possible.
As of late 2005, approximately 248 libraries in Georgia were taking part
in this unique network that provides shared services to patrons across
the state, referred to as the Public Information Network for Electronic
Services (PINES).[8] The results of an end user survey in early 2004 produced impressive results, with a large majority of respondents reporting
satisfaction with the services provided by PINES member institutions.[9]

SEMANTIC TECHNOLOGIES AND TOOLS
FOR EXTENDING LIBRARY AUTOMATION CAPABILITIES

As discussed in the previous section, there has been progress toward
addressing gaps in the capabilities of automated systems. However,
most advances have taken place within the context of a single institution
or library (such as MIP at UC Berkeley), or in rare cases, within the context of a regional or institutional grouping of libraries (such as PINES).
It is also important to emphasize that existing library cataloging practices are based on a well-established tradition that has served libraries
and their patrons well. As already noted, those roots originated at a time
when there was no need to catalog electronic resources, and were based
on what David Levy refers to as the "order of the book,"[10] a phrase that
reflects the significance of printed publications and their role in shaping
cataloging and other standard practices in libraries.

What is still needed, therefore, is a more systematic approach toward
applying semantic technologies and tools such that they meet the needs
of a critical mass of libraries and of the patrons of those libraries. Lytras
et al. (2005) suggest that the promise of the Semantic Web in the library
domain can be seen both as an extension of existing metadata-centric
approaches used in digital libraries, and as an opportunity to share
ontologies via the Web and thus facilitate interoperability across nu-

merous information providers, including libraries, archives, and other cultural heritage institutions. Further potential benefits of applying semantic technologies and tools include at least partial automation of tasks such as cataloging, metadata harvesting, digital rights management, information resource version control, and the generation of metrics related to information resource quality, information retrieval accuracy, and the return on investment associated with these and other library investments in semantic technologies and tools.

Above all else, libraries and their patrons can benefit from technical solutions that make it possible to share information and to collaborate in ways that have not been possible before. Chad and Miller (2005) are among those who are seeking to provide online interfaces so that library users can communicate their views more easily, for example, to offer their insight on information resources they have used, as well as information resources that they might like to see the library acquire. Further, Chad and Miller favor a move away from the dominant ILS procurement methodology, characterized as it is by a long selection process resulting in the selection of a single vendor. Instead, an ILS solution more in line with Library 2.0 would be one that "adapts to changing technologies and requirements . . . free to swap components as newer and more appropriate ones become available . . . This library must engage and actively participate with a wide range of technology partners, ensuring that a modular and interoperable set of core systems remains reliable and robust. At the same time, the library must continually seek opportunities to push existing library services across new channels to new users, and to engage with existing and potential users in different ways that make sense to them" (p. 11).

Vendor-Driven Approaches to Library Automation

A short discussion of library automation models as they are currently practiced will help set the stage for analysis of alternative approaches. In a recent Helping You Buy column, Pace (2005) reports the results of a 2005 ILS user survey. One of the things that is most notable about the survey results, according to Pace, is a considerable amount of homogeneity from one ILS vendor to another, causing him to observe that the "commodity-like nature of basic ILS functionality has shifted both the endeavors of library automation companies and the ways in which librarians evaluate new systems" (p. 25). That said, Pace distinguishes between two library automation models that dominate the automation landscape: (1) a centralized model, typically the more expensive of the two models, where the ILS and most other automation services are managed by a single internal body that maintains the servers and other infrastructure; and (2) an application service provider (ASP) model that tends to cost less money because it delegates most of the responsibility for managing the ILS, servers, and infrastructure to a third party.

Hybrid Approaches to Library Automation

Due to the considerable homogeneity in terms of the feature sets available in ILSs, and also because of the cost of purchasing various ILS add-ons and modules, many organizations are considering or already deploying custom solutions that address particular needs as they continue to use their existing ILS to address more traditional library automation functions. Meyer's (2005) coverage of the data management and communication protocol capabilities that are planned for or already included in ERM offerings from the major automation vendors provides insight into the increasing complexity that libraries must content with. The list of data formats[11] being addressed includes MARC, MARC21, MARC-XML, UniMARC, ONIX, COUNTER, SOH, XML, CSV, and MDB, and communication protocols include HTTP, FTP, Web services, SOAP, SIP, SIP2, NCIP, LDAP, SRU/SRW, and Z39.50.

An even more diverse picture emerges when one looks at the types of software solutions that are in use in smaller institutions. For example, the results of the Automation Survey on the Special Libraries Association Web site (2005) lists software from 39 different vendors, and the size of the institutions' collections varies from less than 1,000 records to well over 1 million records. Some institutions report the use only of lightweight database applications such as Microsoft Access or Filemaker Pro, while other institutions report that they use more expensive solutions from companies such as EOS International or Inmagic.

Due to the vastly different approaches to library management and library automation that exist, it is clear that there are areas where semantic technologies and tools could be employed to address information processing gaps in libraries. As with any project, it is critically important that each institution carefully assess its goals and be able to translate those goals into tangible requirements.[12] Table 1 describes various semantic technologies, some of which are already being used, and others that could be employed to facilitate interoperability among various systems in a library environment.

Because there are so many semantic tools that might conceivably be useful as a means of complementing an existing ILS or other software solution in a library environment, Table 2 and Table 3 provide categorized lists of tools to facilitate rapid perusal.

AREAS FOR FURTHER RESEARCH

Gradman (2005) makes a number of observations that both reinforce much of the information presented in this paper and also suggest areas where further research might be needed. First, the current structure of

TABLE 1. Semantic Technologies

Technology	Purpose	Examples
Semantic Markup/Descriptive Markup[1]	Provide semantic cues in a standardized way that specify *what* a particular information resource contains, as opposed to "presentational markup" (HTML) that specifies *how* an information resource should be presented.	XML
Semantic Classification	Define data types and structures.	Document Type Definition (DTD), XML Schema
Metadata	Provide information about a particular data element such as how, when, and by whom it was received, created, accessed, or modified; provide a description of a data element; provide information such as the intended purpose, provenance, or revision history of a data element.	Dublin Core, MARC, Resource Description Framework (RDF)
Web Service	Act as a software agent to perform requests at the behest of other software agents or programs.	Semantic brokers, semantic mappers
Ontology	Act as a controlled vocabulary that describes objects and relationships between objects in a formal way through use of a grammar that expresses meaning only within a specific domain.	OpenCyc, WordNet
Ontology Language	Act as a framework for describing ontologies and provide a means of making assertions about the objects that constitute a particular ontology.	RDF Schema (RDFS), Web Ontology Language (OWL)

[1]Bray (2003), On Semantics and Markup, http://www.tbray.org/ongoing/When/200x/2003/04/09/SemanticMarkup.

TABLE 2. Semantic Tools for Automatic Classification, Cataloging, and Indexing

Category	Category Description	Framework/Project/ Tool Name	Framework/Project/Tool Description
Automatic Classification	Applications that automatically generate categories, clusters, or taxonomies	IDOL[1]	Autonomy markets solutions for automatic categorization, clustering, and taxonomy generation.
		Insight Discoverer[2]	Temis markets automatic information extraction, clustering, and categorization solutions.
		MindServer Categorization[3]	Recommind markets solutions that automatically translate structured and unstructured data to taxonomies, ontologies, or subject heading classifications.
		SmartDiscovery[4]	Inxight markets solutions for data extraction, taxonomy management and categorization, and search.
		Scorpion[5]	Open source software project led by OCLC that automatically classifies electronic resources.
Cataloging and Indexing	Applications that perform metadata extraction, cataloging, and/or OPAC functions	Catalogo[6]	Open source application that performs semi-automated web site cataloging and metadata creation, automated catalog generation, and has a semantic search web interface.
	Applications that perform metadata extraction, cataloging, and/or OPAC functions	CLiMB[7]	The Computational Linguistics for Metadata Building (CLiMB) project produced a toolkit for extracting item-level metadata and building a catalog from that metadata.
		Leeber[8]	Open source, RDF-based cataloging tool and OPAC.
		Lingway KM[9]	Lingway markets an NLP-based indexing and categorization engine.
		Web-based Library Catalog[10]	Open source OPAC.

[1]Autonomy (IDOL) Automatic Classification: http://www.autonomy.com/content/Products/IDOL/f/Classification.html
[2]Insight Discoverer (Temis): http://www.temis-group.com/index.php?id=59&selt=1
[3]MindServer Categorization (Recommend): http://www.recommind.com/index2.php?cat=products&id=categorization
[4]Inxight (SmartDiscovery): http://www.inxight.com/products/smartdiscovery/
[5]Scorpion: http://www.oclc.org/research/software/scorpion/default.htm
[6]Catalogo: http://catalogo.sourceforge.net/
[7]CLiMB: http://www.columbia.edu/cu/libraries/inside/projects/climb/
[8]Leeber: http://leeber.sourceforge.net/
[9]Lingway KM: http://www.lingway.com/en/b1c.htm
[10]Web-based Library Catalog: http://sourceforge.net/projects/webpac/

TABLE 3. Semantic Development Frameworks and Tools for Metadata Management and RDF Manipulation

Category	Category Description	Framework/Project/ Tool Name	Framework/Project/Tool Description
Development Frameworks	Programmatic environments for building Semantic Web applications	IBM Integrated Ontology Development Toolkit (IODT)	IODT is produced by IBM's alphaWorks unit and includes RDFS/OWL parsing and serialization, as well as transformation between RDFS/OWL and other data-modeling languages.
		Jena[1]	Open source (Java) framework that supports RDF, RDFS, and OWL, as well as an RDF query language (RDQL).
		Redland RDF Application Framework[2]	Open source (C) modules for working with RDF, including an RDF parser, RDF query library, and a package that provides bindings for Application Programming Interfaces (APIs) to Redland in a variety of languages.
		Talis Platform[3]	Talis provides a set of components including directory services and data stores built on an extensible Web 2.0 platform that enables participation via a shared content creation and delivery architecture.
		SemanticWorks[4]	Altova markets a visual RDF/OWL editor for producing documents, vocabularies, or ontologies in RDF/XML or N-triples.
		WSMO Studio[5]	Open source Semantic Web Service editor based on Eclipse plug-ins that supports Web Service Modeling Ontology (WSMO) elements such as services, goals, and mediators.
Metadata Management	Applications that facilitate metadata transformations and other operations	SchemaLogic Enterprise Suite[6]	SchemaLogic markets metadata management solutions that use a central repository to manage unstructured information through taxonomic metadata, controlled vocabularies and a semantic mapping schema.
RDF Manipulation	Applications that facilitate editing, browsing, or searching of RDF data	Haystack[7]	Open source Semantic Web (RDF) browser that aggregates RDF data and provides point and click semantic navigation.
		Longwell[8]	Open source suite of lightweight RDF browsers that facilitate search of RDF data in either a user-friendly view or an RDF-aware view.
		RDFizers[9]	Open source tools for translating a number of different data formats to RDF.

[1]Jena: http://jena.sourceforge.net/
[2]Redland RDF Application Framework: http://librdf.org/
[3]Talis Platform: http://www.talis.com/platform/
[4]SemanticWorks (Altova): http://www.altova.com/products_semanticworks.html
[5]WSMO Studio: http://www.wsmostudio.org/
[6]SchemaLogic Enterprise Suite: http://www.schemalogic.com/products-suite.asp
[7]Haystack: http://simile.mit.edu/hayloft/
[8]Longwell: http://simile.mit.edu/longwell/
[9]RDFizers: http://simile.mit.edu/RDFizers/

most bibliographic records, which include layers of information that often are not of very much use to end users, and which sometimes describe different manifestations of the same information resource, is a model that often produces poor search results and is also not well-suited to born-digital electronic resources. Second, many library data models do not translate very well to the Web, particularly when complex entities such as multi-volume works are involved. Third, the massive amounts of data with which libraries must contend can be so unwieldy that many libraries are hesitant to change their current practices. Gradman goes on to say that these observations might partially explain what he sees as relatively slow adoption of the recommendations found in Functional Requirements for Bibliographic Records (FRBR). He proposes that FRBR serve as a meta-ontology for information objects that could be expressed using RDFS or OWL, that would itself serve as the basis for a catalogue implementation in RDF, thus solving the aforementioned problem with bibliographic records and making "all objects, instances, attributes, [and] relations of information objects modeled in catalogues WWW-transparent" (p. 71).

Tillett (2005) also sees considerable potential in FRBR, in that it can help facilitate changes in bibliographic control mechanisms. From Tillett's point of view, more research is needed on user needs and user tasks, and she would like to see more systems that can deliver content from searches of abstracting and indexing services, library catalogs, reference tools, and other repositories. She can also see a need for software that could display information such as topic maps that are based on FRBR relationships.

Like Tillett, Taniguchi (2004) sees the need for renewed focus on user needs and user tasks. Taniguchi observes that attempts to apply conceptual modeling to cataloging, including FRBR, have tended to focus on modifying bibliographic records and databases so that they better address user needs. As an alternative to devoting so much attention to bibliographic records, she suggests that scholars apply conceptual modeling techniques so that the requirements of catalogers can be better understood. For example, conceptual modeling might facilitate the further delineation and definition of tasks that catalogers perform when creating a bibliographic record, and it might then serve as a technique for building a core model that includes event patterns that trigger actions by catalogers, action patterns that apply to each event pattern, as well as the nature of event and action pairs.

In closing, as libraries and the people who work in them continue to evolve their internal practices and the systems that support them, it will be absolutely critical not only to thoroughly understand the nature of the work that is done and will need to be done in libraries, but also to understand the needs of information consumers. Fortunately, numerous semantic technologies and tools exist that can help address gaps in existing library automation systems. As Miller (2005) points out, "Leveraging the approaches typified by Web 2.0's principles and technology offers libraries many opportunities to serve their existing audiences better, and to reach out beyond the walls and Web sites of the institution to reach potential beneficiaries where they happen to be, and in association with the task that they happen to be undertaking. With these approaches, we take our existing wealth of data, and we make it work much harder. We begin to break down the internal silos of the separate systems within a single library, and we connect those components to one another, and to related components and services far beyond the building" (pp. 2-3).

NOTES

1. Berners-Lee, T. (2002). Figure 1 taken from W3C's Web site (http://w3.org/) licensed under Creative Commons Attribution 2.5 License.

2. As noted by Meyer (2005), "Managing electronic resources successfully requires a coordinated effort from many different departments. For example, an e-resource might be selected by a collection manager or bibliographer, purchased in the acquisitions department, implemented by a systems librarian, and evaluated by reference staff."

3. Parker et al. (2004), B-1.

4. As noted by Timothy Jewell et al. in the study Electronic Resource Management: Report of the DLF ERM Initiative, the workflow associated with the management of electronic resources tends to be quite complex. Figure 2 shows only the high level process overview–Appendix B of the Reports shows the entire workflow at a very granular level of detail. Furthermore, Karen Calhoun observes that ". . . selecting, 'acquiring,' and describing Internet resources, can be (and often is) an iterative, highly collaborative, looping process that can involve many individuals from many functional groups. The outputs of the process can also vary-the end result may be MARC records in the catalog, links and summary descriptions on a library Web page, or even records in a non-MARC metadata format (Dublin Core or some locally developed record format)."

5. The relative strengths and weaknesses of OCLC and RLIN were assessed by a Cataloging Functional Workgroup at Rutgers University that was led by Weber in 2002: http://www.libraries.rutgers.edu/rul/staff/groups/tech_serv_oclc-rlin/reports/cataloging_report.shtml.

6. Mimno, Jones, and Crane go on to observe that "Analytical cataloging in particular has been constrained by practical considerations. Cataloging a ten volume work as ten individual records significantly increases the cost of cataloging those items. In ad-

dition to the cost of additional cataloging, the decision of how to catalog multi-volume works has implications for the physical arrangement of books in the library. Do patrons expect to find an individual volume under the classification of the volume itself, or alongside the other volumes in the work? Finer subdivisions, such as chapters within a single volume, are rarely reflected in a typical library catalog beyond a brief table of contents. Digital documents, particularly XML documents, have a very different relationship to the catalog. The very nature of a well-structured XML document makes it easy to describe the parts of a work down to a very narrow level of specificity. Moreover, it is practical to display small segments of larger works and 'collocate' related document sections in the online digital library interface" (271).

7. For additional information about Evergreen functionality, refer to the documentation that is available on the Evergreen wiki: http://www.open-ils.org/dokuwiki/doku.php?id=open-ils.

8. Georgia Public Library Service (2003), PINES (Public Information Network for Electronic Services), http://www.georgialibraries.org/public/pines.html.

9. Georgia Public Library Service (2004), Georgia Library PINES User Survey 2004: Results, http://www.georgialibraries.org/lib/pines/PINESUserSurveyResults-MC.pdf.

10. Even as long ago as 1995, at a time when the World Wide Web was just beginning, David Levy, in his article Cataloging in the Digital Order, Introduction, ¶ 4, observes that in light of changes that the Web was clearly bringing about, cataloging practices would most certainly undergo transformation, based as they were ". . . on a kind of ongoing order-making, invisibly sustaining 'the order of the book.'"

11. ONIX = ONline Information eXchange (http://www.editeur.org/onix.html); COUNTER = Counting Online Usage of Networked Electronic Resources (http://www.projectcounter.org/about.html); SOH = Serials Online Holdings (http://www.editeur.org/onixserials.html); SOAP = Simple Object Access Protocol (http://www.w3.org/TR/soap/); SIP = Session Initiation Protocol (http://www.sipforum.org/); NCIP = NISO Circulation Interchange Protocol (http://www.niso.org/committees/committee_at.html); LDAP = Lightweight Directory Access Protocol (http://www.ietf.org/rfc/rfc2251.txt); SRU = Search/Retrieve via URL, SRW = Search Retrieve Web Service (http://www.loc.gov/standards/sru/).

12. For institutions that would like to review a comprehensive list of requirements based on a review of the needs of numerous libraries, Appendix A: Functional Requirements for Electronic Resource Management" in Electronic Resource Management: Report of the DLF ERM Initiative (2004) provides an excellent example. For insight into the challenges that are typical of a custom development project, refer to Glavica and Pavlinusic (2002), Building WebPAC for Faculty of Philosophy Libraries–experiences and lessons learned, http://webpac.sourceforge.net/.

REFERENCES

Beacom, M. (2000, October 16). Crossing a Digital Divide: AACR2 and Unaddressed Problems of Networked Resources. A paper for the conference *Bibliographic Control for the New Millennium*. Retrieved February 11, 2006 from http://www.loc.gov/catdir/bibcontrol/beacom_paper.html.

Berners-Lee, T. (2002). The Semantic Web. Retrieved July 18, 2006 from http://www.w3.org/2002/Talks/04-sweb/Overview.html.

Berners-Lee, T., Hendler, J., & Lassila, O. (2001). The Semantic Web: A new form of Web content that is meaningful to computers will unleash a revolution of new possibilities. *Scientific American*, 35-43. Retrieved January 6, 2006 from http://www.scientificamerican.com/print_version.cfm?articleID=00048144-10D2-1C70-84A9809EC588EF21.

Boydston, J. & Leysen, J. (2002). Internet Resources Cataloging in ARL Libraries: Staffing and Access Issues. *The Serials Librarian, 41(3/4)*, 127-145. Retrieved December 12, 2005 from The Haworth Press Online Catalog (DOI: 10.1300/J123v41n03_11).

Bray, T. (2003, April 9). On Semantics and Markup. *ongoing*. Retrieved February 18, 2006 from http://www.tbray.org/ongoing/When/200x/2003/04/09/SemanticMarkup.

Breeding, M. (2005, May). The Systems Librarian: Looking toward the future of library technology. *Computers in Libraries, 25(25)*, 39-42. Library Technology Guides: Key resources and content related to Library Automation. Retrieved February 5, 2006 from http://www.librarytechnology.org/ltg-displaytext.pl?RC=11414.

Breeding, M. (2005, January). The Systems Librarian: Re-Integrating the Integrated Library System. *Computers in Libraries, 25(25)*, 28-31. Library Technology Guides: Key resources and content related to Library Automation. Retrieved February 4, 2006 from http://www.librarytechnology.org/ltg-displaytext.pl?RC=11340.

Calhoun, K. (2000, 14 December). Redesign of Library Workflows: Experimental Models for Electronic Resource Description. A paper for the conference *Bibliographic Control for the New Millennium*. Retrieved February 11, 2006 from http://www.loc.gov/catdir/bibcontrol/calhoun_paper.html.

Cameron, R. (2002). Bibliographic Protocol: Fine-Grained Integration of Library Services with the Web. *The Serials Librarian, 41(3/4)*, 201-215. Retrieved December 12, 2005 from Haworth Press Online Catalog (DOI: 10.1300/J123v41n03_17).

Chad, K. & Miller, P. (2005, November). Do libraries matter? The rise of Library 2.0. Version 1.0. Retrieved July 2, 2006 from http://www.talis.com/downloads/white_papers/DoLibrariesMatter.pdf.

Cibbarelli, P. (Ed.) (2003, January). ILS Marketplace: CIL's Quarterly Series on Library Automation Markets: Public Libraries. *Computers in Libraries, 23(1)*, 31-36. Retrieved February 18, 2006 from Computer Database (Gale Group) (purl: rc1_CDB_0_A96644493&dyn=11!xrn_11_0_A96644493).

Clark, K., Parsia, B., & Hendler, J. (2004, 21 May). Will the Semantic Web Change Education? *Journal of Interactive Media in Education, 2004(3)*, 1-16. Retrieved February 23, 2006 from http://www-jime.open.ac.uk/2004/3/.

Georgia Public Library Service (2004). Georgia Library PINES User Survey 2004: Results. Retrieved March 1, 2006 from http://www.georgialibraries.org/lib/pines/PINESUserSurveyResults-MC.pdf.

Georgia Public Library Service (2003). PINES (Public Information Network for Electronic Services). Retrieved March 1, 2006 from http://www.georgialibraries.org/public/pines.html.

Glavica, M. & Pavlinusic, D. (2002, September). Building WebPAC for Faculty of Philosophy Libraries–experiences and lessons learned. Retrieved March 3, 2006 from http://webpac.sourceforge.net/.

Gradman, S. (2005). rdfs:frbr-Towards an Implementation Model for Library Catalogs Using Semantic Web Technology. *Cataloging & Classification Quarterly, 39(3/4)*, 63-75. Retrieved December 12, 2005 from The Haworth Press Online Catalog (DOI: 10.1300/J104v39n03_05).

Hisle, L. (2005). The Changing Role of the Library in the Academic Enterprise. *Information Services Staff Speeches and Presentations, Connecticut College, Year 2005*. Delivered at the ACRL National Conference in Minneapolis, Minnesota. Retrieved July 21, 2006 from http://digitalcommons.conncoll.edu/isstaffsp/1.

Jewell, T., Anderson, I., Chandler, A., Farb, S., Parker, K., Riggio, A., & Robertson, N. (2004). *Electronic Resource Management: Report of the DLF ERM Initiative)*. Retrieved November 18, 2005 from http://www.diglib.org/pubs/dlfermi0408/.

Kelly, D. (2005). Business Intelligence: The Smart Way to Track Academic Collections. *EDUCAUSE Quarterly, 4*, 48-53. Retrieved February 2, 2006 from http://www.educause.edu/ir/library/pdf/EQM0547.pdf.

LaJeunesse, B. (2006, March 3). Evergreen–Staff Documentation. Retrieved March 5, 2006 from http://www.open-ils.org/dokuwiki/doku.php?id=evergreen-user:evergreen_end-user_documentation. (3 March 2006).

Levy, D. (1995). Cataloging in the Digital Order. Retrieved December 12, 2005 from http://csdl.tamu.edu/DL95/papers/levy/levy.html.

Lytras, M., Sicilia, M., Davies, J., & Kashyap, V. (2005). Digital libraries in the knowledge era: Knowledge management and Semantic Web technologies. *Library Management, 26(4/5)*, 170-175. Retrieved July 16, 2006 from the Emerald database (DOI: 10.1108/01435120510596026).

Marshall, C. & Shipman, F. (2003). Which Semantic Web? *HT '03, August 26-30, 2003, Nottingham, United Kingdom*, 57-66. Retrieved February 5, 2006 from http://www.csdl.tamu.edu/~marshall/ht03-sw-4.pdf.

Meyer, S. (Ed.) (2005). Helping You Buy: Electronic Resource Management Systems. *Computers in Libraries, 25(10)*, 19-24. Retrieved February 18, 2006 from Computer Database (Gale Group) (purl: rc1_CDB_0_A138966479&dyn=8!xrn_5_0_A138966479).

Miller, D. (2005). XOBIS–An Experimental Schema for Unifying Bibliographic and Authority Records. *Cataloging & Classification Quarterly, 39(3/4)*, 285-303. Retrieved December 12, 2005 from The Haworth Press Online Catalog (DOI: 10.1300/J104v39n03_18).

Miller, P. (2005). Web 2.0: Building the New Library. *Ariadne, 45*. Retrieved December 12, 2005 from http://www.ariadne.ac.uk/issue45/miller/.

Mimno, D., Jones, A., & Crane, G. (2005). Finding a Catalog: Generating Analytical Catalog Records from Well-Structured Digital Texts. *JCDL'05, June 7-11, 2005, Denver, Colorado*, 271-279. Retrieved February 18, 2006 from http://www.cs.umass.edu/~mimno/papers/JCDL2005/f74-mimno.pdf.

Pace, A. (Ed.) (2005). Helping You Buy: Integrated Library Systems. *Computers in Libraries, 25(8)*, 25-32. Retrieved February 18, 2006 from Computer Database (Gale Group) (purl: rc1_CDB_0_A136343208&dyn=13!xrn_6_0_A136343208).

Parker, K., Robertson, N., Anderson, I., Chandler, A., Farb, S., Jewell, T., and Riggio, A. (2004). Report of the DLF Electronic Resource Management Initiative, Appendix B: Electronic Resource Management Workflow Flowchart, B-1-B7. Retrieved November 19, 2005 from http://www.library.cornell.edu/cts/elicensestudy/dlfdeliverables/fallforum2003/Workflow_final.doc.

Passin, T. (2004). *Explorer's Guide to the Semantic Web*. Greenwich, CT: Manning Publications Co.

Solo Librarians' Listserv (2005). Survey of Library Automation Systems in Use at Various Libraries. Retrieved March 31, 2006 from http://www.sla.org/division/dsol/resources/autosurv.htm.

Taniguchi, S. (2004, April). Design of Cataloging Rules Using Conceptual Modeling of Cataloging Process. *Journal of the American Society for Information Science and Technology, 55(6)*, 498-512. Retrieved February 3, 2006 from the Wiley Interscience database (DOI: 10.1002/asi.10404).

Tillett, B. (2005). FRBR and Cataloging for the Future. *Cataloging & Classification Quarterly, 39(3/4)*, 197-205. Retrieved December 12, 2005 from The Haworth Press Online Catalog (DOI: 10.1300/J104v39n03_12).

University of Maryland Libraries (2000). Technical Services Program Review: Cataloging First Time In: Report of Findings as of October 30, 2000–Part 9. Retrieved December 12, 2005 from http://www.lib.umd.edu/TSD/PROGRAMREV/catfirst_pt9.html.

Warren, P. & Alsmeyer, D. (2005). Applying semantic technology to a digital library: a case study. *Library Management, 26(4/5)*,196-205. Retrieved February 2, 2006 from the Emerald database (DOI: 10.1108/01435120510596053).

Weber, M. et al. (2002). Technical Services Evaluation of OCLC and RLIN: "Report of the Cataloging Functional Working Group." Retrieved December 12, 2005 from http://www.libraries.rutgers.edu/rul/staff/groups/tech_serv_oclc-rlin/reports/cataloging_report.shtml.

doi:10.1300/J104v43n03_07

PART II:
SEMANTIC WEB PROJECTS AND PERSPECTIVES

RDF Database for PhysNet and Similar Portals

Thomas Severiens
Christian Thiemann

SUMMARY. PhysNet (www.physnet.net) is a portal for Physics run since 1995 and continuously being developed; it today uses an OWL-Lite ontology and mySQL database for storing triples with the facts, such as department information, postal addresses, GPS coordinates, URLs of publication repositories, etc. The article focuses on the structure and the development of the underlying ontology; it also gives a de-

A major part of this work has been done at the Institute for Science Networking ISN (www.isn-oldenburg.de) with support of the European Physical Society EPS (www.eps.org).

[Haworth co-indexing entry note]: "RDF Database for PhysNet and Similar Portals." Severiens, Thomas, and Christian Thiemann. Co-published simultaneously in *Cataloging & Classification Quarterly* (The Haworth Information Press, an imprint of The Haworth Press, Inc.) Vol. 43, No. 3/4, 2007, pp. 127-147; and: *Knitting the Semantic Web* (ed: Jane Greenberg, and Eva Méndez) The Haworth Information Press, an imprint of The Haworth Press, Inc., 2007, pp. 127-147. Single or multiple copies of this article are available for a fee from The Haworth Document Delivery Service [1-800-HAWORTH, 9:00 a.m. - 5:00 p.m. (EST). E-mail address: docdelivery@haworthpress.com].

tailed overview of an online web-based editorial tool, to maintain the facts database. doi:10.1300/J104v43n03_08 *[Article copies available for a fee from The Haworth Document Delivery Service: 1-800-HAWORTH. E-mail address: <docdelivery@haworthpress.com> Website: <http://www.HaworthPress. com> © 2007 by The Haworth Press, Inc. All rights reserved.]*

KEYWORDS. Semantic Web, RDF, ontology, OWL, world modeling, field-specific portal

INTRODUCTION

Scientists use the Internet to increase the visibility and impact of scholarly and scientific outputs, such as publications, research projects, and teaching material. Discipline specific portals like PhysNet[1] can aid scientists in these goals, by covering a specific research field, Physics in this case, and serving the needs of their target group. The underlying motivation of such a portal service is to bring scientists together, presenting the combination of their research interests, and can result in innovative findings. PhysNet is a leading project in Physics information that demonstrates the use of semantic web technologies and distributed user driven services by providing access to information on self archiving publications and about institutional contact data.

We are running and continuously enhancing the PhysNet portal under the auspices of the European Physical Society (EPS) since 1995. PhysNet is a bouquet of services such as lists of Physics-related institution links (PhysDep), topic specific collections of journals and working groups (PhysTopic), etc. The bouquet contains several search engines on grey literature, open access publications, and self archived publications (Severiens, 2000).

PhysNet was from its beginning developed as a distributed service (Hilf, 2001), which means that on the one hand the editorial team maintaining the content is distributed all over the world and on the other hand the service itself is mirrored on several hosts to offer an unbiased and highly available service. This results in a thorough coverage, good topicality, and further offered information. PhysNet is a maintained and open environment for new developers and team members to set up additional mirroring servers, and for further patronizing societies. The basic principles can be found in the charter.[2]

This article focuses on the data model being used to store the knowledge of the portal and on the used techniques to allow a distributed maintenance of this kind of content.

SEPARATION OF DATA AND VIEW

To offer additional, more interactive and sophisticated services and interfaces to PhysNet, it was requested to separate the knowledge from its representation. Having already information on over 1,000 institutions in the system, this was no triviality.

Until late summer 2004 PhysNet was a huge collection of HTML files containing the actual data, i.e., institution names, their locations and homepage and publication list URLs, embedded within the view, i.e., the HTML markup. The coarser geographical structure (continents, countries) was given by the links between the HTML files, the finer geographical structure (states, cities) was stored in HTML description lists as well as the institutional structure. While a human user could easily identify cities in, e.g., PhysDep service due to the bold printing and recognize the structure of a physics department's institutes due to the different indention, a machine had to infer this information in the same way by interpreting the visualization of the data instead of having precise metadata. Furthermore, small typing errors made while maintaining the lists destroyed even this weak metadata.

Therefore, and to be able to extend PhysNet with other services than just providing URLs, in October 2003 we started examining the structure of the PhysNet data in order to extract it into a database with clear metadata. As one can easily recognize by browsing through PhysDep or PhysDoc, the PhysNet data shows a very simple structure. Starting at the root node "PhysNet World" one has to select a continent and a country until a list of cities is displayed. Each institution is either associated with another institution or with a city or country, etc. This identifies the PhysNet data to be a tree structure, thus XML seems to be the most appropriate data model to use. But a more detailed look shows that certain nodes do have more than one parent. For example, Turkey is counted as a country of Europe as well as a country of Asia, or the "University of California in San Diego" is associated with the city of San Diego but also with the institution "University of California" which is associated with the state California. Therefore, the PhysNet data is actually a graph for which RDF (Manola, Miller, McBride, 2003) is the perfect data model. RDF allows for easy storage by using serialized RDF triples in MySQL databases while RDF Schema combined with OWL Lite provides an adequate language for defining the metadata. On the other hand, while XML allows for editing the data by just using a simple text editor, the RDF graph is more complex, which is the reason that one has to use a more sophisticated editor in order to be able to manage the data amounts and structures as we have to handle with in PhysNet.

The decision for RDF triples as the data model was motivated by a number of reasons:

- The data model should be able to encode all implicitly encoded information of the existing HTML files of PhysNet and combine those parts of information, which was redundantly typed into the files (e.g., sub-institutions of institutions located in more than one city). The fact that the information is a graph, not a tree of hierarchical information, gave a first hint on RDF.
- The data model should be open for any kind of future developments. Semantic encoding in a triples collection and definition of an ontology is perfectly fitting this requirement as it only may request new predicates for the triples to be defined in the ontology.
- It should be possible to mirror and run the database at selected mirror sites. This asked for development of a database structure, which is not essentially requesting a specific implementation of a database software. Our implementation uses only one table with three columns for the data and one other table of the same structure for the metadata.

We were aware of the disadvantages this solutions has:

- Due to the fact that the triples are unsorted, operations on the database are slow by default, even if for most of the requested operations quick solutions could be found. To offer an acceptable performance to those users operating on the database directly it is essential to hold it in the main memory of the server. Due to the effect that nearly all interaction with public users are running on static HTML files (views) generated every night, the resulting load of the server is low.
- Offering more interactive views like WebServices or XQuery based networking, it could be requested to transfer the knowledge into a native RDF or RDF-XML database to increase the speed of the interface. In 2004, when a decision on the architecture had to be made, RDF databases were still in early development stage and too unstable, from our point of view, to trust them. We wanted to make sure that we will always be able to change or expand the data model and technology.

THE PhysNet ONTOLOGY

In the following we will describe the metadata we created for storing the data presented in PhysNet. The ontology defining the predicates in the triples follows the conventions of RDF Schema (Brickley, Guha, 2000) and OWL Lite (Dean, 2003), but the related RDF-editor recognizes a few semantic extensions which will be introduced in this section and specified later on. This part will be pretty formal and detailed but only by that the reader may be able to set up related services of his own.

Figure 1 shows a diagram representing the class hierarchy in the ontology. Each arrow pointing from class A to class B states that class A is a subclass of class B, thus inherits all properties of class B. However, to improve readability, some simplifications had been made: We omitted the namespace prefixes, as we will do throughout most of this article, and the class `physnet:Object`, which is just a simple (abstract) base class without any properties that is used to make the hierarchy graph a tree. All classes that seem to have no superclasses (base classes) are actually a subclass of `physnet:Object`. Classes which names are printed in italic are defined with the namespace prefix `physnet_abs` while all other classes are defined with `physnet` except for `PACSCode` which is defined with the namespace prefix `pacs` (for Physics and Astronomy Classification System).[3] Similarly, all properties tagged by `[abs]` are defined with `physnet_abs` while all others are defined with `physnet` except for `parent` in `pacs:PACSCode` which belongs to the namespace `pacs`.

All classes and properties defined with `physnet_abs` are considered to be abstract. The concept of abstract classes is an extension to RDF Schema and OWL Lite. The RDFEditor will not offer an option to create an instance of such a class nor offer to assign a value to such a property. While the concept of class inheritance and abstract classes is familiar from other object-orientated environments, the concept of property inheritance and abstract properties might be new to the reader. In the diagram, we list the properties of each class under the class name. In each line, the name of the property, its range (type) and cardinality is given. Since we use OWL Lite, the only cardinality restrictions available are "unlimited" ($0..*$), "max. 1" ($0..1$), "at least 1" ($1..*$), and "exactly 1" ($1..1$). If a property is a subproperty, the name of its superproperty is given in parentheses before the colon.

As already mentioned, the PhysNet data contains a lot of hierarchical structure. To represent this in the editor and to simplify navigating through the data, we introduced the abstract class `physnet_`

FIGURE 1. Class hierarchy in the PhysNet ontology.

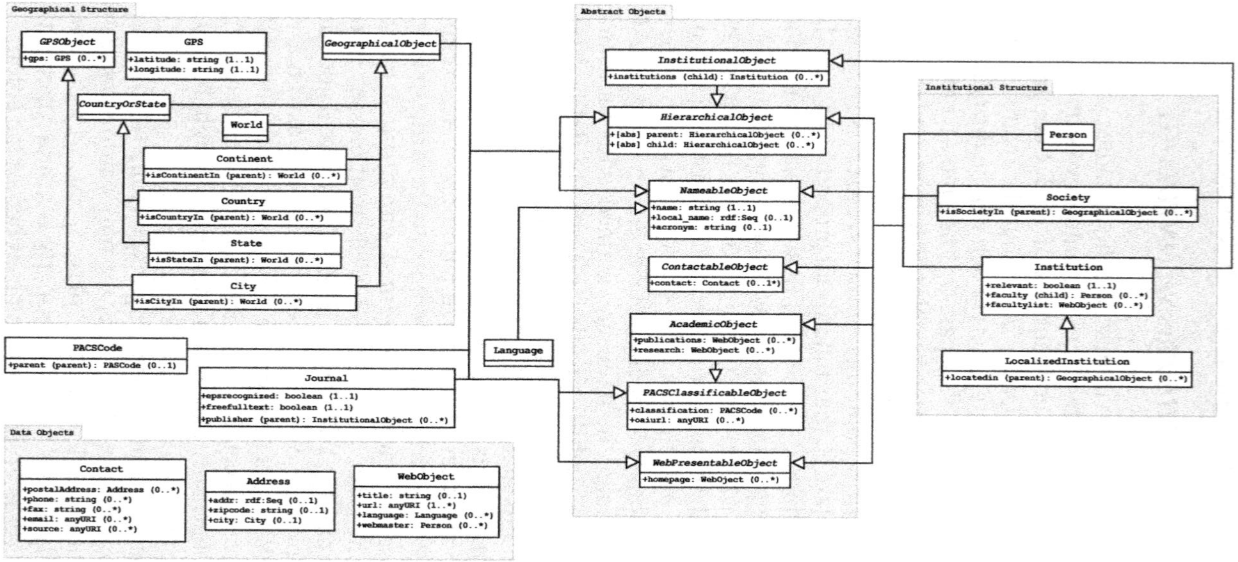

`abs:HierarchicalObject` with the two abstract properties `physnet_abs:parent` and `physnet_abs:child`. Both properties have the range `HierarchicalObject` and any assignment of a value "Instance B" to `parent` (`child`) on "Instance A" states that "Instance B" is considered to be a parent (child) of "Instance A" in the logical hierarchy. The RDFEditor uses these special semantics to provide a display of the hierarchical neighborhood around one particular instance instead of listing all instances of a certain type or other matching criteria and thus drastically simplifies navigation inside the PhysNet data graph.

Another semantic extension of the RDFEditor is the `physnet_abs:NameableObject` which provides the properties `physnet:name`, `local_name` and `acronym`. This class is meant to be a base class representing any type of object that can have a name. The RDFEditor recognizes such instances and displays them using their name rather than their RDF-URI. Note that in contrast to `HierarchicalObject` the properties of `NameableObject` are non-abstract. While `name`, `local_name` and `acronym` will always have simple strings as values, the different types of objects in the hierarchy might be restricted to different parent or child objects which requires them to define a new property derived from `parent` or `child` but further restrict the range of that property.

The simplest example of using the `HierarchicalObject` and the `NameableObject` is representing the PACS tree by using one instance of `PACSCode` for each code. `PACSCode` defines a new property `pacs:parent` derived from `physnet_abs:parent` that has `PACSCode` as range. The PACS code and text is stored in the `name` property. This design results in a subgraph of `PACSCode` instances in the PhysNet data graph. Practically, since we represent the official PACS tree, this subgraph is of course a tree.

Another class derived from those two abstract classes is `GeographicalObject` which serves as a base class for any object representing geographical structure, in particular `World`, `Continent`, `Country`, `State`, and `City`. Each one of them defines a subproperty of `parent` that states the containment of one geographical instance in another. `Country` and `State` are not direct subclasses of `GeographicalObject` but are derived from `CountryOrState` because we needed cities to be located in countries as well as in states, but there is no way in RDF Schema to specify that values on a specific property might be of either type A or type B. `City` is also a subclass of the abstract `GPSObject` which adds the `gps` property to all instances of City to which one can assign a GPS instance containing the longitude and latitude of the city. While GPS data was first gathered for cities only, currently the exact positions of single institutions are collected. Using this information PhysNet will be able to calculate the distances between cities and offer searches like "Show all institutions 50 km around city A or institute B independent of borders of countries or continents." Currently we are evaluating whether this kind of service should be implemented on the database level, many databases already implement these algorithms, or on the service level, which would allow us to stay independent of the selected database software.

As shown in the lower left corner of the diagram, we defined three pure data objects representing contact information, postal addresses, and metadata about Websites. Address is a simple structure that can be used to represent a complete postal address. The first address lines containing recipient and street name are stored using an RDF Sequence container. The zipcode is stored in a simple string and the city property refers to an instance of City in the PhysNet data. Therefore the country can be inferred by following the isCityIn property of the value on city. The Contact class provides properties to store postal addresses and other contacts like e-mail and phone. The source property is not an actual data field shown on PhysNet but is used to specify the URL of the Website(s) from which the contact information was taken. A data validation script, that continuously checks for broken links in the PhysNet data, uses this value to verify that the contact information is still up to date. The WebObject is used to represent the content, PhysNet was launched for: web links. Each instance must have a value on url giving the actual URL and may optionally provide further information on title, language and webmaster.

All objects that might have a contact or a homepage have to be an instance of the abstract class ContactableObject or WebPresentableObject which provide the two properties contact and homepage. Another class referring to WebObject is the abstract class AcademicObject defining the two properties publications and research which are meant to store the links provided in PhysDoc, while the information given on the property homepage is used in the PhysDep lists. Every AcademicObject is also a PACSClassificableObject. This abstract class was introduced to add the property classification to Institution in order to be able to associate PACS codes with institutions. It evolved to a base class for any object that can be associated with any astronomy or physics related field and now provides also the `oaiurl` property, where URLs of OAi data-providers[4] are stored.

Introducing the abstract class `InstitutionalObject` leads us to the description of the institutional structure in the PhysNet data graph. Each institution like universities, departments, research groups or independent research institutes is represented by an instance of `Institution` and due to the `institutions` property inherited from `InstitutionalObject` each such institution can have "child institutes." Using this property, departments can be associated with universities and research groups with departments. Different universities have different types of institutional structure, thus we did not add any more specific meaning to the `Institution` object and left the recognition of the type of the actual instances to the PhysNet user. Therefore there is no technical difference between, e.g., the "University of Göttingen," the "Physics Department" and the "Institute for Theoretical Physics" although the structure stored in the PhysNet data graph and shown together with the institution's name in PhysDep or PhysDoc implies significant differences between the three institutions. However, `Institution` provides the mandatory `relevant` property whose value is used to evaluate whether an institution is doing mainly Physics related research or not. Thus, in the above example, "University of Göttingen" would have a `false` value on `relevant` while the other two would have a `true` value. This implementation allows field specific robots to extract the relevant starting URLs for building up field specific learned search engines.

The institutions represented by `Institution` are actually interpreted to be some sort of child institutions located in a bigger institution. For universities or independent research institutes we use instances of `LocalizedInstitution` that adds the `locatedIn` property to specify a `GeographicalObject` in which this institution is located. This property, as a subproperty of `HierarchicalObject`'s `parent`, connects the institutional structure graph with the geographical structure graph.

Another element of the institutional structure is the `Person` class used to represent specific persons that may have a homepage or publication list. `Persons` can be inserted into the PhysNet hierarchy by adding them as values to the `faculty` property of some `Institution` instance. Furthermore, `Person` instances can be used to store contact information about a Webmaster of a Website using the `webmaster` property of `WebObject`. The validation script that checks for broken links uses the `email` value of the `Contact` instance on the `Contact` property of the `Person` instance on the `webmaster` property of the instance of the `WebObject` storing the broken link, to send a predefined e-mail asking for the new URL of the Website.

The `Society` class is the last element of the institutional structure and is used to represent physical societies. The property `isSocietyIn` connects to the geographical structure and is used to specify the country or continent the society is associated with. Technically there is no difference between an instance of `Society` and `LocalizedInstitution` in the PhysNet data, but instances of `Society` are also displayed in the Societies listing of the PhysNet service while instances of `LocalizedInstitution` are shown in PhysDep and PhysDoc only. Even semantically there is sometimes little difference between societies and what we understand as localized institutions, as there are some societies like the "Max Planck Society" that supervise several research institutes but there are also institutes like the Italian "Istituto Nazionale di Fisica Nucleare (INFN)" which are split up into several small research institutes spread out over a whole country and may be seen as a society as well.

Finally, to represent journals as shown in the PhysNet's Journals list, we defined a class `Journal`, that adds the boolean properties `epsrecognized` and `freefulltext` to the inherited properties from `NameableObject`, `WebPresentableObject` and `PACSClassificableObject`. These two properties are used to generat the lists of only EPS recognized journals and journals with free full text available. Since many journals are published by physical societies or institutes, we also derived Journal from `HierarchicalObject` and introduced the `publisher` property, which connects to the institutional structure.

RDF ONLINE-EDITOR

As mentioned above, we need an adequate editor to manage the data stored in the RDF graph. During the design phase of the editor we were thinking whether it would be better to build an editor which exactly fits the structure of the PhysNet data or offers the full flexibility of RDF. We decided to go for more flexibility and created RDFEditor being able to edit any RDF graph described by normative RDF Schema and OWL Lite while still offering convenient data entry forms due to support plugins. The plugins offer a convenient method to initiate a whole set of operations on the RDF graph.

As described in the preceding section, the Webmaster's e-mail address for some Webpage is stored in a `Contact` instance associated with a `Person` which is associated with the respective `WebObject`. Adding a new link with Webmaster e-mail address in pure RDF is a tedious task of creating three RDF objects and linking them together correctly. That is the way the RDFEditor offers the full flexibility of RDF to the user, but in this case it was more than convenient to create a plugin that displays a simple form with input fields for URL and e-mail address and takes care of the creation and linking of the RDF objects.

The same plugin, called PhysNetToolbox, offers a form for entering contact information including postal address, thus combining the creation of a `Contact` and `Address` instance in one step. However, the price for simplicity is the loss of flexibility as with using only the PhysNetToolbox there is no possibility to create more than one postal address per contact or to insert more than three name and street lines to a postal address. But then, one can use the basic RDF editing capabilities of RDFEditor to enter the data as needed. This combination of being able to handle RDF on its basic level and the support for user-defined plugins makes RDFEditor a very powerful tool.

Furthermore, we had to decide on the platform on which to implement the editor. Since some countries in PhysDep and PhysDoc are not maintained by us but by volunteers from all over the world, we needed a system that allows editing the PhysNet data from various places. We decided to make the RDFEditor completely Web-based so that the only thing one needs to use it is a Web browser.

RDFEditor can handle multiple users and for each of them certain editing restrictions can be enforced. It is possible to create an account for somebody who is responsible for the data of the, e.g., German PhysDep list and who can only edit RDF objects that are children (in the sense of the `child` and `parent` properties of `HierarchicalObject`) of the `Country` instance "Germany."

The Data Model

The data model that is processed by RDFEditor can in theory be any RDF graph. It requires the graph to be serialized into RDF triples and stored in a MySQL database. However, the internal design of the RDFEditor allows for other input/output modules such as XML import or export.

The data model has to be described using OWL Lite which must be provided as an RDF graph also stored in a MySQL database. This description is interpreted to be normative, thus RDFEditor does not allow for the creation of classes that are not defined in the metadata. Almost every feature of RDF Schema and the cardinality restrictions of OWL Lite are supported, the only exception is that RDFEditor does not allow for resources that are instances of more than one class. This, however, enforces object-orientated design of the metadata. Furthermore, RDFEditor implements some additional semantic features that are described in the following (see also Figure 2).

 # Definition of a World

'physnet:world','rdf:type','physnet:World'
'physnet:world','physnet:name','PhysNet World'

 # Definition of Europe

'physnet:1080985493971846894281','rdf:type','physnet:Continent'
'physnet:1080985493971846894281','physnet:name','Europe'
'physnet:1080985493971846894281','physnet:isContinentIn','physnet:world'

 # Definition of Asia

'physnet:1080985492911746798533','rdf:type','physnet:Continent'
'physnet:1080985492911746798533','physnet:name','Asia'
'physnet:1080985492911746798533','physnet:isContinentIn','physnet:world'

 # Definition of Turkey

'physnet:109108474884939277521','physnet:name','Turkey'
'physnet:109108474884939277521','physnet:local_name','_:109108474884238966480'
'physnet:109108474884939277521','rdf:type','physnet:Country'
'_:109108474884238966480','rdf:type','rdf:Seq'
'_:109108474884238966480','_:1','Türkiye'

 # Location of Turkey

'physnet:109108474884939277521','physnet:isCountryIn','physnet:1080985492911746798533'
'physnet:109108474884939277521','physnet:isCountryIn','physnet:1080985493971846894281'

Abstract Classes and Properties: In general, any of the classes defined in the metadata can be created by using the RDFEditor and values can be assigned to any properties defined in the metadata. Since this is sometimes not intended, the RDFEditor offers to specify an abstract namespace prefix. All classes that are defined using that namespace prefix will not be shown in the RDFEditor's class list as well as properties defined using that namespace prefix will be hidden in the RDFEditor's resource edit panes.

FIGURE 2. RDF triples and graph to describe that Turkey is located in Europe and Asia, which are continents of the world, and that Turkey has a local name "Türkiye."

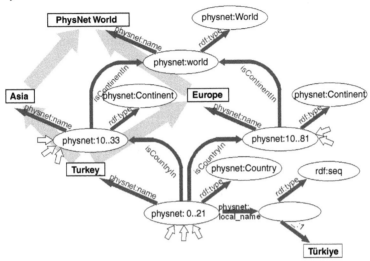

Instance Names: RDFEditor allows for specifying the name of a class and one of its properties. All instances of this class are then considered to have a name given as the (only) value of the specified property. This name is used to represent the instance in listings or titles, etc. If no such class is specified, all RDF instances are listed using their URI which often is a cryptic value.

Hierarchy: Data stored in RDF graphs often show some sort of hierarchy, which can be exploited to simplify navigation in the graph. In the configuration of RDFEditor the name of a class and two of its properties can be given. All instances of this class are then interpreted as nodes in the hierarchy, while values on the two properties are interpreted as pointers to parents or children of a particular instance. With this information given, RDFEditor is able to replace the generic resource list, which simply lists all instances in the data model, with a hierarchical resource list which lists parents and children of one particular instance and allows for traversing through the graph along the hierarchy edges (parent/child properties).

Special Datatype Interpretation: The RDFEditor offers one simple HTML text input for every value assigned to a property. However, sometimes it is more convenient or necessary to provide different input fields. If the range of some property is xsd:boolean, values on that property are shown as a two-radio-button group rather than a text input field where one would have to write either "true" or "false." If the range of some property is rdf:password, a HTML password input field is shown to hide the content from the screen and the contents of this field are stored MD5 encoded instead of plain text.

The User Interface

The RDFEditor's web-based user interface is modular. Every browser window is considered to be a *frame* containing several user interface components, which are presented in the following. Throughout, the RDF term *type* is used instead of the object-orientated term *class*, and *resource* is used instead of *instance*.

Generic and Hierarchical Resource List: The generic resource list simply lists all resources which exist in the currently edited data model and match certain filter criteria. A variant of the resource list is the hierarchical resource list which shows parents and children of a specific resource. The relations "parent" and "child" must be defined in the metadata as explained above.

For each resource its type and its URIref or name is displayed. The URIref (or name) is a link which performs an action depending on the context of the resource list. The resource list in the main editor frame (Figure 3) sets the currently edited resource in the resource edit pane to the resource which URIref (or name) has been clicked.

The hierarchical resource list (Figure 4) additionally shows an arrow ("->") before each resource. By clicking this link you can follow the hierarchy, i.e., the resource which parents and children are shown is set to the resource which arrow has been clicked. On the right side of the hierarchical resource list a "Change resource" button is presented ([. . .]) which asks the user for an URIref and sets the resource list's resource to the one specified by the user. Next to it the hierarchical resource list offers a button to switch to a generic resource list (" [non-hier] " in the title row). The resource list which is shown after pressing this button offers a button to switch back to the hierarchical resource list.

The list of resources shown by a resource list can be restricted using a filter. By clicking the magnifying glass in the title bar one can open the resource list's filter setting dialog (Figure 5). The RDFEditor distinguishes two different kinds of filters: type filters and property value filters.

FIGURE 3. Screenshot of RDFEditor currently editing the resource "Institute for Science Networking."

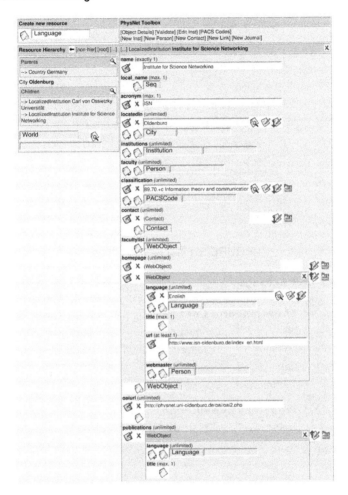

The type filter is set in the upper half of the filter settings dialog. The resource list will display only those resources the type of which is among the selected ones.

The property value filters are configured in the lower half of the filter settings dialog. By clicking the "New property value filter" button a new filter can be created. Existing property filters can be deleted by

FIGURE 4. Hierarchical resource list.

Resource Hierarchy	[root] [...]
Parents	🔍
--> Continent Europe	
Country **Germany**	
Children	🔍
--> City Berlin	
--> City Bochum	
--> City Braunschweig	
--> City Frankfurt am Main	
--> City München	
--> Society German Physical Society	
--> Society Hermann von Helmholtz Society	
--> Society Max Planck Society	

FIGURE 5. Filter setting dialog.

Filter Settings

Show resources of type

☐ City ☐ Language ☐ State
☐ Continent ☐ LocalizedInstitution ☐ World
☑ Country ☐ Person
☐ Institution ☐ Society

Property value filtering

✗ | name ▼ | regexp ▼ | (United|land)

clicking the "Delete property value filter" button which is shown left to each filter. For each filter three input elements are displayed. The left drop-down box shows a list of properties defined in the metadata. The right drop-down box offers "regexp" and "equal."

If "regexp" is selected in the right drop-down box, the value given in the text field is interpreted as a regular expression and the filter rejects all resources which do not have at least one value on the selected property that matches the regular expression. If "equal" is selected the filter rejects all resources which do not have at least one value on the selected property which exactly matches the string entered in the text field. The comparisons are case-sensitive.

The filter configured in Figure 5 matches all resources of type "Country" which have a value on the property "name" that contains either the string "United" or "land."

Resource Edit Pane: The resource edit pane (Figure 6) is the facility for editing a resource. The type and the identity of the resource are shown in the title bar (the name of the resource is displayed instead of its URIref if the editor is configured for nameable objects). By clicking the red cross in the title bar the whole resource can be deleted from the RDF data. This results in the erasure of all triples which subject or object matches exactly the URIref of the shown resource.

The type of a resource can be changed by clicking its type in the title bar. However, this feature is to be used with caution because it may re-

FIGURE 6. Resource edit pane.

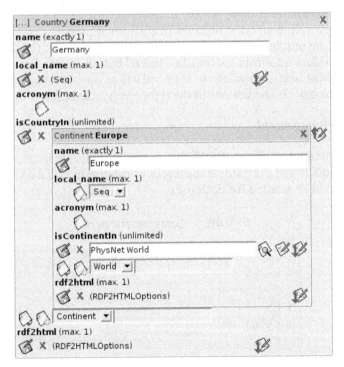

sult in non-metadata-conform data since it only changes the type of the resource regardless to whether the properties values are stored for in the data are still defined with the new type.

Left to the resource edit pane's title is a "Change resource" button ([. . .]) which, similarly to the hierarchical resource list's equivalent, asks the user for an URIref and changes the edited resource to the one specified by the user.

The pane lists all properties which can be applied to the resource and the values on that properties. If a value is a literal value, a text field is displayed. If a value is the URIref of another resource, i.e., a reference, the pane may show a sub-resource-edit-pane showing the referenced resource.

Next to the property name the cardinality is displayed. Possible values are "unlimited," "max. 1," "at least 1" and "exactly 1."

If the resource is not editable by the currently logged in user, the resource edit pane shows only the plain data without any edit options. That means, most of the buttons are not shown.

Container Edit Pane: The container edit pane (Figure 7) is a specialized resource edit pane which is designed for editing rdfs:Containers. In general, it behaves like a normal property except that the values are numbered. The buttons to the left of the input fields insert or delete values into/from the list (the "Insert" button creates a new value on the current index, all values next to and below the button are shifted one index number). The buttons to the right change the order of the values.

User Management

As mentioned above, RDFEditor supports multiple users. Access to data models and even single resources or subgraphs of a data model can be denied or granted for each user.

FIGURE 7. Container edit pane.

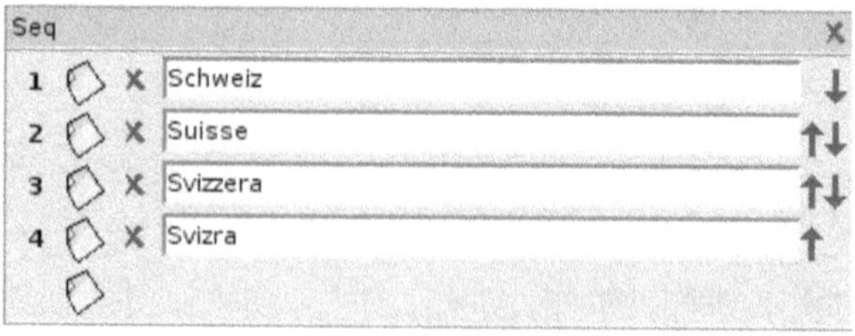

Figure 8 shows an example user which has access to the data model "myDatamodel" but is not allowed to edit resources below the resource "mydata:world." In the example data model the resource "mydata:germany" is a child of "mydata:europe" which is a child of "mydata:world." Eddie is allowed to edit "mydata:germany" because it is explicitly mentioned in "allowedResources." Also the whole subtree below "mydata:germany" (which contains for example "mydata:berlin") can be edited by Eddie while "mydata:europe" and other subtrees below "physnet:world" (for example "mydata:asia") will appear read-only to Eddie.

OUT VIEW AND NEXT STEPS

In 2005 and 2006 we successfully transferred the knowledge of PhysNet from static HTML files into the database of RDF triples. Meanwhile, the knowledge within the database is continuously being updated and enriched. A semi-automatic tool was developed, which

FIGURE 8. User with restricted write access.

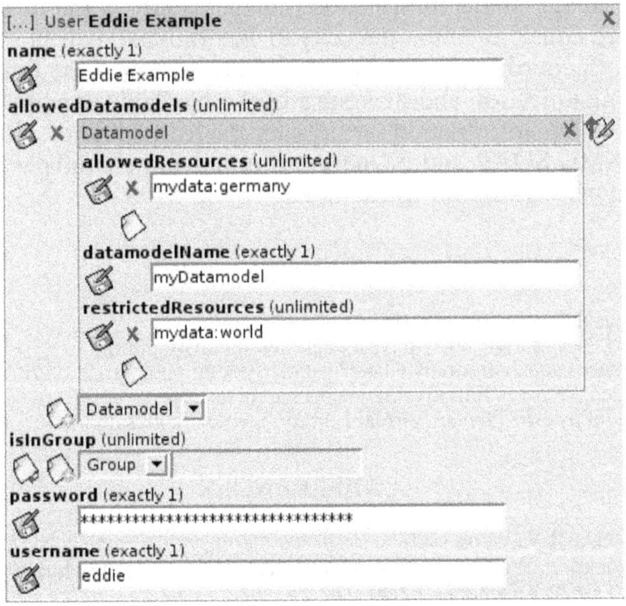

checks for broken links and outdated information like phone numbers and other fragile information, e.g., in the `ContactableObjects`.

For summer 2006 we are planning a tutorial workshop with the goal to increase the number of editors and further optimize the RDFEditor tool. This is desirable because topic related services require a granularity of the institution on at least working group level.

One problem occurs to be serious but independent of the data model: PACS classification is frequently updated as a result of upcoming new fields and research topics in Physics. A unique migration path is not always given, resulting in a high amount of intellectual work being left after automatic migration to the latest version of PACS. Currently PhysNet is still using PACS 2003 instead of the latest 2006 version of the classification.

Networking with other portals is currently one of the most relevant topics. As an example, let us have a view into ViFaPhys,[5] the Physics Virtual Library. Their collection of web resources, of PACS classified online and offline journals would perfectly fit into a topic specific portal service like PhysTopics. On the other hand, their service lacks a well-maintained list of institutions, like PhysNet offers.

Networking with similar portals from other research fields may result in new and innovative services. Sharing common parts of information, like the geographical information (independently of the field the continents are equal, even the majority of institutions, their postal address, their GPS coordinates, etc., are identical), will increase interdisciplinary communication and make use of the available synergies in maintaining online information services for the learned fields. WebServices using XML SOAP and XQuery are promising candidates for the requested networking infrastructure.

NOTES

1. PhysNet: www.physnet.net.
2. PhysNet charter: www.physnet.de/PhysNet/charter.html.
3. Physics and Astronomy Classification System: publish.aps.org/PACS/.
4. Open Archives Initiative: www.openarchives.org.
5. ViFaPhys the Physics Virtual Library: www.vifaphys.de.

REFERENCES

Brickley, D., R.V. Guha (2000). *Resource Description Framework (RDF) Schema Specification*, World Wide Web Consortium, March 27, 2000. http://www.w3.org/TR/2000/CR-rdfschema-20000327/.

Dean, M., G. Schreiber, F. van Harmelen, J. Hendler, I. Horrocks, D. L. McGuinness, P. F. Patel-Schneider, L.A. Stein (2003). *OWL Web Ontology Language Reference*, World Wide Web Consortium, March 31, 2003 (work in progress), http://www.w3.org/TR/owl-ref/.

Hilf, E. R., M. Hohlfeld, T. Severiens, K. Zimmermann (2001). Distributed Information Services in Physics in High Energy Physics Libraries Webzine [ISSN 1424-2729] Issue 4 / June 2001.

Manola, F., E. Miller, B. McBride (2003). *RDF Primer*, W3C Working Draft, October 10, 2003, http://www.w3.org/TR/rdf-primer/.

Severiens, T., M. Hohlfeld, K. Zimmermann, E. R. Hilf (2000) PhysDoc–A Distributed Network of Physics Institutions Documents–Collecting, Indexing, and Searching High Quality Documents by using Harvest D-Lib Magazine, Vol. 6 No. 12, December 2000.

doi:10.1300/J104v43n03_08

Biomedicine and the Semantic Web:
A Knowledge Model for Visual Phenotype

John Michon

SUMMARY. Semantic Web tools provide new and significant opportunities for organizing and improving the utility of biomedical information. As librarians become more involved with biomedical information, it is important for them, particularly catalogers, to be part of research teams that are employing these techniques and developing a high level interoperable biomedical infrastructure. To illustrate these principles, we used Semantic Web tools to create a knowledge model for human visual phenotypes (observable characteristics). This is an important foundation for generating associations between genomics and clinical medicine. In turn this can allow customized medical therapies and provide insights into the molecular basis of disease. The knowledge model incorporates a wide variety of clinical and genomic data including examination findings, demographics, laboratory tests, imaging, and variations in DNA sequence. Information organization, storage and retrieval are facilitated through the use of metadata and the ability to make computable statements in the visual science domain. This paper presents our work, discusses the value of Semantic Web technologies in biomedicine, and identifies several important roles that library and information scientists

This work was supported in part by grant 1K08EY014665-01 from the National Eye Institute.

[Haworth co-indexing entry note]: "Biomedicine and the Semantic Web: A Knowledge Model for Visual Phenotype." Michon, John. Co-published simultaneously in *Cataloging & Classification Quarterly* (The Haworth Information Press, an imprint of The Haworth Press, Inc.) Vol. 43, No. 3/4, 2007, pp. 149-160; and: *Knitting the Semantic Web* (ed: Jane Greenberg, and Eva Méndez) The Haworth Information Press, an imprint of The Haworth Press, Inc., 2007, pp. 149-160. Single or multiple copies of this article are available for a fee from The Haworth Document Delivery Service [1-800-HAWORTH, 9:00 a.m. - 5:00 p.m. (EST). E-mail address: docdelivery@haworthpress.com].

can play in developing a more powerful biomedical information infrastructure. doi:10.1300/J104v43n03_09 *[Article copies available for a fee from
The Haworth Document Delivery Service: 1-800-HAWORTH. E-mail address:
<docdelivery@haworthpress.com> Website: <http://www.HaworthPress.com>*

KEYWORDS. Ontologies, biomedicine, Semantic Web, personalized
medicine

BIOMEDICAL KNOWLEDGE

Health care and biomedicine are among the largest and most complex
areas of human knowledge. All of us are potential patients and it is generally assumed that a long, healthy lifespan is an important and desirable component of quality of life. Information is at the heart of clinical
practice and serves as the basis for therapeutic decisions. Biomedical
information has important economic as well as personal implications,
since most developed countries spend 8-15% of their economic output
on health care with lesser amounts spent on biomedical research. Health
care queries are also common for most search engines, and sites devoted
to this area are among the most popular on the Web.

The scale and scope of biomedical information is extraordinary. The
scale extends from molecules measured in microns up to the entire
global population. Intermediate levels include molecular assemblies,
cells, tissues, organs and organ systems, individual patients, and many
sublevels of analysis. There is also analysis across levels. For example,
a single DNA mutation leads to a single change in the hemoglobin protein in the blood in sickle cell anemia. This causes red blood cell mal-
formation and a variety of clinical manifestations including anemia,
kidney failure, and painful joints. The scope extends beyond biology to
the cognitive and social sciences including economics, sociology, and
psychology. Another characteristic is the rapid accumulation of new information, driven in part by improved technology. The vast complexity
of biological systems ensures that biomedical information stores will
continue to increase in many areas at an exponential rate. The risk is that
separate "silos" of information will be created, with little ability to relate findings in one area to those in others to produce knowledge useful
to human health.

Information in both basic sciences and clinical medicine is very expensive to create. The United States spent $1.7 trillion on health care in

2003, or 15.3 percent of Gross Domestic Product.[1] The fraction spent on information creation and management, such as patient examinations, laboratory tests, and imaging cannot be precisely measured. However, it is likely that it is in the hundreds of billions of dollars. On the research side the National Institutes of Health budget for fiscal 2006 is over $28 billion and there are substantial research expenditures in the private sector that are at least as large. Capturing the value present in this information to improve both human health and our fundamental understanding of disease is therefore an important priority. Clinical information is primarily unstructured, consisting of free text with only limited use of classification and coding schemes. This makes it difficult to use automated techniques to extract knowledge from biomedical sources. Research information is generally better organized, but is often stored in a relational database structure. The schemas that arrange relational databases are typically hidden and difficult to develop or extend, and so their use across the Web is limited. Because unorganized or hidden information is essentially lost to further use, this puts a premium on making the meaning of information explicit and computable over an open network such as the Web.

The problem of managing biomedical knowledge is made more acute by the increasing use of high-throughput experimental techniques. These generate massive data sets which challenge our ability to interpret and use the information contained within. As an example, a reference human genome sequence has recently been created. This describes the basic DNA building blocks which form the structural and functional plan for human organisms. Called the Human Genome Project, this effort has generated enormous data sets which are just the beginning of further studies which seek to understand the genomic basis of human disease. Having a reference genome is useful, but all of us (except identical twins) are genetically unique. Only 0.1% of the genome (or one out of every 1,000 DNA units) varies between individuals. In a genome of 3 billion units, however, this means that there are an average of 3 million differences between any two individuals. Many of these differences have medical implications and characterizing the association between them and disease susceptibility is a major task for both researchers and clinicians.

The undiscovered links between genes and disease have led to many efforts, both public and private, to sequence the entire genome of individuals. This allows the specific differences between them and the reference human genome to be characterized. With all of this dedicated effort, including analysis of non-human model organisms, the amount of DNA sequence data is doubling every 1.4 years. Further, the biomedical literature is expanding at a rapid rate. The major online repository of the biomedical literature is PubMed,[2] which contains more than 10 million records dating back to 1966. Because of the current growth rate of biomedical research, 400,000 new citations per year–or a new article every 3.3 seconds–are being added. In areas of explosive research advances, the number of articles is increasing exponentially. Abstracts in genomics are now doubling every 1.2 years, with a doubling time of only a little over 6 months exists in the related field of proteomics.

GENOTYPE AND PHENOTYPE

All biological properties arise as a result of *genotype* (the full complement of an individual's genetic material) acted upon by environment to create *phenotype*, the observable biological characteristics of a person (Figure 1).[3]

Genotype can be explicitly defined because of the digital, discrete nature of DNA. Once the locations on the human genome and the types of change has been specified, there should be no ambiguity about genotype. Phenotype, however, is a much more fluid concept and can consist

FIGURE 1. Relationship of Genotype and Phenotype

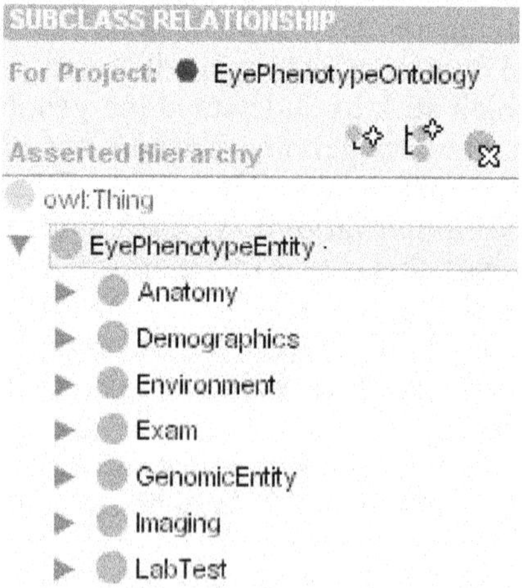

of nearly any descriptive term or concept that can be imagined. In routine clinical use, phenotype can range from simple, atomic declarations ("male," "age = 38 years") to complex compound sentences ("loss of visual field despite intraocular pressure less than 15 mm Hg"). Identifying associations that link genotype and phenotype therefore requires that phenotypes can be explicitly and carefully defined and characterized. In this way clinicians who see patients with a specific pattern of findings can query whether a genomic basis for them has been identified. Conversely, researchers investigating genome variants may be able to assess their possible clinical effects.

There are two major components to making phenotype more explicit and available for computation: cataloging phenotypic observations and determining the correlation of these observations. For example, diabetics cannot effectively use the glucose in the foods that they eat and often have a high blood sugar as a result. This single feature can manifest as hunger (due to cellular starvation), frequent urination (due to the high blood sugar), and thirst (due to the frequent urination). Encoding these observations in a computable format will be required to fully link phenotype to the underlying genotypic data that is being generated in such large amounts.

CLASSIFICATIONS IN BIOMEDICINE

Biomedicine has long used various classification systems. Perhaps the first in widespread use was the International Classification of Disease (ICD), now one of the most widely used statistical classification systems in the world. Codified in 1900 and updated every decade, ICD was designed to foster international comparisons in the representation and analysis of morbidity and mortality data. Typical ICD categories are "myocardial infarction" (heart attack), or "bacterial pneumonia." Many other systems describing different aspects of medical care exist. For example, the Diagnostic and Statistical Manual (DSM) is used in mental health, while the Current Procedural Terminology (CPT) encodes surgical procedures. Newer classifications describe molecular phenomena, including the Gene Ontology.[4] All of these give only a partial picture of biomedical reality.

The Unified Medical Language System[5] (UMLS), developed by the United States National Library of Medicine, is a compendium of many of these medical classifications which also provides a mapping structure between them. UMLS contains a large database of biomedical concepts in their various names and the relationships among them. It is built from the electronic versions of many different thesauri, classifications, code sets, and other health-related sources. UMLS currently contains over 1 million concepts and 5 million concept names, all of which are from over 100 controlled vocabularies and classification systems. What the UMLS and other systems lack is a knowledge model that accurately ascribes meaning to biomedical information sources.

Knowledge models facilitate knowledge processing, sharing and reuse and serve as a store of knowledge for reasoning. Most importantly, an appropriate model will allow inference over existing data sets to create new knowledge. For example, if it is known that Peter and Jennifer share the same biological parents and that Peter is a male and Jennifer is a female, then the two are brother and sister. In a biomedical example, if protein A is known to interact with protein B, and protein B is a cancer-related growth factor, then protein A might be involved in tumor growth. Thus a well-constructed knowledge model can *organize* as well as *extend* existing information resources.

THE SEMANTIC WEB AND BIOMEDICINE

Creating a Web in which computers themselves are aware of the meaning of information is an important goal.[6] The burden of routine information processing is usually on humans. It is desirable for machines to find, organize, infer, and suggest relationships among information resources. This saves human attention for creativity, intuition, and judgment which are tasks that people are far better suited for than computers. It is particularly desirable that information stores be both machine-readable and Web-accessible. In most cases the sheer volume of data will preclude human analysis. This means that metadata markup will be required for efficient processing. This can be conferred by using a series of Web standards collectively termed the Semantic Web. The Semantic Web is based on a series of nested tools which have the ability to endow information with meaning. The eXtensible Markup language (XML) allows data description tags to be extended and customized according to domain user's specifications. This is important in medical domains in which highly specialized concepts and attributes exist, and in which new ones are being regularly created. XML imposes structure on data and allows a logical tree to be built that represents data elements and attributes. XML has been a major advance but it is a syntactic standard and lacks a data model. A related application, the Resource Description Framework (RDF), has also been developed as a standard way of using XML to encode and exchange metadata. In this context a resource can be used to represent anything, from a physical entity to an abstract concept. The advantages of encoding medical data using XML and RDF are manifold.

RDF provides a simple data model that is analogous to human language. RDF is composed of triples which form a directed labeled graph. An RDF statement combines a specific resource (subject) with a property type (predicate) and its value (object). Labels on both nodes and edges may be URIs (Uniform Resource Identifiers), unique Web addresses that any of the members of the triple may occupy. RDF allows objects and values to have a dual identity, and each to carry a URI so that they may be found on the Web.

OWL, the Web Ontology Language, further provides a language for defining structured, Web-based knowledge models. OWL has the ability to be distributed across multiple computer systems, is compatible with Web standards, and is open and extensible.

A KNOWLEDGE MODEL FOR VISUAL PHENOTYPE

Vision and visual science are important both medically and economically. Visual impairment has a high prevalence in the United States. Blindness or low vision affects 3.3 million Americans aged 40 or above. This number is projected to reach 5.5 million by the year 2020.[7] Visual disability also increases significantly with age, particularly in people over age 65. Those 80 years of age and older currently comprise eight percent of the population, but account for 69 percent of blindness. As our society ages, the burden of visual loss is expected to grow dramatically. Eye disease has a profound impact on quality of life, which carries both economic and social costs. The National Eye Institute estimates the annual cost of vision impairment and eye disease to the United States is $68 billion.[8]

A knowledge model of visual phenotype would therefore assist the integration of visual science research with patient care. Characteristics associated with either good or bad clinical outcomes could be identified and serve as the basis for additional research. Further, machine understanding of metadata semantics could allow automated inference and categorization based on clinical findings. The knowledge model we have created combines several features that make it a particularly advantageous tool for the visual sciences:

- Its semantics are *understandable by both humans and machines*, the latter property being critical in allowing inference to be performed over the data contained within.
- It is *extensible* so that the visual science community can expand, modify, and customize its contents.
- It can accept and *integrate existing clinical informatics standards* such as UMLS, SNOMED, and ICD-9 as well as molecular standards such as the Gene Ontology (GO), GenBank, and MGED.
- It has been created using *official Web standards* and other open source programs and will integrate easily with other Web-based protocols, tools, and resources.

The knowledge modeling tool Protégé was used to create classes and subclass hierarchies to reflect the important properties of the visual system that manifest clinically as ocular phenotype. Protégé is a uniquely valuable tool for creating such a model.[9] Protégé uses frame-based modeling primitives similar to other tools of the Semantic Web and can produce output as RDF and OWL. Protégé has an extensible architecture that allows for integration with other applications.

The foundation classes in the knowledge model are shown in Figure 2.

The most general class is EyePhenotypeEntity which can describe any concept in the phenotype domain. The major classes that comprise this superclass are Anatomy, Demographics, Environment, Exam, GenomicEntity, Imaging, and LabTest. All of these have many subclasses and finer divisions to more fully specify the characteristics of each phenotype (also see Figure 3). Each class has a series of properties and possible values that may be associated with it (for example, the class "right eye" may have a property "visual acuity" with a value of "20/20"). Classes, properties, and values are all extensible and can be modified according to clinical and scientific consensus. Thus the knowledge model should become a standard tool of the visual science community and not reflect any specific individual view of the visual science domain.

Figure 3 shows an expansion of the Imaging subclass. The full range of imaging modes for the eye as well as image properties and values can be described using the knowledge model. Output can be generated as a series of RDF/OWL statements. These can be combined with other in-

FIGURE 2. Classes in Visual Phenotype Knowledge Model in Protégé

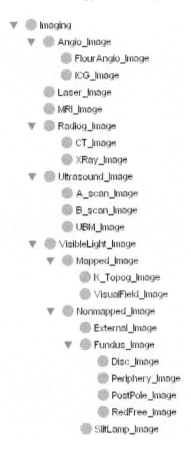

formation to create new statements that are inferred and are not expressed originally, but are implicit. Class definitions were also mapped to the extent possible to existing classifications, including the Foundational Model of Anatomy, the Gene Ontology, SNOMED, and ICD.

Why not choose a simple relational database (RDB) model as a Web backend to organize and store visual phenotype information? RDF is more flexible and uses a graph model instead of a series of relational tables. The graph can be traversed to define relationships between resources using the object-based model. RDBs deal poorly with hierarchy. Optional and variable relationships are inadequately handled in the

FIGURE 3. Example of Imaging Class and Subclass Structure in Protégé

relational model. In addition, RDBs are not document-centric, which is the predominant metaphor of the Web. Since documents may have irregular structure, larger grained data and mixed content, RDBs may be poorly suited for this task, thus Web servers with DB backend. At the same time RDF has many similarities to RDBs. For example, a resource may be thought of as a record (tuple or row), a column as a property type, and an individual cell as a property value. RDF is also an open system and can be used to join multiple RDBs that may be proprietary and platform-dependent, e.g., electronic medical records or billing systems. Perhaps the most compelling reason to forgo RDBs in favor of RDF is the latter's extensibility,[10] i.e., it is much easier to change the data model than is possible with RDBs, which are usually optimized for high performance with fairly simple data models and large transactional volumes.

Evaluation of the knowledge model was carried out according to established principles. Attention was paid primarily to design and structural validity since a full-scale evaluation was difficult in light of time and budgetary constraints. In addition, comparison-based evaluation was impossible because of the non-existence of comparable efforts to date. The axes along which an evaluation were performed included: (1) clinical need; (2) workability; (3) extensibility; (4) backward compatibility (interoperation with existing components); and (5) representation of the domain it seeks to model.[11]

The clinical need is compelling for the reasons cited above. Visual loss is prevalent and causes a great deal of personal distress besides its financial impact. Our system is workable, with a simple Web-based interface that can associate phenotypic descriptors with any set of metadata variables. This work is also highly extensible in that the ontology and the tools we have created to make it operational may be extended to accommodate new information resources and new clinical criteria for assessing patients. This frame-based ontology embraces the object model allowing for class-based inheritance and graph-based representation and traversal to allow logical inferences to be made. The use of Protégé likewise allows customization of data acquisition forms.

CHALLENGES

A primary challenge is to develop a biomedical Semantic Web that can store and represent large amounts of knowledge. Knowledge models in each domain area must be constructed and new and existing information marked up to reflect its semantics. Model building is both a social and a technical process. Domain experts need to agree on the names and relationships of essential concepts and then work with information scientists and other technical experts to commit the ontology to a computable format. Information markup will likewise present many challenges since laborious manual enrichment of existing data stores will not be feasible in most cases. Automated extraction and semantic assignment of useful information is difficult because these documents are expressed in natural language.

A further challenge is our dependence on standard disease diagnoses, which are often incomplete and imprecise, to represent human phenotypes. These are based on clinical traditions which may vary between medical specialties and in different geographic locations. As genotyping studies accelerate, we need greater systemization to match the higher data throughput that will occur.

The role of library and other information scientists may be crucial for the success of this effort. Physicians, allied health care workers, and researchers are generally naïve when it comes to classification and categorization issues. They are often too busy with their primary duties. Creating, implementing, and testing knowledge models for the large and diverse number of biomedical domains will be a cooperative process between information scientists and domain experts. Understanding the principles of knowledge modeling, the tool sets available for this work and codifying expert knowledge will challenge information scientists and demand that they learn a fair amount of biomedicine. However, the results will justify the efforts if we can capture more of the value inherent in biomedical information and use it to improve human welfare.

We have created a model of human phenotype in the visual sciences since it is a confined, well-studied domain. This will enhance our ability to integrate genomic data with clinical data for prediction of disease risk and recommendations for specific therapies. This can serve as a foundation for a knowledge base of the human visual system that can be accessed and used by clinicians, laboratory scientists, and others to aid both patient care and basic research. It also serves as an example that may be followed in other biomedical domains.

The further value of structured data in biomedicine may include improved workflow and content management. It could also facilitate measurement of outcomes, foster quality assurance, and improve medicolegal documentation.

Thus the integration of genomic data with rich clinical data sets, expressed semantically and in computable format, could be a powerful tool for the prevention of blindness in the future.

NOTES

1. National Center for Health Statistics: http://www.cdc.gov/nchs/fastats/hexpense.htm.

2. PubMed: http://www.ncbi.nlm.nih.gov/entrez/query.fcgi?db=PubMed.

3. Genotype is the full complement of genes that an individual possesses. Environment acts upon this raw material to produce the observable characteristics of every organism, the phenotype.

4. Ashburner M, Ball CA, Blake JA et al. Gene ontology: tool for the unification of biology. The Gene Ontology Consortium. *Nat Genet*, May 2000, 25 (1):25-9.

5. Unified Medical Language System: http://www.nlm.nih.gov/research/umls/.

6. Berners-Lee T, Hendler J and Lassila O. The Semantic Web. *Scientific American.*, May 2001. Available online at: http://www.sciam.com/2001/0501issue/0501berners-lee.html.

7. NEI Statistics and Data: http://www.nei.nih.gov/eyedata/.

8. National Eye Institute: Statistics and Data: http://www.nei.nih.gov/eyedata/hu_estimates.asp.

9. Noy NF, Sintek M, Decker S, Crubézy M, Fergerson RW and Musen MA. *Creating Semantic Web Contents with Protege-2000*. IEEE Intelligent Systems 2001;16 (2):60-71 (March/April 2001).

10. Staab S, Erdmann M, Maedche A and Decker S. An extensible approach for modeling ontologies in RDF(S). In *ECDL 2000 Workshop on the Semantic Web*.

11. Friedman CP et al. Evaluation and Technology Assessment. In Shortliffe and Perreault, Medical Informatics, Computer Applications in Health Care and Biomedicine. New York, Springer, 2001.

doi:10.1300/J104v43n03_09

Towards an Infrastructure
for Semantic Applications:
Methodologies for Semantic Integration
of Heterogeneous Resources

Anita C. Liang
Gauri Salokhe
Margherita Sini
Johannes Keizer

SUMMARY. The semantic heterogeneity of Web information in the Agricultural domain presents tremendous information retrieval challenges. This article presents work taking place at the Food and Agriculture Organizations (FAO) that addresses this challenge. Based on the analysis of resources in the domain of agriculture, this paper proposes (a) an application profile (AP) for dealing with the problem of heterogeneity originating from differences in terminologies, domain coverage, and domain modelling, and (b) a root application ontology (AAO) based on the application profile which can serve as a basis for extending knowledge of the domain. The paper explains how even a small investment in the enhancement of relationships among vocabularies, both metadata and domain-specific, yield a relatively large return on investment. doi:10.1300/J104v43n03_10

This material was prepared by Ms. Gauri Salokhe and other staff of the Food and Agriculture Organization of the United Nations (FAO) for *Cataloging & Classification Quarterly (CCQ)* (Vol. 43; No. 3/4), specifically for the corresponding monograph *Knitting the Semantic Web*, and is reproduced here with the permission of the FAO.

[Haworth co-indexing entry note]: "Towards an Infrastructure for Semantic Applications: Methodologies for Semantic Integration of Heterogeneous Resources." Liang, Anita C. et al. Co-published simultaneously in *Cataloging & Classification Quarterly* (The Haworth Information Press, an imprint of The Haworth Press, Inc.) Vol. 43, No. 3/4, 2007, pp. 161-189; and: *Knitting the Semantic Web* (ed: Jane Greenberg, and Eva Méndez) The Haworth Information Press, an imprint of The Haworth Press, Inc., 2007, pp. 161-189.

Available online at http://ccq.haworthpress.com
doi:10.1300/J104v43n03_10

KEYWORDS. Application profiles, information integration, information management, metadata, ontologies, semantic standards

INTRODUCTION

The information resources available from the fora of international agriculture related arena differ in degree of the subject coverage (e.g., some resources, such as AGROVOC, principally concern generic agriculture, food safety, etc.), sub-discipline (e.g., nutrition, animal and plant health), type (e.g., databases, images, news announcements), and content (e.g., journals, institutions, expert information, project descriptions, thesauri). No single search engine can retrieve a comprehensive set of the resources relevant to a user's needs given the distributed, heterogeneous nature of the resources comprising this domain.

Users looking for specific information may not get what they need because of the lack of meaning given to the words used on searching (e.g., "rice" may be ambiguous, so the result page might contain biased or inaccurate statements about the topic).

The World Wide Web (WWW) needs to transform itself into a system for disseminating knowledge that can be interpreted not only by humans but also and especially by computers, to handle the huge quantity and heterogeneity of information published on the Web intelligently and efficiently. This implies an evolution to a Web that is first and foremost meaning based rather than form based. An intelligent WWW, that is, one using semantic technologies, could then process the query *cereal crop researchers in France*. Based on its "understanding" of the query (e.g., through a process of resolving the query terms into concepts and matching those concepts to an ontology over which reasoning can be performed), it could conduct not only a comprehensive search, but also retrieve/suggest related concepts and resources, irrespective of the actual terms and language of the query.

AGRIS[1] is the international information system for the agricultural sciences and technology, created by the Food and Agriculture Organization of the United Nations (FAO) in 1974, to facilitate information exchange and to bring together world literature dealing with all aspects of agriculture. AGRIS is a cooperative system in which participating countries input references to the literature produced within their boundaries and, in return, draw on the information provided by the other participants.

This paper discusses the rationale and the methodologies for developing semantic standards in the domain of Agriculture. In particular, we propose two inter-related activities: firstly the creation of an *AGRIS Application Profile* (AAP) to address the problem of semantic heterogeneity of exchanging metadata on document-like information objects, and secondly, from the AAP, we derived a corresponding ontology, the *AGRIS Application Ontology* (AAO). The application ontology upon which the application profile is based makes explicit the semantics that already exists within the application profile, and may be further enriched with additional semantics through the introduction of schemes, thesauri, and other terminologies. The semantic richness of the application ontology varies according to the extent to which additional concepts and relations have been incorporated into the ontology. We refer to this AAO alternatively as a root ontology, since it serves as a starting point for further semantic extensions.

Developing and applying standards for resource description is a prerequisite for creating the infrastructure for a network of information services that can alleviate the semantic heterogeneity of the diverse and distributed services providing information resources in the Agricultural domain. Moreover, this emphasis on meaning over form allows for the development of "smart" applications for areas such as content management (e.g., automatic mark-up of documents), knowledge management (e.g., expert locators, concept-based search), and advisors/recommenders (e.g., mediators).

SEMANTIC WEB

In his vision of the Semantic Web, Tim Berners-Lee (Berners-Lee 2000) outlines an architecture for the Web that is multi-layered and machine processable, as depicted in the much-reproduced image in Figure 1. The layers with which we will principally be concerned are the resource description framework layer ("RDF + rdfschema") and the ontology layer ("Ontology vocabulary"). The XML layer will be touched upon insofar as it addresses the issue of content.

The XML Layer: Content of a Resource

The XML layer is concerned with the description of what a document or resource is about. Inasmuch as data that is proprietary to an application has limited use, the XML layer provides for standardized means of

FIGURE 1. Layers of Concern for the Development of Semantic Standards in the Agricultural Domain

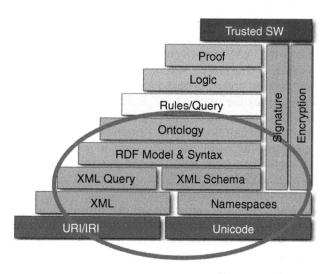

describing content in order to free up that content for use by any number of applications.

Granularity

Domain-specific XML tags can be used to mark up the content of a resource at various levels of granularity ranging from the level of the resource itself (i.e., to describe what the resource is about using descriptor terms or abstracts) down to the level of the section or passage within the document (if it is a text), to the sentence-level, to the level of a single term (i.e., to describe what the term means or refers to). In the case of structured data such as databases, the database itself might be described, or the fields of the database might be semantically indexed.

The level of granularity at which data is indexed is directly related to the types of queries the user can ask and the types of results that can be retrieved. If resources are marked up coarsely, such as at the level of the website (or individual pages on a website) or metadata record, then the user's query, normally in the form of one or more keywords, will retrieve a set of links that either contain or are associated with (via, for example, matching strings in the resource's metadata) the user's keywords. This option limits resources to those that can be identified via a URL or metadata records retrieved via a SELECT SQL query.

In contracts, at finer-levels of marking up information, such as the chapter of a book, or a passage, the results retrieved can be more directly targeted to the user's query, more so than matching keywords against metadata describing a document or URL, which may not contain the information needed by the user. For instance, if the user is looking for information on the health hazards to humans of pesticide use in Africa, she might indeed find a document indexed with (or having significant frequencies of occurrences of) "pesticides," "health hazards," and "Zambia," but the document might be about the removal of these substances, or the amount sold of those types of substances, or regulations about their use, etc., rather than about the ways in which they are hazardous. This is because there is little or no indication of what the relationship is between the terms used to describe a given resource and the resource itself, or among the terms themselves. When information is described below the level of the resource, retrieval results may match user queries more effectively. So an article containing a section on pesticides, health hazards, and Zambia would be indexed differently, and ranked at a higher position than one containing one section on pesticides and health hazards and another on Zambian culture. At the finest level of mark-up, where individual words are indexed, the system "understands" the meaning of each term in a sentence, as well as its relation to other terms. In such a system, the user can issue a well-formed question as a query, and the result elicited would be in the form of an individual sentence, based on an analysis of the user's query and a search for the best match among the sentences within the resources. For example, it would be possible for the user to input "What are the health hazards of pesticides used in Zambia?" and for a direct response to be in the form of a sentence drawn from resources, e.g., "Pesticide use in Zambia are associated with the following toxic effects."

Within the domain of agriculture, content description is initially envisaged at the metadata level, within the RDF layer (cf. next section), using controlled vocabularies. Thus, what can be retrieved are resources such as experts, software, and DLIOs (as opposed to individual answers, discussion threads, or text passages). This is mainly for practical reasons, given that there already exist numerous bibliographical databases that contain descriptions of bibliographic metadata using controlled vocabularies. The database structures can be studied to develop the initial version of the AAP and the AAO, while the controlled vocabularies can serve as the basis of further developing the AAO. However, it must be stressed that this is a starting point, and that more sophisticated systems can be developed once the AAO has been extended using vocabularies containing rich semantics.

The RDF Layer: Metadata of a Resource

The RDF layer contains information about a resource, viewed externally, that is, from outside the resource, and includes information such as its title, author, and publisher. This information that describes a resource is called metadata. Standardized XML tags can be used to mark up metadata. For resource description, there already exist standards such as the Dublin Core Metadata Element Set[2] (DCMES). The Agricultural Metadata Element Set[3] (AgMES), which complements the DCMES, has also become a standard commonly used in the domain of Agriculture, with its specific emphasis of agricultural vocabularies and terminologies (cf. Salokhe et al. 2004). What distinguishes, however, the lower XML layer, which merely describes a resource, from the RDF layer (Figure 2) is that the latter is able to express relations between resources.

In contrast to the WWW, where associations, i.e., hyperlinks between resources are meaningful to the extent that they are interpretable by humans (e.g., while a human could understand why a string *Mahatma Gandhi* would be hyperlinked to an image of the Indian flag, to a computer, such a relation would be indistinguishable from any other text that was hyperlinked to an image). RDF provides a standardized format for uniquely defining resources and a well-defined syntax for making statements about those resources. Figure 3 exemplifies the type of statements that RDF allows about a resource.

As mentioned, for developing an integrated information service for the domain of Agriculture, resources will be described using an *application profile* (AP), metadata elements that are drawn from one or more standardized metadata element sets that may also be extended and customized to the types of resources to be provided by the information service. This will allow resources to be described using standard mark-up languages that are independent of local platforms and applications and can enhance the possibility of semantic interoperability of resources within the domain. In Methodologies for Semantic Integration, we specify a methodology to develop an AP.

FIGURE 2. Section of Metadata Record Expressed in RDF

```
<rdf:Description rdf:about="http://www.fao.org/ag-pub/citation/1">
   <rdf:type rdf:resource="http://purl.org/agmes/1.1/citation"/>
   <ags:citationTitle rdf:resource="http://www.fao.org/ag-pub/citationTitle/1"/>
   <ags:citationNumber rdf:resource="http://www.fao.org/ag-pub/citationNumber/1"/>
   <ags:citationIdentifier rdf:resource="http://www.fao.org/ag-pub/citationIdentifier/1"/>
</rdf:Description>
<!-- Start description of the first resource -->
<rdf:Description rdf:about="http://www.fao.org/ag-pub/XM20053081089">
   <dc:title xml:lang="en">Application of a novel disposable film culture system</dc:title>
   <dc:creator rdf:resource="http://www.fao.org/ag-pub/creator2"/>
   <dc:creator rdf:resource="http://www.fao.org/ag-pub/creator3"/>
   <dc:creator rdf:resource="http://www.fao.org/ag-pub/creator4"/>
   <dc:publisher rdf:resource="http://www.fao.org/ag-pub/pub2"/>
   <dc:date rdf:resource="http://www.fao.org/ag-pub/date2"/>
   <ags:subjectThesaurus rdf:resource="http://www.fao.org/aos/2005/cabt#SQ00095"/>
   <ags:subjectThesaurus rdf:resource="http://www.fao.org/aos/2005/cabt#NT05852"/>
   <dcterms:abstract xml:lang="en">To overcome various disadvantages [...etc]</dcterms:abstract>
   <dc:identifier rdf:resource="http://www.ingentaconnect.com/content/cabi/ivp/"/>
   <dc:type rdf:resource="http://purl.org/dc/elements/1.1/type/JA"/>
   <dc:language xml:lang="en-US">en</dc:language>
   <agls:availability rdf:resource="http://www.fao.org/ag-pub/availability/2"/>
   <ags:citation rdf:resource="http://www.fao.org/ag-pub/citation/1"/>
</rdf:Description>
</rdf:RDF>
```

FIGURE 3. [resource] –dc:title–> v[dc:title]

Subject	Predicate	Object
http://http//www-smi.stanford.edu/pubs/SMI_Reports/SMI-97-0685.pdf	http://purl.org/dc/elements/1.1/title	"A Study of Collaboration Among Medical Informatics Research Laboratories"

The Ontology Layer: Modelling the Domain

In the RDF layer, resources are defined by virtue of their relation-ships to other resources. In addition, the ontology layer offers the possi-bility of reasoning within the domain through precise specifications of concepts, relations, and rules, thereby creating the possibility of infer-ring new data from existing data. In other words, an ontology provides a knowledge model of a given domain that can interface with the RDF layer via mappings to its metadata elements. The model is made explicit via a knowledge representation language. Although many such languages exist, we use OWL Web Ontology Language,[4] the W3C standard knowledge representation language that offers rich semantics and is native to the Web (i.e., is serialized in XML).

For the domain of Agriculture, we distinguish two levels of knowledge to be represented: (1) One consists of the root ontology, where concepts, relations, and rules corresponding to the resource metadata will be specified for and mapped to the elements comprising the aforementioned application profile. (2) The other consists of all other ontologies derived from knowledge organisation systems such as thesauri and terminologies that can extend the root ontology. These other knowledge organization systems may provide a set of valid metadata values for resource attributes, or they may comprise an entire (sub) ontology in their own right that can extend the root ontology.

METHODOLOGIES FOR SEMANTIC INTEGRATION

In the previous section, we discussed the parts of the Semantic Web architecture that can aid the development of a semantic integration solution for Agriculture. In this section, we present our rationale methods, and steps for the development of those components.

AGRIS Application Profile

Definition and Rationale

An application profile (AP) is a flexible, platform- and architecture-independent, information exchange format to facilitate the exchange of information resources via the Web for a given project or application. It consists of specific data elements (encoded in XML tags), drawn from one or more namespaces (i.e., named collection of elements and attributes), combined together and optimised for a given domain (cf. Heery et al. 2000). By reusing elements specified in already-existing metadata standards, such as the DCMES, AgMES, and the Australian Government Locator Service[5] (AGLS), the AP transcends proprietary systems and organizational boundaries, and thus creates the possibility of improving management of and accessibility to domain-specific information materials (cf. Onyancha et al. 2004).

Figure 4 shows the use of an AP as a common exchange layer to resolve the heterogeneity among information systems, and as a basis for the development of value-added services.

FIGURE 4. Interoperability Between Datasets Allow for Creation of Value-Added Services and Systems

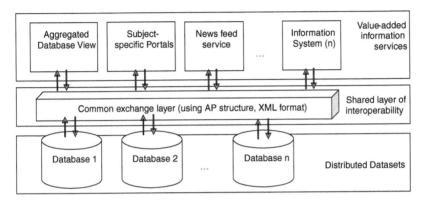

An AP prescribes the vocabulary, content, and structure rules that can be used to share information between heterogeneous datasets without requiring any change to the local system. With the possibility of using tools such as XSL Transformation (XSLT),[6] the information extraction and conversion becomes a simple yet extremely important task towards facilitating interoperability. The fact that the resource itself does not have to be attached to the metadata makes it easy to control access rights on it.

The following steps briefly describe the process (Figure 5) of generating valid AGRIS XML records from proprietary XML-enabled databases:

1. Identify the fields in the catalogue of the local database that will match the AGRIS AP XML DTD elements and schemes. Export the desired fields into well-formed XML documents from the local system.
2. Map, normally with the help of cataloguers or librarians, fields from the local database to the fields of the AGRIS DTD.
3. Create an XSLT stylesheet is then used to encode the mapping document produced by the cataloguers.
4. Convert the well-formed XML documents in step 1 to AGRIS AP XML resources by means of an XSL processor.
5. Validate the generated XML documents against the AGRIS AP XML DTD by means of XML parsers.

FIGURE 5. Converting from a Proprietary XML Enabled Dataset to the AP

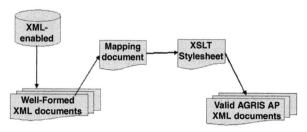

The next section describes the methodology adapted for developing the AGRIS Application Profile.

Methodology for the Development of the AGRIS Application Profile (AAP)

The creation of the AAP involved several phases.

Phase 0. Definition of the AGRIS Application Profile (AAP) Project, Its Goal, and Its Scope

The first and foremost task is to specify the long-term objectives. These were to:

1. Develop a platform independent exchange format that can alleviate the semantic heterogeneity characterizing the resources provided by the 200-some information systems identified thus far;
2. Conduct the foundation work enable information service providers of agricultural resources to achieve digital information management standards for the next generation Semantic Web.

Our solution for goal one is to provide a format, such as XML, that will not bind resource centres to any specific information system, yet allow them to share their data, regardless of the platforms and technologies they are using. These resources can remain distributed and can use either Hypertext Transfer Protocol (HTTP) or Web Services[7] to perform multi-host searches, or they can be centralized to a single database. If they remain distributed, Web Services is recommended both for scalability and for automatic discovery of resources, especially for the future, when the adoption and implementation of semantic technologies (presumably) becomes more widespread. The second goal, which depends on the first, as well as on the development of the agricultural metadata and subject ontologies (defined in Phase 2), provides a means of converting data into machine-processable smart data, a prerequisite for transformation of the WWW into the Semantic Web.

As shown in Phase 1, a review of the resource types identified by the initial surveys of the agricultural information services indicated that in all likelihood, it will need to be extended to include not only document-like information objects[8] (DLIOs) but other entities such as institutions, individuals, and projects, and even services provided by collaboration software and texts generated by means of those services.

Phase 1. Assessment of the Information Objects

The major objective of this phase was to specify the range of resource types comprising the agriculture domain. Within the domain of Agriculture, the following resources have been identified thus far:

- Internet portals, link collections, personal web pages, web pages of institutions and organisations
- databases: institutes, experts, literature, press articles, multimedia files, bibliographic data, projects, events
- publications: journals, newsletters, book excerpts, online texts
- collaboration software: discussion fora, calendars, event notification service, etc.

Once the actual resource types to be accounted for had been determined, for example, through user surveys, Web logs, etc., each needed to be analyzed to determine the properties characterizing it. Such analyses established the initial requirements for specifying an application profile for the agricultural domain. Note that different types of resources will be described using different criteria. For example, part of an adequate description of a book should include information such as its title and its identifier, which usually is expressed as an ISBN. An adequate description of a journal article should include not only the title of the article and its ISSN but also the title of the serial. In contrast, to describe an individual, information such as the employing institution, the individual's title, research areas, and e-mail address, might be deemed crucial.

Phase 2. Assessment of the Existing Metadata Standards and Creation of the AP

As shown above, different types of resources exist within the domain of Agriculture: DLIOs; non-DLIOs such as persons, institutions, events, and projects; and services provided by collaboration software. Because many of the resources are in fact document-like resources found in digital library collections, a natural starting point from which to create the AP was the set of elements, refinements, and schemes recommended by the DCMES. It is clearly defined yet shallowly scoped to serve the aim of wide applicability, i.e., cross-domain description, discovery, and retrieval of information objects. It is also extensible in that additional elements, refinements, or schemes may be added. However, this extensibility has to be controlled as it can be counterproductive to achieving the aim of interoperability. This phase also includes the identification of other entity types for which suitable metadata standards must be found or developed. For instance, to describe persons, the suitability of standards such as vCard and FOAF can be assessed.

Phase 3. Developing New Properties

The AgMES was developed because there are no standards registered metadata schemes that adequately support our information needs. AgMES provides a namespace for declaring additional resource description metadata elements for our domain.

The first step in this phase was to identify a set of necessary properties for agriculture resources–independent of any given standard. We posed the following questions to achieve this goal:

1. Is the elements/refinement/scheme really required to support:
   - resource description?
   - resource discovery?
   - interoperability?

Then, with the properties evaluated as necessary (for description and searching), another series of questions helped on the identification of the need for a new element:

2. Once it is determined that the need for a given property exists, then:

- Can the need be solved with a scheme value for an existing DC element? If yes, then create an AgMES scheme for an existing DC element, or else
- Can the need be solved with a refinement for an existing DC element? If yes, then create an AgMES refinement for an existing DC element, or else
- Can the need be solved by a qualifier from an existing non-DC set? If yes, then use that as a qualifier for the DC element, or else
- Can the need be solved by an element from an existing non-DC set? If so, then use that element, or else
- Create a new EEMES element (and, if necessary, a scheme).

The iterative fashion was adopted based on the original guidelines from Stuart Sutton.

The task of trying to match each property to an existing element, refinement, or scheme was meant to avoid reinventing the wheel. One consequence was that all declared elements, refinements, and schemes in AgMES have ended up looking like a hodgepodge. To make sense of them, they need to be seen along with their DC "parent element." Two further steps were necessary for completing this phase.

    a. Provide the ISO/IEC 11179 metadata[9] for each element, refinement, and scheme in the AgMES namespace.

Once the elements, refinements, and schemes were given entry into the AgMES, they were then described using the ISO/IEC 11179 standard for the description of metadata elements. The use of the ISO/IEC 11179 helps to improve consistency with other communities and augments the scope, consistency, and transparency of the AgMES.

Ten attributes were used to define the elements; and they are presented in Table 1. The terms **Name** and **Label** are not as they appear in ISO/IEC 11179 and were modified to adhere to the terminoloy currently being used in the XML community. This approach was taken to facilitate the assimilation of this set into the XML and RDF communities.

    b. Create the data model of the AP.

The next step involved taking each of the terms and defining them in the context of Agriculture. APs allow us to provide application specific definitions as long as they do not change the concepts themselves. For each element, we provided definition, cardinality, and data type information by giving some examples of best practice guidelines. These guidelines try to cover as many scenarios as possible but are not exhaustive for practical reasons and suggest the use of schemes whenever possible; for example, the ISO639-2 scheme to indicate the language, when necessary. This process was applied to all the elements and refinements (Table 2).

Phase 4. Create an XML DTD or Schema

The guidelines were then converted into an XML DTD which is used to validate all the XML-based inputs to the AGRIS Network. The XML DTD provides the logical structure of the record (the sequence and/or nesting of elements), the obligation (if a term is mandatory or optional), and the cardinality (how often can a term appear in one record, 0, 1, or more times).

TABLE 1. List of Attributes, from the ISO/IEC 11179 Metadata Standard, Used to Describe the Elements

Attribute Name	Definition
Name	The unique identifier assigned to the data element.
Label	Label assigned to the data element.
Version	The version of the data element.
Registration Authority	The entity authorized to register the data element.
Language	The language in which the data element is specified
Definition	A statement that clearly represents the concept and essential nature of the data element
Obligation	Indicates if the data element is always or only sometimes required (mandatory, optional, conditional)
Data type	Indicates the type of data that can be represented in the value of the data element
Maximum Occurrence	Indicates any limit to the repeatability of the data element.
Comment	A remark concerning the application of the data element.

TABLE 2. List of Additional Attributes Used to Describe the Elements

Attribute Name	Definition
Element Refined	The name(s) of element(s) refined.
Scheme	The applicable schemes for encoding the values of the term.

Phase 5. Test the Schema, and the Application Profile, with Real Data

The application profile was then made available as both a document and also as an XML DTD, which was necessary for validating XML inputs. The guidelines were then applied by a test information provider for subsequent refinements of both the document and the DTD.

The technical implementers, i.e., those who would be responsible for converting their proprietary databases to the AP format, were provided with documentation on how to handle the conversion. Each implementer was given one-to-one feedback to help them successfully implement the exchange standard.

AGRIS (International Information System for the Agricultural Sciences and Technology) Application Ontology

Defining and Providing a Rational for the AGRIS Application Profile (AAP) Ontology

An ontology is a shared model of a given domain whose basic components consist of a vocabulary of terms, a precise specification of those terms, and the relations between them. Although an ontology has a structure similar to that of a taxonomy, the real power of an ontology comes from the ability to go beyond the information encoded in the structure to generate new information through inferencing. Using an ontology creates a separate knowledge layer distinct from any local information technology, information architecture, or application. It is more scalable than traditional methods of integration, where fields from separate data sources are mapped to each other. In traditional methods, the addition of a single database to be mapped to n databases requires n mappings from each field in the new database to each corresponding field(s) in the other n databases. Moreover, drawing the correspondences between fields from the new database to those in the others requires an understanding of the semantics of each field in each database. Thus, the task of integrating every new database to the system, or indeed, making a change to any one of the databases, becomes more and more unwieldy, increasing by an order of magnitude the number of mappings to be carried out.[10] However, when the knowledge layer is abstracted away from the details of a specific application, each new system has only to perform a single mapping in order to communicate with the other systems. This facilitates management of and communication among otherwise heterogeneous systems.

Mapping the Application Profile to the Application Ontology

The Agriculture Application Ontology (AAO) is the root ontology of the system. The representation of resource metadata elements as an ontology is motivated by the recognition that, as far as a resource metadata is concerned, the normally underexploited semantics existing between extrinsic descriptors of resources could be used to enhance the user's information retrieval/knowledge acquisition experience. For example, nearly all bibliographic metadata contain the following assertions.

[resource] dc:creator *v*[dc:creator] or [resource] dc:subject *v*[dc:subject]

where *v* represents the *value* of the property.

A simple but useful inference that can be drawn from these assertions is:

v[dc:creator] hasWrittenOn/hasPapersAbout dc:subject

An application such as a search engine could make use of such meanings not asserted by the metadata or the resource (e.g., to make suggestions to the user, to enhance the user's learning experience, etc.). Yet, rarely do bibliographical information retrieval systems take advantage of the ability to make these kinds of inference.

Other metadata standards describing other types of resources (e.g., events, experts, etc.) are treated analogously.

Figure 6 depicts the three-tiered organization outlining the relationships between the resource, the metadata elements from, in this case, the AP, and then the application ontology.

The resource metadata is marked up using the AP. The AP elements and the relations between them correspond to concepts and relations in the application or root ontology that make it possible to generate new information through the extraction of inferences. For instance, a search for a certain journal could also yield, by inference, the e-mail address of the institution responsible for that journal. Indeed, in the future, with the use of the W3C OWL standard, this inference could be made even if the information about the e-mail address and the journal were on different websites.

Query: search for "Food, Nutrition and Agriculture" Journal

Inference: contact e-mail of the "Food, Nutrition and Agriculture" Journal

FIGURE 6. The Three-Tiered Relation Between Resource, Metadata, and Ontology

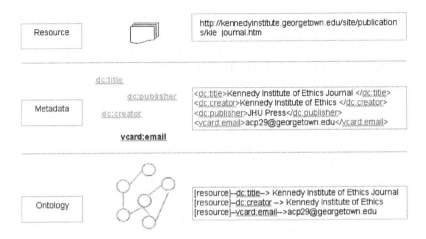

In the domain of food, nutrition, and agriculture, FAO has developed a multilingual metadata ontology containing few concepts (corresponding to the metadata elements), some relationships between them (such as "has_author," "publication_date," "has_subject," etc.), and many instances which correspond to the metadata records of a bibliographical database (see Figure 7).

Extending the Agriculture Application Ontology (AAO)

The AAO root ontology formalizes the metadata element semantics (e.g., title, creator, publisher), thus enhancing the value of catalogued resources. Additionally, the ontology can be further developed: subclass concepts, already formalized in the root ontology can be added. For instance, the dc:title concept subsumes the more refined concept dcterms:alternative. The root ontology can also be extended through the incorporation of controlled vocabularies. These vocabularies may simply consist of a flat list of terms, such as language codes. Any controlled vocabulary, specifically a thesaurus, can be viewed as a sub-domain ontology or domain-specific ontology that can extend the foundation/root ontology. These extension types are elaborated in the next two sections.

FIGURE 7. Metadata Ontology for the Food, Nutrition and Agriculture Online Catalogue

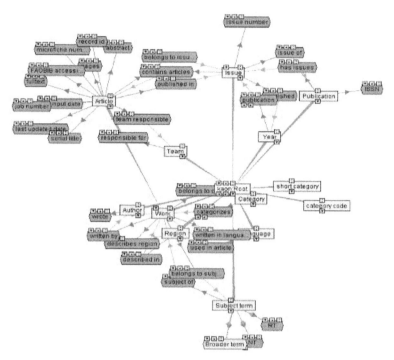

Concepts Refinements. As previously indicated, Dublin Core is being used as the basis of the AAO root ontology. The low level and simplistic design of the Dublin Core, allows for interoperability and allows it to be extensible to domain specific needs. Within Agriculture, the following extensions have been identified, as shown in Figure 8.[11]

Controlled Vocabularies. Controlled vocabularies are terminologies consisting of a set of terms and associated meanings that have been standardized for describing and searching resources. They often represent the intellectual work of experts and/or standards bodies that can and should be reused to avoid reinventing the wheel and to increase the possibilities for interoperability. This paper is concerned with controlled vocabularies that can be used as valid metadata values and those with richer semantics useful for development of sub-ontologies.

FIGURE 8. Additional Refinement of Concepts

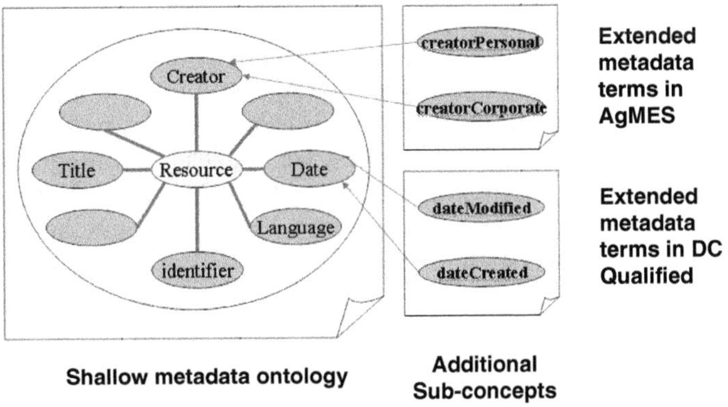

Shallow metadata ontology

Additional Sub-concepts

The main distinguishing features are that such controlled vocabularies they tend to occur as a flat file containing standardized names or symbols. They are extremely important because they provide *valid values*. Controlled vocabularies extend the root ontology inasmuch as they supply a list of valid values for specifying resource attributes. Examples include language codes, identification types for bibliographical resources, etc.

Vocabularies that contain rich semantics are often accompanied by prose definitions where the semantics is implicit, i.e., interpretable exclusively by humans, as in a glossary or dictionary, or where the relations among terms or concepts are (more) explicit and thus (more) amenable to machine processing, as in a taxonomy. In contrast to our discussions thus far on the AAP and the corresponding AAO, where we have been concerned with the extrinsic properties of resources (e.g., title, author, publication type), these kinds of vocabularies tend to describe the concepts and relations that make up a given domain, that is, those that describe the content of resources. Vocabularies such as thesauri are a good starting point for ontology development because they already are to some degree of machine readable. These vocabularies are extremely important for the development of *sub-ontologies*, and we can attach them to the root ontology via the dc:subject concept.

Several vocabularies may exist that are of relevance to the domain. That is, one provider might use *GMO crop* while another might use *novel food* to refer to the same concept. The subject sub-ontology can act as a mediating structure for multiple thesauri within the same or overlapping domains. Because it is concept- and not string-based, terminologies can map their specific terms to the corresponding concepts within the ontology. Further, with the help of domain experts, relations can be drawn between each uniquely defined concept. Consequently, providers can maintain the use of their terminologies while also being semantically interoperable with other vocabularies by integrating them based on a common semantic structure that can specify both terminological relationships (such as synonymy) and taxonomic and other semantic relationships (such as part-of).

Methodology for Ontology-Building

AGRIS Application Ontology. The AAO is based on elements constituting the AAP. Indeed, an ontology already exists for the Dublin Core Metadata Element Set (cf. Kamel-Boulos et al. 2001) that can be used both as a model and as a starting point for the construction of the AAO. Therefore, the construction of this ontology should not create significant problems. Figure 9 shows the correspondences among the concepts derived from resource, the AAP, and the AAO.

Sub-ontology: Agricultural Subject Ontology. This involves at least two strata of ontologies: the core domain and component sub-domains.

Phase 1. Gather and Characterize Existing Terminological Resources in the Domain

In keeping with the principle of reuse (and in the service of interoperability), the first step is to identify the lexical resources that can furnish the raw materials, i.e., terms and meanings, from which to build the ontology (cf. Soergel et al. 2004). These lexical resources may involve semantics of varying degrees of explicitness (e.g., a word list only identifies concepts without definitions or relations; a taxonomy has some semantics expressed through terms connected via a hierarchy), that may or may not be machine-interpretable (e.g., a glossary is intended for human interpretation; a database scheme can be "understood" and used by a computer). They include glossaries, wordlists, thesauri, taxonomies, subject classifications, XML DTDs, and database schemes as well as ontologies. Figure 10 shows how these resources fall along a continuum, according to the explicitness of their semantics and their amenability to machine interpretation.

FIGURE 9. Corresponding Concepts in the Resource, Application Profile, and Application Ontology

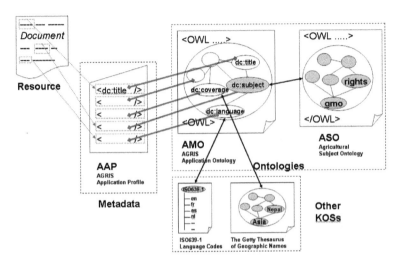

The degree to which the resource covers the domain in question, as well as the sub-domains covered, should also be assessed. For instance, a dedicated Aquatic Sciences and Fisheries Thesaurus[12] (ASFA Thesaurus) would obviously be relatively coextensive with the domain whereas a thesaurus such as AGROVOC, which is a general agricultural thesaurus, would contain only parts, scattered throughout the thesaurus that were relevant. Other information that should be determined are:

- Number of concepts/terms
- How concepts and/or equivalence classes are identified
- Semantic relations, hierarchical and associative (e.g., RT)
- Number of top-level terms
- Depth of trees
- Classes v. individuals
- Annotations

Thus far, in agriculture, over 40 terminological resources,[13] whose content is of varying degrees of relevance to the domain, have been identified. These include, among others the AGROVOC Thesaurus, the

NAL Thesaurus from the National Agricultural Library of United States, the CAB thesaurus.

With the help of subject matter experts (SMEs), those parts that are relevant to the domain and need to be incorporated into the ontology would need to be identified. Based on the findings in Phase 1, the next phase can be implemented.

Phase 2. Analyze Data Models

This phase requires analysis of each of the individual terminologies to establish the correspondences to be made to the data model of the ontology. Thus, for example, for thesauri, the following correspondences hold:

- terms are treated as strings not concepts;
- concepts correspond to classes and are not equivalent to subjects, topics, or domains;
- BT/NT are converted to superclass/subclass relations;
- RT is generalized to top-level conceptual relations (in fact concept-to-concept relations will be represented in a hierarchical manner; see Figure 11);
- an individual is distinct from and a member of a class;
- USE/UF may or may not correspond to synonymy relations.

Note that other terminologies may have other correspondences, e.g., in an XML DTD, elements may correspond to concepts; in a glossary, each term might correspond to a concept while relations to other terms or concepts might be derived from informal definitions.

FIGURE 10. Terminological Resources on a Continuum of Semantic Explicitness.

Wordlist ꜐ glossary ꜐ taxonomy ꜐ thesaurus ꜐ db scheme ꜐ axiomatized theory

Increasing semantic explicitness

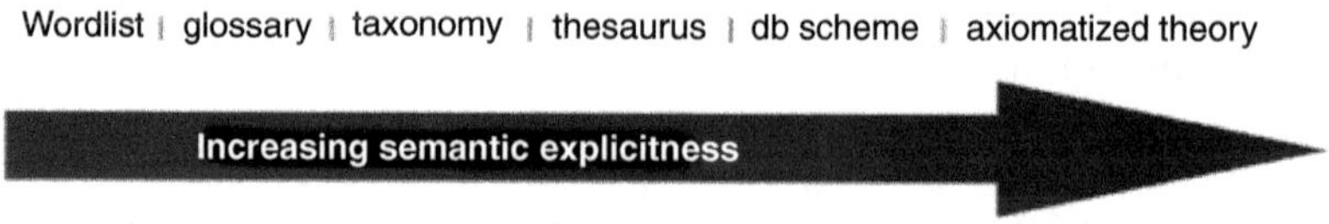

(Based on McGuinness 1999.)

FIGURE 11. Hierarchical Organizations of Concept Relationships

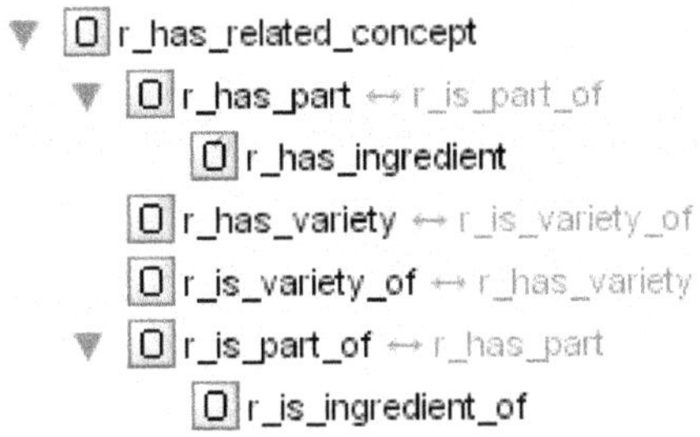

▼ ☐ r_has_related_concept
   ▼ ☐ r_has_part ↔ r_is_part_of
      ☐ r_has_ingredient
     ☐ r_has_variety ↔ r_is_variety_of
     ☐ r_is_variety_of ↔ r_has_variety
   ▼ ☐ r_is_part_of ↔ r_has_part
      ☐ r_is_ingredient_of

Phase 3. Convert Mapped Data Models into OWL

This stage involves the transformation of the correspondences made in Phase 2 to a knowledge representation language. Each transformation should retain information about the source terminology. For instance,

AGROVOC Thesaurus: *fires* ==> <owl:class rdf:id="fires@agrovoc">

NAL thesaurus: *fires* ==> <owl:class rdf:id="fires@NALThes">

Phase 4. The Core Subject Ontology: Capturing Knowledge from Subject Matter Experts (SMEs)

In this phase, SMEs are given a set of key questions or use cases to identify fundamental entities, roles, components, functions, and relations for building the ontology. The objective of this stage is to specify the domain-specific concepts and relations at the highest level of abstraction. The ontology that is developed at this stage then can serve as the foundation for the hierarchies identified and extracted in the next phase.

Phase 5. Identify Hierarchies Within Terminologies

Once the resources have been identified, they need to be classified according to the degree of explicit structure contained in the resource. Terminologies containing hierarchical structures can be (re)used to build the structure of the ontology while those with semantics meant for human interpretation such as glossaries can serve to provide synonyms and annotations.

Phase 6. Alignment

These top terms along with their hierarchies are then aligned to the core domain ontology created in Phase 4. If a corresponding class does not exist, and the term is pertinent to the domain, enrich the relevant part of the core domain ontology to create a place for alignment. Figure 12 shows a graphic of how alignment is done.

Phase 7. Merging

Merging is the process of integrating corresponding concepts from the source terminologies. For example, the concept {climatic change} is homonymous in the AGROVOC, CAB Thesaurus, and NAL Thesaurus and UNBIS Thesaurus, to the concept {climate change}, i.e.,

AGROVOC:[14] climatic change   **CAB Thesaurus:**[15] climatic change
NAL Thesaurus:[16] climate change   **UNBIS Thesaurus:**[17] climate change

Thus, the four sources are realized in the core domain ontology as lexicalizations of the same concept. Tools[18] are available to help SMEs with this process.

In other cases, homonymous terms may refer to different concepts. In AGROVOC, *euthanasia* refers to *putting animals to death*, while in the CAB Thesaurus, the context in which it occurs suggests that it refers to the *putting a human to death*.

AGROVOC: **CAB Thesaurus:**
  Euthanasia   *Euthanasia*
  USE Destruction of animals   UF: mercy killing
                                     RT: health protection; pain

For synonyms referring to the same concept, e.g., *GMO crop* and *novel food*, a SME is required to make the determination.

Phase 8. Enrich Through Annotations

Multilingual labels, synonyms, comments, identifier numbers are then mapped to the appropriate concepts.

FIGURE 12. Aligning Hierarchies from Different Terminologies to the Core Domain Ontology

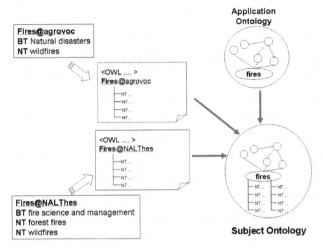

Phase 9. Post-Processing

Once alignment and merging has taken place, the resulting structure should be checked for inconsistencies. The exposure of such inconsistencies is facilitated using tools[19] built for such purposes.

XThes: DisjointClasses (a:female a:male)

XThes: Class (a:Sam partial a:female)

XThes: Class (a:Sam partial a:male)

$\rightarrow$ Inconsistent

CONCLUSION

The overall architecture integrating the AP and the root ontology is depicted in Figure 13. However, there are two principal architectures that combine these two components. Owners of distributed databases map records to and expose content in the AP format. This metadata is

FIGURE 13. Integrating the Ontology Layers with the Metadata Layers

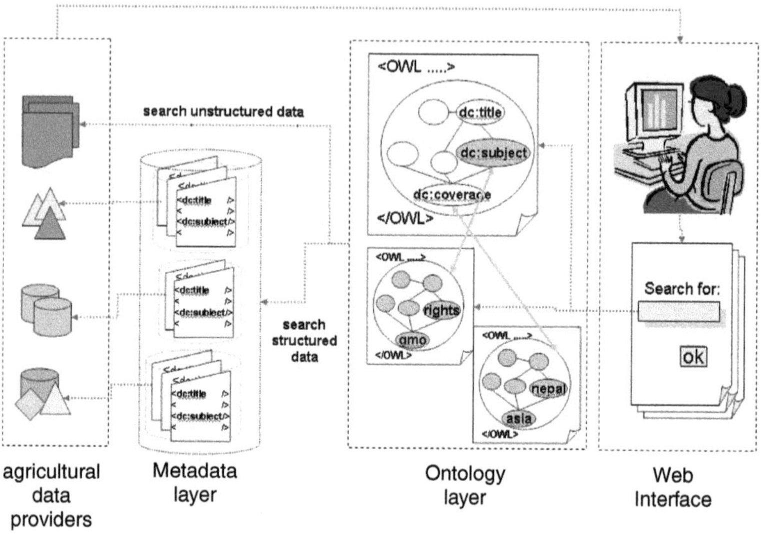

sent to a centralized database or it is made available on individual
websites. The former is called the mediator approach while the latter is
the federated multi-host approach. Both metadata and subject ontologies
are made available in a pre-defined location, although in the future, they
may be located in a registry of ontologies and accessed via Web services.

In the mediated approach, all metadata is stored in a single centralized
location. Queries are first pre-processed (e.g., parsed, spellchecked, normalized for singular/plural forms) and then interpreted via the AO,
where they are resolved to concepts or instances. These concepts or instances are then matched to the relevant fields within the central database. Note that, as mentioned, the AO itself may be centralized or
distributed.

In contrast to the Mediated approach, in a federated architecture, databases are stored locally and made available for WWW access. As in
the mediated approach, queries would undergo pre-processing and interpretation via the AO. But rather than conducting a search on a single
database, the interpreted query would be sent via Web services to databases hosted on multiple distributed servers and a search executed on

each of those databases. Thus, there are two dimensions to the building of the architecture: the centralization (or not) of the data, i.e., resources, and the centralization (or not) of the domain knowledge that describes those resources.

This article has reviewed how semantic standards promise to be an effective approach to resolving the problems posed by semantic heterogeneity and how they can be the source of applications that help users find and discover information efficiently and effectively. The development of semantic technologies is an ongoing process, whereby any given stage can be the source of application development. The richer the semantics, the greater the possibilities are for developing smart applications.

Our work efforts have required time commitments from project staff, but it has not been so demanding that it has interfered with daily routine information management related activities in the department. In other words, our work achievements did not require an unreasonable amount of time, and the results thus far indicate that the time investment was extremely worthwhile. It is not the case that large expenditures of time and effort are necessary to develop or to enjoy the advantages of semantic technologies, nor is it the case that structured indexed data are necessary to realize the benefits. As we have shown, even a small investment in the enhancement of relations between vocabularies, both metadata and domain-specific, yields a relatively large return on investment. There are several scenarios of varying complexity that enable information providers within the agricultural domain to exploit semantic technologies to provide information effectively and allow their users to access it easily.

NOTES

1. The AGRIS Network http://www.fao.org/agris/.
2. Dublin Core Metadata Initiative http://www.dublincore.org/.
3. Agricultural Metadata Element Set http://www.fao.org/aims/agmes_elements. jsp.
4. Cf. the OWL Web Ontology Language Overview (http://www.w3.org/TR/2004/REC-owl-features-20040210).
5. AGLS: http://www.naa.gov.au/recordkeeping/gov_online/agls/cim/cim_manual. html.
6. XSL Transformations (XSLT) Version 1.0 http://www.w3.org/TR/xslt.
7. Web services http://www.w3.org/2002/ws/.

8. A DLIO is a unit that is comparable to a paper document. The term is used to indicate resources such as websites, presentation files, photos, etc., but may not cover, for example, organizations or projects.

9. ISO/IEC standard http://metadata-standards.org/11179/.

10. $n\_P\_2 = \dfrac{n!}{(n-2)!}$

Where n = number of databases that want to share information with each other.

11. AgMES extensions for DC elements http://www.fao.org/aims/agmes_elements.jsp.

12. Aquatic Sciences and Fisheries Thesaurus http://www4.fao.org/asfa/asfa.htm.

13. Knowledge organizations systems (KOS) currently in use within the Agriculture and related domains http://www.fao.org/aims/kos_list_type.htm.

14. AGROVOC Thesaurus: http://www.fao.org/aims/ag_intro.htm.

15. CAB Thesaurus http://www.cabi-publishing.org/.

16. NAL Thesaurus http://agclass.nal.usda.gov/agt/dne/search.shtml.

17. UNBIS Thesaurus http://unhq-appspub-01.un.org/LIB/DHLUNBISThesaurus.nsf.

18. Multiple Ontology Management Tools: Prompt (http://protege.stanford.edu/plugins/prompt/prompt.html) and Chimaera (http://www.ksl.stanford.edu/software/chimaera).

19. For instance, the OWL plug-in in Stanford's Protégé tool is able to highlight logical inconsistencies in an ontological structure.

REFERENCES

Berners-Lee, T. (2000). *Semantic Web on XML*. Keynote presentation for XML 2000. Slides available at: http://www.w3.org/2000/Talks/1206-xml2k-tbl/slide1-0.html. Reporting available at: http://www.xml.com/pub/a/2000/12/xml2000/timbl.html.

Heery, R. and Patel, M (2000). *Application profiles: mixing and matching metadata schemas*. Ariadne, N. 25, September 2000. Available at: http://www.ariadne.ac.uk/issue25/app-profiles/intro.html.

Kamel-Boulos, M. N., Roudsari, A. V. and Carson (2001). Towards a semantic medical web: HealthCyberMap's Dublin Core ontology in Protégé-2000. In *Fifth International Protégé Workshop, SCHIN, Newcastle, UK, July 2001*.

McGuinness, Deborah L. (2002). Ontologies come of age. In Dieter Fensel, Jim Hendler, Henry Lieberman, and Wolfgang Wahlster (eds.), *Spinning the Semantic Web: Bringing the World Wide Web to Its Full Potential*. MIT Press.

Onyancha, I., Weinheimer, J., Salokhe, G., Katz, S., and Keizer, J. (2004). Metadata Exchange without pain: the AGRIS AP to harvest and exchange quality metadata, In *Proceedings of the International Conference on Dublin Core and Metadata Applications (DC2004)*.

Salokhe, G., Pastore, A., Richards, B., Weatherley, S., Aubert, A., Keizer, J., Nadeau, A., Katz, S., Rudgard, S., and Mangstl, A. (2004). FAO's role in Information Management and Dissemination–Challenges, Innovation, Success, Lessons Learned. In *Quarterly Bulletin of the International Association of Agricultural Information*

Specialists (IAALD) 1019-9926, v. 49 (no. 3/4) p. 73-83. Available at: http://www.fao. org/docrep/008/af238e/af238e00.htm.

Soergel, D., Lauser, B., Liang, A., Fisseha, F., Keizer, J., and Katz, S. (2004). Reengineering Thesauri for New Applications: the AGROVOC Example, *Journal of Digital Information vol.4, n.4.* Available at: http://jodi.tamu.edu/Articles/v04/ i04/Soergel/.

Sutton, Stuart A. (2000). see: http://www.schemas-forum.org/workshops/ws2/ws2-presentations/DC-Ed/index.htm.

Volz, R., Studer, R., Maedche, A., and Lauser, B. (2003). Pruning-based Identification of Domain Ontologies. In *Proceedings of I-KNOW '03. Graz, Austria, July 2-4, 2003.* Available at: http://i-know.know-center.tugraz.at/previous/i-know03/papers/ kc/volz.pdf.

doi:10.1300/J104v43n03_10

FOAF:
Connecting People on the Semantic Web

Mike Graves
Adam Constabaris
Dan Brickley

SUMMARY. This article introduces the Friend Of A Friend (FOAF) vocabulary specification as an example of a Semantic Web technology. A
real world case study is presented in which FOAF is used to solve several
specific problems of identity management. The main goal is to provide
some basic theory behind the Semantic Web and then attempt to
ground that theory in a practical solution. doi:10.1300/J104v43n03_11 *[Ar-
ticle copies available for a fee from The Haworth Document Delivery Service:
1-800-HAWORTH. E-mail address: <docdelivery@haworthpress.com> Website: <http://www.HaworthPress.com> © 2007 by The Haworth Press, Inc. All
rights reserved.]*

KEYWORDS. Semantic Web, FOAF, Friend Of A Friend, Social Networks

INTRODUCTION

We often think of the Web as a collection of documents that we look
at and absorb through our Web browser. Much of the current Web con-

The authors would particularly like to thank Jane Greenberg and Eva Méndez for
their invaluable input and editorial guidance.

[Haworth co-indexing entry note]: "FOAF: Connecting People on the Semantic Web." Graves, Mike,
Adam Constabaris, and Dan Brickley. Co-published simultaneously in *Cataloging & Classification
Quarterly* (The Haworth Information Press, an imprint of The Haworth Press, Inc.) Vol. 43, No. 3/4,
2007, pp. 191-202; and: *Knitting the Semantic Web* (ed: Jane Greenberg, and Eva Méndez) The Haworth Information Press, an imprint of The Haworth Press, Inc., 2007, pp. 191-202. Single or multiple copies of this
article are available for a fee from The Haworth Document Delivery Service [1-800-HAWORTH, 9:00 a.m. -
5:00 p.m. (EST). E-mail address: docdelivery@haworthpress.com].

sists of documents marked up in HTML. As a markup language, HTML is designed to create a human-oriented digital representation of a document or some other piece of information. The explosive growth of the Web and its increasing importance in nearly every aspect of our lives suggests that HTML has been very effective as a medium for content delivery. Fundamentally though, HTML marks up a document for display, not semantics. As humans, we have the cognitive ability to translate display into semantics. We can look at a Web page, read the words, look at the pictures, notice the way the text has been laid out and formulate an understanding of what the page is about. In theory, a computer could also be programmed to read the words, look at the pictures, and notice the way the text has been laid out. In practice, however, it has proved to be very difficult for a computer to take all that information and make the jump to actually understand. For the original architects of the Web, this limitation did not go unnoticed (Berners-Lee, 1994a).

The World Wide Web is built upon the foundation of the Universal Resource Identifier (URI) (W3C Technical Architecture Group, 2004; Berners-Lee, 1994b). The URI is not a new concept. We encounter universal identifiers outside of the Web on a daily basis when we pick up a book (ISBN), buy groceries (bar code), call a friend (telephone number), and pay our bills (mailing address). The Web uses a specific kind of URI called a Uniform Resource Locater (URL), which will be familiar to anyone who has typed a Webpage address into their browser. What the Web adds, by means of the hyperlink, is the ability to link any document on the Web to any other document. Most often, this appears to the user as a clickable link. It is understood that what is at the other end of that link has some relation to the page that is currently being viewed. However, the linking system designed for the Web does not have any mechanism to precisely determine what the relationship between those two documents is. It is only the context in which the link appears that defines the relationship between the two linked documents.

Prior to the Web's proliferation in society, the bibliographic community had been addressing many of the same issues that would soon come to the attention of the conventional Web's architects. Namely, the International Federation of Library Associations' development of the Functional Requirements for Bibliographic Records (FRBR) (1998) recognized the importance to users in making not only the entities on either end of a link explicit, but also in defining the relationship between those entities. The Web, by design, is a decentralized architecture meant as a generic content delivery system. As a result, it is difficult to define and maintain an authoritative list of entities and relations.

The Semantic Web follows the same basic principle of linking documents together, but while the conventional Web is meant largely for human consumption, the Semantic Web is designed to be machine-readable (Berners-Lee, Hendler, & Lassila, 2001). It extends the notion of the URI to encompass far more than just documents. In fact, the real power of the URI is that it can point to anything. While the physical representation of a URI is, of course, a collection of bits somewhere on a server, conceptually a resource can be anything, not just documents or images. URIs can be used to represent events, geographic locations, books, people and even insubstantial concepts such as ideas and relationships between objects.

Having a URI is not enough to create a web, though. A URI is only a point in space, which must be connected to other points if it is to be useful. In order to provide a mechanism for making these connections, the Semantic Web community has developed the Resource Description Framework (RDF). Simply stated, RDF provides a method of connecting URIs in a way that is meaningful. More specifically, RDF attempts to address the fundamental limitation of the conventional Web by helping computers understand what a document is about. Every entity, even real world entities and the relationships between them, can be given a URI. In light of the decentralized, open nature of the Web, this means that anyone can give an entity a URI and explicitly state, through another URI, how that entity relates to other entities.

This all sounds somewhat abstract and so, it is our intent through this paper to ground some of the theory discussed so far in a real world case study. We use various Semantic Web technologies, primarily a vocabulary specification called Friend Of A Friend (FOAF), to address some specific problems of identity management in a large organization. By building upon the basic architecture of RDF, it is possible to describe real world entities and how they relate to each other to begin adding functionality to the framework.

FRIEND OF A FRIEND

The Friend Of A Friend (FOAF) project (http://www.foaf-project.org) was created in 2000 using RDF to publish and exchange descriptions of people and the things they make and do. The FOAF vocabulary specification (Brickley & Miller, 2005) defines some basic kinds of entities (Person, Organization, Group, Document) and the relationships that commonly exist between them. For example, a person can be a member of a group, a document can be created by an organization, and a person can know another person. In particular, FOAF was initially designed as a Semantic Web update to the very popular idea of a personal homepage. In the conventional Web, a person's homepage typically provides some basic contact and biographical information, perhaps a photograph, resume, calendar, or any other information that defines who one is and what they do. However, encoded as HTML, this information is only meaningful to a person. HTML gives the computer just enough information to control how the data should be displayed. The final step of deciphering what the information means requires a human user. FOAF takes all this data and encodes it in such a way that a computer can understand what it means. A very simple FOAF document might look something like this:

```
<foaf:Person>

  <foaf:name>Dan Brickley</foaf:name>

  <foaf:mbox rdf:resource="mailto:danbri@danbri.org" />

  <foaf:img rdf:resource="http://example.org/dan.jpg" />

  <foaf:homepage rdf:resource="http://danbri.org/" />

</foaf:Person>
```

While the specifics of the machine-readable RDF syntax used in the example above are beyond the scope of this article, a human readable translation would be: "There is a person with the name 'Dan Brickley,' an e-mail address of danbri@danbri.org and who has a depiction located at http://example.org/dan.jpg. Dan's homepage is at http://danbri.org."

To take this example a step further, consider the decentralized nature of the Web: anyone can create a URI, and anyone can link to that URI from anywhere else in the world. Documents and information get broken up, spread out, passed around and as a result, from the machine's perspective, the Web starts to look like a jumbled mess of pages and links with little discernible order. It becomes increasingly difficult to determine which pieces of information belong to which. This is where the URI becomes important. If some real world entity is given a URI, then all the information about that entity, scattered throughout the Web can be brought back together.

A person is a complex entity, and a single FOAF file is not going to completely describe an individual. One might have a personal homepage, a business homepage, a personal description in an online forum, and any number of other places on the Web that contains information about who they are and what they do. When everyone agrees to refer to an entity (e.g., a person or a monograph) in the same way, we can be certain that we really are talking about the same entity. One of the ways FOAF has of referring to people indirectly is via their e-mail address. An e-mail address, like an ISBN or URL, is a universally unique identifier—it can only refer to one person. If a computer looks at two different FOAF documents and sees that the person described by each document has the same e-mail address, it can draw the conclusion that those two documents are really about the same person. The result is that the computer can successfully merge the two documents in a meaningful way. There are some limitations to this approach. For instance, the FOAF vocabulary specification does not require that a person's e-mail address be present in their description. In practice it seems, most occurrences of FOAF data on the Web do contain an e-mail address (Finin, Ding, Zhou, & Joshi, 2005). In the cases where an e-mail address is not present, it may be possible to use another URI, such as a personal homepage, to connect two FOAF descriptions.

This process of disambiguation is familiar to many librarians, especially catalogers. A classic example is that of Mark Twain. It is important to know that a book authored by Quintus Curtius Snodgrass and one authored by Mark Twain are by the same author. This is accomplished through the use of the Library of Congress Name Authority File. The Semantic Web does not have a central authority to provide this kind of service, and so it must rely on a more decentralized approach. By comparing e-mail addresses present in FOAF files, a computer can distinguish which FOAF data belongs to which person.

FOAF is not limited to simply merging multiple FOAF documents, though. FOAF describes people and activities, and one activity people often do is to write books. In the same way that FOAF can be used to describe people, a similar tool, the Dublin Core (DC) (DCMI Usage Board, 2005), can be used to describe books. When DC metadata about a book is encoded using RDF, an author's FOAF document can be merged with their article's DC document.

For example, an author might keep an extensive personal FOAF profile, with contact information and a current list of publications, each being represented by a URI such as an ISBN. Since this information is likely to need updating often, it is best managed by the author. A library might keep their own catalog information stored in an RDF format. By merging the author maintained FOAF file with the library maintained DC file, a complete, up to date list of the author's contact and publication information could be generated on the fly by a computer. What is exciting and important to point out here is that neither the author nor the publisher need to be aware of each other. The Semantic Web lets anyone say anything about any resource. By using machine processable data (RDF) and standard identifiers (ISBN) the information can be merged by anyone in whatever fashion suits their needs. Opening up one's data to the Semantic Web creates the possibility that it may be used in new and potentially useful ways which were never envisioned. For example, an author's book signing schedule could be tied to a local library's online catalog. For authors represented in the library's collection, the catalog might choose to list any book signings within ten miles.

The same principle of merging multiple information sources could be applied to anything that might relate to a person, even other people. From these explicitly defined relationships, it is possible to computationally create a web of trust (Golbeck & Parsia, 2006). Establishing a system of trust in the Semantic Web will make it easier for computers to determine which information comes from an authoritative source and which does not.

MODELING ORGANIZATIONAL STRUCTURE IN FOAF

Most organizations have at least some data about their members in electronic format, whether it is a custom designed relational database or, for much larger organizations, an online directory server that can be queried using a technology such as LDAP (Lightweight Directory Access Protocol). LDAP directories, having evolved in a straight line from telephone directories, have a record-oriented structure. Similar remarks apply to the sorts of record-based informational structures often found in relational databases. These sorts of resources are well understood and mature, and already enjoy industry wide acceptance. So why would anybody want to duplicate this information using the FOAF vocabulary?

In large, diverse organizations or organizations that have grown quickly and haphazardly, the data might be stored in many different places. Even in cases where information about people is stored electronically, well organized and well maintained, the individual data sources are likely to be incomplete. These data sources evolve over time to fit the immediate needs of those that use the data most often. To pick a concrete example, consider when an employee wants to find out who in the organization is responsible for the maintenance of a specific application. A departmental LDAP server usually will not hold information about a particular chain of responsibility for some service or application. This information may already be recorded in a relational database or spreadsheet file. However, in many cases, the only recourse might be to the oldest form of information retrieval: ask someone who has been around for a while. This is not an intolerable situation to be in. After all, it is the situation people have been in throughout recorded history, but it is natural to think that with information technology at our disposal, we could do a better job of managing this information.

The main benefit of modeling information that comes from a number of sources in RDF is most evident when you want to compile a more comprehensive view of the data. Each individual data source supplies only a partial view of the whole. RDF provides a method of weaving those partial views into a coherent whole. Discovering and querying all these sources of information can take quite a bit of time, and may require going to a number of different servers and using several different query languages. In such a situation, it makes sense to create a single source, with a single method of querying. A well-designed repository of RDF information can be queried with an RDF query language such as SPARQL (Prud'hommeaux & Seaborne, 2006). Applications that require this information can employ a single technique, rather than cobbling the information together from multiple places using multiple techniques.

FOAF is an especially attractive vocabulary here because it is primarily used for describing people and the relations between them. In cases where the defined FOAF vocabulary does not suffice to completely describe a person, it can often be extended in fairly natural ways to cover an individual organization's needs. For instance, by adding a property that describes who a person reports to, the structure of the organization can be modeled. Because FOAF is based on RDF, it also provides a solid foundation for integrating new sources of data as they are discovered or created. The following section presents one particular application of FOAF in context of a large organization's IT department.

CASE STUDY: STATE UNIVERSITY IT DEPARTMENT

As the Knowledge Management group in the IT department at UNC Chapel Hill, we found ourselves needing a more complete picture to be able to survey the structure of the organization, find out who knows what, and who knows who. A primary function of our group is maintaining documentation about various systems and processes. Doing this job well requires the ability to identify places where documentation is needed and to obtain the source information from the most knowledgeable individual, when possible. An organizational chart exists with names in boxes to represent groups, and lines connecting the boxes to represent the reporting structure of the organization. An organizational chart, however, is not easily "queryable" by a machine, and it is difficult to add data to. To solve these specific information needs, we decided, in effect, to construct a giant FOAF description of the IT department.

The source material consists of the campus-wide LDAP directory, an HR database containing information about the reporting structure (who reports to whom), and various other relational databases. Of these sources, the most valuable is the LDAP directory, because an LDAP entry for a person contains the same sort of information found in basic FOAF documents (e.g., first or given name, last or surname, full or "common" name, e-mail address, and telephone number). Most of the organizational structure is at least implicitly represented in the HR database. It also bears mentioning that the information stored in various heads–what people in the organization know–was crucial to putting the final system together. The challenge is to weave together these various sources of information into a coherent model; each of the systems involved is designed to serve its own purpose, none of which match our own particular goals.

Our goal was to aggregate all of these data sources into a single queryable data source. In the FOAF model, people are resources, and a resource needs an identifier. As explained earlier, FOAF uses e-mail addresses as identifiers for people, but not every system from which we pull data uses e-mail addresses, and the same person is liable to use different e-mail addresses (aliases, home vs. work, etc.) in different places. In order to aggregate the different sources of information, we needed a way to identify individuals across the different data sources. Like many large organizations, our university assigns each member a unique identifying number, and most of the systems use that identifying number somewhere. Therefore, the problem of missing or multiple e-mail addresses was largely solved by using this identifying number as a URI of sorts.

The end result is a reasonably simple, standardized, and extensible representation of the IT department's structure and the people that it comprises. It is now possible for us to run queries in seconds to answer questions that used to involve several phone calls. The biggest payoffs will probably come after the information contained in this system is made available to additional applications, which may have a different set of information needs. Take, for example, the various computer systems and servers an IT department maintains for the university. An RDF vocabulary could be created to describe these systems and the relationships between them, much like the FOAF vocabulary describes the relationships between people. This repository of systems information could be combined with the necessary data from the larger FOAF repository. A system using the combined data would be able to automatically discover who needs to be notified when a particular database server becomes unavailable and notify them. Another area of integration that would seem to offer immediate benefits are event based systems, such as calendar applications. Once an organization has undertaken the initial effort of connecting its people on the Semantic Web, other opportunities for linking resources together will become evident.

In our particular case, we have used FOAF in a relatively confined and controlled environment to accomplish some very specific goals of integrating multiple data sources and modeling the organizational structure in a machine-readable fashion. What of the unpredictable, distributed environment of the Web, though? A recent study (Ding, Zhou, Finin, & Joshi, 2005) found over 1.5 million FOAF documents on the Web. Many of these documents are automatically generated from user data by existing social networking websites. LiveJournal (http://www.livejournal.com), a popular blogging website, for example, creates a FOAF document for each user. Other community websites that create FOAF documents include My Opera (http://my.opera.com/community/), Tribe.net (http://tribe.net), and the business oriented Ecademy (http://www.ecademy.com/).

With so many large islands of FOAF data available on the Web, the next step is to begin connecting those. Leigh Dodds and Morten Frederiksen created the FoaF explorer (http://xml.mfd-consult.dk/foaf/explorer/), which can be used to browse a large collection of FOAF documents using a human friendly interface (see Figure 1).

Edd Dumbill has built an Internet Relay Chat bot called FOAFBot (http://usefulinc.com/foaf/foafbot), which can answer some basic ques-

FIGURE 1. Example FOAF File Displayed in FOAF Explorer

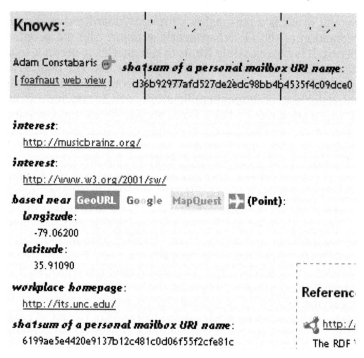

tions about who a person is and even what they look like. In addition, FOAFBot provides provenance data, which can be useful in determining the authority of the information it provides. Of particular interest to academic researchers, Aleman-Meza et al. (2006) used existing FOAF data collected through Swoogle (http://swoogle.umbc.edu/), a Semantic Web search engine, to determine conflicts of interest among researchers and reviewers in the field of computer science. Such research and development activities illustrate the potential in making meaningful connections between people on the Semantic Web.

CONCLUSION

From the abacus to supercomputers, humans have long been fascinated with the idea of getting machines to help us do things. Adding semantics, or meaning, to the conventional Web makes it easier to automate various information management tasks. We have focused on just one Semantic Web technology, FOAF, and shown how it can be applied to specific real world problems. While the benefits of this approach are indeed identifiable, the true benefits will be seen further down the road when more data is introduced into the Semantic Web.

As has been previously discussed, on the Semantic Web, anything can be considered a resource. People are perhaps the most important resource, for all other resources, both in this world and on the Web, are created, managed, and ultimately destroyed by people. It makes sense, then, to begin knitting the fabric of the Semantic Web with the common thread of people. FOAF provides the tools necessary to begin constructing this web of people, to which other resources and information can be added and, in turn, they themselves added to.

REFERENCES

Aleman-Meza, B., Nagarajan, M., Ramakrishnan, C., Ding, L., Kolari, P., Sheth, A. et al. (2006). Semantic Analytics on Social Networks: Experiences in Addressing the Problem of Conflict of Interest Detection. Presented at the 15th International World Wide Web Conference (WWW2006), Edinburgh, Scotland, UK. Retrieved June 17, 2006 form: http://www2006.org/programme/files/pdf/4068.pdf.

Berners-Lee, T. (1994a). Retrieved June 17, 2006 from: http://www.w3.org/Talks/WWW94Tim/.

Berners-Lee, T. (1994b). Universal Resource Identifiers in WWW: A Unifying Syntax for the Expression of Names and Addresses of Objects on the Network as used in the World-Wide Web. Retrieved June 17, 2006 from: http://www.w3.org/Addressing/rfc1630.txt.

Berners-Lee, T., Hendler, J., & Lassila, O. (2001). The Semantic Web. *Scientific American 284*(5) 34-43. Also available online at: http://www.sciam.com/article.cfm?articleID=00048144-10D2-1C70-84A9809EC588EF21.

Brickley, D., & Miller, L. (2005). *Friend of a Friend Vocabulary Specification.* Retrieved June 18, 2006 from: http://xmlns.com/foaf/0.1/.

Ding, L., Zhou, L., Finin, T., & Joshi, A. (2005). How the Semantic Web is Being Used: An Analysis of FOAF Documents. *Proceedings of the 38th International Conference on System Sciences.* Retrieved June 17, 2006 from: http://csdl2.computer.org/comp/proceedings/hicss/2005/2268/04/22680113c.pdf.

DCMI Usage Board. (2005). DCMI Metadata Terms. Retrieved June 17, 2006 from: http://dublincore.org/documents/dcmi-terms/.

Finin, T., Ding, L., Zhou, L., & Joshi, A. (2005). Social Networking on the Semantic Web. *The Learning Organization, 12,* 418-435.

Golbeck, J., & Parsia, B. (2006). Trust Network-Based Filtering of Aggregated Claims. *International Journal of Metadata, Semantics and Ontologies, 1,* 58-65.

IFLA Study Group on the Functional Requirements for Bibliographic Records. (1998). *Functional requirements for bibliographic records: Final report.* München: Saur. Also available online at: http://www.ifla.org/VII/s13/frbr/frbr.pdf.

Prud'hommeaux, E., & Seaborne, A. (Eds.). (2006). SPARQL Query Language for RDF. Retrieved June 19, 2006 from: http://www.w3.org/TR/rdf-sparql-query/.

W3C Technical Architecture Group. (2004). Architecture of the World Wide Web, Volume One. Retrieved June 17, 2006 from: http://www.w3.org/TR/webarch/.

doi:10.1300/J104v43n03_11

Advancing the Semantic Web
via Library Functions

Jane Greenberg

SUMMARY. This article explores the applicability of primary library functions (collection development, cataloging, reference, and circulation) to the Semantic Web. The article defines the Semantic Web, identifies similarities between the library institution and the Semantic Web, and presents research questions guiding the inquiry. The article addresses each library function and demonstrates the applicability of each function's policies to Semantic Web development. Results indicate that library functions are applicable to Semantic Web, with "collection development" translating to "Semantic Web selection"; "cataloging" translating to "Semantic Web 'semantic' representation"; "reference" translating to "Semantic Web service"; and circulation translating to "Semantic Web resource use." The last part of this article includes a discussion about the lack of embrace between the library and the Semantic Web communities, recommendations for reducing this gap, and conclusions. doi:10.1300/J104v43n03_12 *[Article copies available for a fee from The Haworth Document Delivery Service: 1-800-HAWORTH. E-mail address: <docdelivery@haworthpress. com> Website: <http://www.HaworthPress.com> © 2007 by The Haworth Press, Inc. All rights reserved.]*

KEYWORDS. Semantic Web, library functions, collection development, cataloging, reference, library outreach, circulation, Semantic Web planning and policies

---

[Haworth co-indexing entry note]: "Advancing the Semantic Web via Library Functions." Jane Greenberg. Co-published simultaneously in *Cataloging & Classification Quarterly* (The Haworth Information Press, an imprint of The Haworth Press, Inc.) Vol. 43, No. 3/4, 2007, pp. 203-225; and: *Knitting the Semantic Web* (ed: Jane Greenberg, and Eva Méndez) The Haworth Information Press, an imprint of The Haworth Press, Inc., 2007, pp. 203-225. Single or multiple copies of this article are available for a fee from The Haworth Document Delivery Service [1-800-HAWORTH, 9:00 a.m. - 5:00 p.m. (EST). E-mail address: docdelivery@ haworthpress.com].

Available online at http://ccq.haworthpress.com
© 2007 by The Haworth Press, Inc. All rights reserved.
doi:10.1300/J104v43n03_12

INTRODUCTION

The modern library of today, in all its shapes, forms, and constituent services, is often defined by the following primary functions: *collection development, cataloging, reference,* and *circulation.* The size of a library generally dictates if these functions are carried out in separate departments, or combined with other library operations. For example, cataloging generally forms a separate unit or division in large academic libraries, while it is often outsourced or combined with other functions in smaller public or corporate libraries. The library functions, identified here, are supported by protocols that have developed over time, and they are applicable to both physical and digital libraries. Most important, these library functions fulfill patent objectives that are integral to a successful library operation.

Primary library functions may also be valuable for developing the Semantic Web. This hypothesis is put forth because there are many similarities between the Semantic Web and the library. This hypothesis is also put forth because the Semantic Web community and the library community have *not* fully embraced one another, despite the similarities and pertinent connections. History tells us that solutions to past challenges are often useful for solving new, similar problems. For example, computer simulation techniques historically developed for training air force pilots have proved useful for training commercial pilots, and these techniques have improved flight safety in both realms (Rolfe & Staples, 1986). Given that the library and the Semantic Web are cultures devoted to increasing information access and knowledge discovery, it makes sense to explore the foundations of the library (the more established institution) and consider what primary functions may help advance the Semantic Web initiative. Said more forcefully, the library has been society's chief information custodian for the last several hundred years; and, if the Semantic Web is to evolve into a chief and trusted information network, affording services and performing tasks for both humans and machines, we need to examine the applicability of the library's primary functions to the Semantic Web.

This paper addresses this need and explores the applicability of library functions to the Semantic Web. This inquiry is a discussion based on rudimentary deduction, which is supported by an analysis of various library guidelines and policies. The article begins by defining the Semantic Web and identifying similarities between the library institution and the Semantic Web. The article then presents research questions guiding the inquiry, followed by a discussion of each function and how each function's polices can assist Semantic Web development. The last part of the article includes a discussion about the lack of embrace between the library and the Semantic Web communities and recommendations for improving this gap, followed by research conclusions.

THE SEMANTIC WEB: STATUS AND PLANNING

The Semantic Web, representing Berners-Lee's initial vision of the World Wide Web (Web), is an extension of the Web where "information is given well-defined meaning, better enabling computers and people to work in cooperation" (Berners-Lee et al., 2001). The goal is to construct a *network* of structured, sharable semantics that is accessible, understandable, and manipulable by computer agents. Computer agents (Semantic Web agents), acting on behalf of people or other computer agents, will traverse the semantic network, find and manipulate information, perform desired tasks, and offer services. A high level example is that a Semantic Web agent should be able to plan your family vacation to Las Vegas (e.g., purchase the airline tickets, book your hotel, and purchase tickets to a performance for a night-on-the-town) (McIlraith et al., 2001).

As with many significant developments, Berners-Lee's vision of the Semantic Web has been shaped by historical developments and ideas, such as Vannevar Bush's conceptualization of the Memex; J. C. R. Licklider's work at ARPA that led to ARPANET; and Ted Nelson's coining of hypertext and project Xanadu (Greenberg et al., 2003). Berners-Lee's conception of the Semantic Web was developed amidst technological capabilities stemming from ARPA and the Internet, an infrastructure *realistic* for contemplating an environ where "machines become capable of analyzing all the data on the Web . . . the content, links, and transactions between people and computers" (Berners-Lee, 1999). The information infrastructure in which Berners-Lee's ideas evolved is remarkably different than the environment available to earlier visionaries having similar ideas. For example, the state-of-the-art technology was microform (film and fiche) when Vannevar Bush conceived his idea of the Memex (Bush, 1945).

Although technological infrastructure is a significant factor underlying the conceptualization and potential of the Semantic Web, *technological infrastructure* alone is not sufficient for rapid and robust growth. In some respects, we can argue that the Semantic Web is evolving slowly compared to many other fast paced developments in our technologically intensive, highly connective, and increasingly wireless world. Consider the pace at which cell phone technology and functionalities have developed. A probable factor, contributing to this slowness, is the fact that requirements for building a fully functional Semantic Web have not been articulated in a detailed strategic plan or policy. Rather, Semantic Web development is being guided by the famous layer-cake graphic that appears in nearly every article that defines the Semantic Web,[1] several key documents outlining underlying principles (Koivunen & Miller, 2001), and the *top of the mountain view* of what the Semantic Web will or can be (e.g., Berners-Lee et al., 2001).

One reason for this predicament (the absence of a detailed plan) is that the original design of the Web–as the Semantic Web–was initially derailed, due to the rapacity with which Hypertext Markup Language (HTML) was adopted for Web development. HTML primarily focuses on tagging documents for appearance and format display; it is relatively simple compared to the intellectual task of the tagging required for the Semantic Web; and it has enabled the Web to mushroom at an unpredictable and exponential rate. Another reason for the absence of a detailed plan is that most Semantic Web efforts have focused on infrastructure and enabling technology development (e.g., Resource Description Framework (RDF) and the Web Ontology Language (OWL)) (Greenberg & Roberson, 2002). Building a network of shared semantics that is understandable and accessible by agents (people and machines) requires time and thinking.

This paper demonstrates that the library institution and the Semantic Web have many similarities, and that greater attention to functional planning and policies, as evidence in the library community, may accelerate Semantic Web development and contribute to its sustainability. In presenting this thesis it is important to acknowledge that there is, indeed, interest in semantic tagging, and it appears to be increasing via folksonomies and social tagging projects (e.g., Flickr,[2] Del.icio.us,[3] and Facebook[4]). One may add to this recent partnerships between academic and research libraries and information industry leaders (Google, Yahoo!, and Microsoft), where digital content and associated metadata are key commodities. These developments are unprecedented and represent aspects of Miller's "Library 2.0" (2006), including a move toward a more *semantic* Web.

Despite these recent developments, there is still an absence of plans and policies guiding Semantic Web development. It's possible that members of the Semantic Web community view planning and policy development as an impediment to the open spirit of the Semantic Web or considered too labor intensive to produce, although literature and discussion does not reveal this opinion. Another more likely reason is that members of the Semantic Web initiative have not had the time to consider the benefits of shared planning and policy development, due to other pressing foci and activities. Regardless of the reason for the absence of Semantic Web plans and polices, I firmly believe that librarians have a responsibility to share, with all information communities, including the Semantic Web, their knowledge of library practices and functions that have allowed the modern library to operate successfully over the last century. One way to do this is through sharing policies and practices. I also believe that it is the responsibility of those wanting to build a Semantic Web to look beyond modern library limitations, and inquire about the functions that have sustained and allowed this chief custodian of information to thrive for the last few centuries. Helping to validate this inquiry, it seems prudent to first consider the similarities between the library and the Semantic Web.

SIMILARITIES BETWEEN THE LIBRARY AND THE SEMANTIC WEB

Many clichés defining the Web either distinguish it from the library or point to similarities. For example, the "Internet [Web] has been described as a library with all the books tossed on the floor" (Wilson, 2000) or "the Web is like a virtual library"–the latter statement marshals little support when considering the full scope and anarchy of the Web. The Semantic Web part of the larger Web is, however, quite similar to the library for the following reasons:

- The library and the Semantic Web have each developed, in part, as a response to an abundance of information.
- The library and the Semantic Web have mission statements grounded in service, information access, and knowledge discovery.
- The library and the Semantic Web have advanced as result of international and national standards.
- The library and the Semantic Web have grown due to a collaborative spirit.
- The library and the Semantic Web have become a part of society's fabric–although less so for the Semantic Web.

The following discussion shows these similarities to be quite strong, further justifying the need for an inquiry on the applicability of library functions for developing the Semantic Web.

Response to Information Abundance

Today's familiar modern physical library has it roots in the Renaissance. It grew, in part, to accommodate the enormous number of publications produced with the development of the printing press (Miksa, 1996). The digital library also developed in response to the increase in digital information (Chepesuik, 1997). Similar to the development of the modern library, the idea of the Semantic Web was initiated as a means to more effectively manage and take advantage of the increased amount of digital data.

Missions Grounded in Service, Information Access, and Knowledge Discovery

Most libraries have some form of a *mission statement* articulating their goal to provide high quality library services, enhance access to information of "enduring and contemporary value," and support research and communication.[5] These goals are evident in both physical and digital library initiatives; and, in the academic world, they are integrated with the larger institutional mission (Snow, 2004). The library's definitive goal is to support knowledge discovery for advancement of citizens and society.

> . . . by creating a setting conducive to learning, discovery, and cultural excitement, we help community members meet academic and personal goals that extend knowledge and promote achievement in the individual and in the community.[6]

> We strive to inform, enrich and empower every person in our community by creating and promoting easy access to a vast array of ideas and information, and by supporting an informed citizenry, lifelong learning and love of reading.[7]

The Semantic Web's homepage provides a succinct definition of the Semantic Web that is characteristic of a mission statement.

The Semantic Web provides a common framework that allows data to be shared and reused across application, enterprise, and community boundaries. It is a collaborative effort led by W3C with participation from a large number of researchers and industrial partners. It is based on the Resource Description Framework (RDF).[8]

This statement highlights such components as a common framework, shared data (information), and collaboration; and it parallels the library's standardization and sharing of bibliographic data, resource circulation, and collaborative activities. The Semantic Web Activity Statement[9] provides a more in-depth view of the Semantic Web's mission by stating its goal to "to create a universal medium for the exchange of data . . . global sharing of commercial, scientific and cultural data." The Semantic Web's overriding goal to imbue computer and human agents with *intelligence*, which is very similar to the library's goal of *advancing knowledge*.

Advancement via International and National Standards

The library community's response to the increased amount of information has also led to development of cataloging codes; formalized classificatory and verbal systems; and encoding/communication standards (International Bibliographic Description (ISBD) and MAchine Readable Cataloging (MARC)). The Web and digital library growth has also motivated rethinking and revision of cataloging standards, models, and codes, as evidenced by the development of the many metadata schemes, Functional Requirements for Bibliographic Records (1998), and Resource Description and Access (RDA) drafts.[10]

The Semantic Web has followed a similar path as evidenced by a collection of information standards: eXtensible Markup Language (XML), RDF, OWL, Friend Of A Friend (FOAF), and Simple Knowledge Organizations System (SKOS). The word "standard" is used loosely here, because these developments do not have standard numbers, rather they exists as W3C formal recommendations.

Collaborative Spirit

Collaboration has been, and continues to be, necessary for library and the Semantic Web development. Library standards, primarily cataloging standards, have developed via national and international collaboration. For example, the American Library Association, Association of Library Collections and Technical Services, Cataloging and Classification Section (ALA/ALCTS/CCS), includes many committees that propose and review cataloging polices and standards, and which interact with international organizations (e.g, IFLA and the Dublin Core Metadata Initiative). Collaboration extends to all library functions, such as collection building and collection use/access via consortiums and cooperative systems.

Collaboration is a key part of Semantic Web development, as indicated on the Semantic Web's homepage referenced above (. . . "a collaborative effort . . . "). All of the enabling technologies/standards listed above (RDF, OWL, FOAF, and SKOS) have been developed through working groups and public calls for comment. Additionally, the Semantic Web supports a number of working groups exploring a variety of topics, such as Semantic Web Best Practices and Deployment Working Group,[11] which offers hands-on guidance for Semantic Web application developers. The World Wide Web Consortium (W3C), the home of the Semantic Web, is, itself, a collaborative effort involving academic, research, and industry members, and it has set a path of collaboration underlying the Semantic Web initiative.

A Part of Society's Fabric

The library is an institution, an operation, and a part of society's fabric. That is, the library (*all* types combined–public, academic, corporate, and special) is made available to all economic classes and strata of society. The library touches millions of people everyday in their daily activities in the work place, after work, and in the comfort of their home, as they connect to the library virtually, or physically interact with library materials by reading, listening, and/or viewing. The Semantic Web intends to be a part of society's fabric, although it's less so than the library at this point because it is relatively small. It has already permeated society through the popular press and high impact articles such as the Berners-Lee et al. (2001) piece in *Scientific American*. If the current Web is any indication of the extent of the Semantic Web's reach, which seems quite logical, the Semantic Web (or what ever the Semantic Web morphs into) will surely impact millions of people's lives daily, and become a major thread of society's fabric.[12]

INQUIRY

This article explores the applicability of four primary library functions (collection development, cataloging, reference, and circulation) to the development of the Semantic Web. The inquiry is a discussion based on rudimentary deductive reasoning (without formal logic), and supported by an analysis of various library guidelines and policies. The deductive analysis is supported by the "library and Semantic Web similarities" presented above. The analysis was undertaken because of these obvious similarities and because it has been hypothesized that primary library functions may also be valuable for developing the Semantic Web. As a first step in testing this hypothesis, the inquiry presented here asks the following two questions:

- Which basic library functions of *collection development*, *cataloging*, *reference*, and *circulation* apply to the development of the Semantic Web?
- If these basic library functions are applicable to the Semantic Web, how can they guide Semantic Web development?

APPLICABILITY OF LIBRARY FUNCTIONS
TO THE SEMANTIC WEB

This section discusses the goals and objectives of the four primary functions underlying the modern library. The discussion also explores the applicability of each function to the Semantic Web, based on the above analysis of library and Semantic Web similarities.

Collection Development

Collection Development in the Library

The goal of collection development is to build and maintain a coherent collection that services a designated constituent/patron population. Collection development activities are generally guided by a written collection development policy that may be viewed as a contract between the library and its users. Collection development policies document the library's intent to grow the collection, identify collection strengths and limitations, and guide library staff, particularly bibliographers, in their collection development work. Guidelines also include selection criteria about preferred subjects and formats.

Collection development policies are not permanent, rather they need to be reviewed and revised, as user populations change and present new demands. Consider how inner city populations change, with new immigrant population influxes, and more established immigrant populations migrating to the suburbs. New areas of study and emerging disciplines also have a major impact on collection development polices, particularly for university and college libraries. Finally, collection development can help libraries with administrative activities by including procedures for acquisitions, gifts, weeding, replacing lost items, and collection evaluation.[13]

Semantic Web Selection

The Semantic Web initiative, as a whole, does not identify a specific type of user, although individual Semantic Web projects are often initiated to service specific populations or topics. (The word "project/s" is used hereafter for refer to Semantic Web undertakings and initiatives that are part of the larger Semantic Web.) For example, MusicBrainz,[14] a community music metadatabase, is for people interested in both music resources and building a comprehensive music information site; and the Semantic Web Environmental Directory,[15] a distributed directory, is for environmental organizations wanting to disseminate and maintain organizational and project information.

A useful question to ask, as part of this current analysis, is: *Can library collection development policies inform Semantic Web development?* Inquiry into this topic indicates that a *Semantic Web selection policy* may help a Semantic Web project carry out the following:

- Articulate the intent of a project; and, in turn, a policy could help a project determine the degree to which Web resources and data need to be semantically encoded.
- Clarify the type of format(s) that will be tagged and made accessible for a project.
- Identify the strengths and limitations of a project.
- Guide managers with project development and evaluation, including the acquisition and removing (weeding) of project resources or data.
- Guide project employees (e.g., collection developers and metadata creators) in their selection and tagging of resources.

- Provide information useful to vendors who want to develop effective Semantic Web tools.
- Assist related projects with their selection and develop policies.
- Explain factors and means by which a project's scope may change.

Following this last point, it's likely that Semantic Web selection policies will require review and revision for the following key reasons: the development of new and related projects–some of which may be competitors; the identification of new user agents (computer and human); and the development of new technologies and machine capabilities.

Based on knowledge about the library community's experience developing library collection development policies, it's likely that Semantic Web selection policy development will require time and patience, particularly given the absence of examples specific to the Semantic Web. The wide availability of library collection development guidelines and resources, such as *Guidelines for Writing Collection Development Policies* (Dartmouth College, 2000) provide a useful framework for developing Semantic Web selection polices. And, if Semantic Web selection policies were to develop at any noticeable rate, a master guideline specific to writing a Semantic Web selection policies could be developed to assist future projects.

Cataloging

Library Cataloging

The goal of cataloging is to make library collection materials findable and discoverable so they can be used. Charles A. Cutter's (1904) objectives for a library catalog, printed in the 4th edition of his *Rules for a Dictionary Catalog*, are among the most influential statements impacting cataloging. Cutter's objectives state that a library should:

1. Enable a person to find a book when the author, title, or subject is known;
2. Show what the library has by author, subject, and literature genre; and
3. Assist in the selection of a book by its edition and literary or topical composition.

Written a century before the development of the Web, Cutter's objectives are still applicable to library operations today, and thus influence current cataloging activities. Cutters' *Rules for a Dictionary Catalog* also includes principles to meet the stated objectives. For example, subject specificity is expressed by informing catalogers to "enter a work under its subject-heading, not under the heading of a class which includes that subject" (e.g., "Put Lady Cust's book on the cat under Cat, not under Zoology or Mammals, or Domestic animals."). Throughout cataloging history, there are other principles such as the "Statement of Principles" (Paris Principles) (International Federation . . . , 1963) that have had a major impact on cataloging policy and practice.

Jumping a century beyond Cutter to today, digital resource cataloging (metadata creation) is being guided by principles and objectives documented in a variety of metadata schemes (Greenberg, 2005). Underdevelopment are the *Rules for Description and Access (RDA)*, which includes a draft statement of objectives (RDA . . . , 2005). RDA may have the most impact on cataloging in the 21st century, although it is far too early to tell. Part 2 of RDA's draft statement of objectives includes a series of statements about the catalog record's responsiveness to user needs. For example, descriptive data (metadata) created using RDA should enable a user to "identify the resource described" and select appropriate resources "with respect to content, format, etc." Additional objectives address access points, representation of entities identified in Functional Requirements for Bibliographic Records (FRBR) (1998), and cataloging quality criteria (e.g., data flexibility, sufficiency, and accuracy). Describing RDA in more detail is well beyond the scope of this paper, but it's important to recognize that RDA intends to provide cataloging guidance well beyond what is presented in communication and encoding standards (e.g., MARC and XM). Moreover, RDA's objectives may help with the development of the Semantic Web.

Semantic Web "Semantic" Representation

Similarities between library cataloging and producing metadata for the Semantic Web are obvious, in that both deal with representation. In fact, the boundary between the employ of representation standards in these two environments (libraries and the Semantic Web) is artificial. Rather, the representation activity takes place along a continuum, with simple bibliographic representation for search and retrieval on one end, and the implementation of formal ontologies and machine supported deductive reasoning on the other (McGuinness, 2003, p. 175). What is missing in the context of the Semantic Web are principles and objectives for using metadata schemes and ontological system. *How should a*

Semantic Web project decide which metadata schema or ontology to use? What level of representation is required to properly represent the information entity so that an agent can successfully manipulate the information and provide a useful service? Similar to the library's community extensive MARC documentation,[16] the Semantic Web provides comprehensive documentation for working with enabling technologies, such as XML, RDF, and OWL. However, the Semantic Web community falls short, currently, in providing documentation to guide the use of metadata standards and ontologies.

Plans, guidelines, and policies are needed stating principles and objectives for Semantic Web representation to ensure good quality "semantics" (e.g., coherent, consistent, accurate semantic representation). A *semantic representation policy* would help secure a robust framework for effective Semantic Web operations. There are many examples cataloging policies[17] that document and detail principles and objectives, and could serve as a model for developing useful policies for the Semantic Web. Similar to the development of a Semantic Web selection policy, the development of a *Semantic Web "semantic" representation policy* would require time, but as more examples are created, a general framework might also be developed to assist future projects feeding into the overall Semantic Web initiative.

Reference

Reference and Outreach

The goal of reference is to provide the library community with effective information services. Reference services include personal interaction; dissemination of documentation (e.g., pathfinders, bibliographies, and guides on collection resources or technology use); signs identifying location and directions; and educative and outreach activities, such as bibliographic instruction (RUSA Access to Information Committee, 2000; University of Texas at Arlington, 2006). The library has an obligation "to provide information service to support the educational, recreational, personal and economic endeavors of the members of their respective communities" (RUSA Access to Information Committee, 2000). In meeting these needs, libraries uphold the American Library Association's Library Bill of Rights,[18] Freedom to Read Statement,[19] and Code of Ethics.[20] Reference services are generally supported by guidelines stating service goals, which are integrated into library access

policies, collection development polices, or the library's mission statement (e.g., Office of the Associate University Librarian, 2006).

   An extension of reference is *outreach*. Libraries plan services that are
of value to their users. Consider a library centrally located in a retirement
community, where the majority of the user population over the age 65.
For this library, it makes sense to conduct bibliographic instruction/out-
reach sessions highlighting collection holdings that address retirement
challenges, healthy living for the elderly, and health issues impacting
seniors. Whereas conducting outreach to highlight collection resources
that help with finding a first professional job would not be that practical,
unless, of course, the grandchildren of the retirees frequent the library to
such an extent that is would be a useful service to provide. Outreach extends to *community outreach*, generally in public through the offering
of classes and other services (e.g., English as a second language classes,
story time for youngsters, reader advisory services, even cooking and
art classes). These items extend beyond reference, but deal with overall
access and use of the library facility, and often promote collection use.

Semantic Web Service

   How, we may ask, is reference applicable to the development of the
Semantic Web? The tie is with "service"–the central pillar of Semantic
Web. The Semantic Web depends on standardized structured metadata
and Semantic Web algorithms capable of reading and manipulating
such data, but the overriding goal is to provide service, to free humans
from mundane tasks that computers can perform–and can perform effectively. Current Semantic Web services facilitate knowledge and service discovery, and more sophisticated forecasted activities include
automatic purchasing of an airline ticket–even an airline ticket from
your preferred carrier (McIlraith et al., 2001).

   To learn and benefit from the experience of reference services, Semantic Web projects might look to RUSA's *Guideline for Information
Services* (RUSA Access to Information Committee, 2000) as a template
for developing *Semantic Web service* guidelines and statements that
could facilitate Semantic Web development. Table 1 and Table 2 pull
examples from Section 1.0 Services and Section 5.0 Evaluation respectively and demonstrate how the statements could be modified to guide
Semantic Web development.

   The reference function, like all library functions, has taken advantage
of technological advances, including those associated with the Web.
One of the most obvious changes is virtual reference–often labeled as

TABLE 1. Library Reference and Semantic Web Project Service Policy Statements

Library Reference Service Statements*	Semantic Web Project Service (SWPS) Statements
RUSA Statement 1.1	SWPS Statement 1
The goal of information services is to provide the information sought by the user. Information service should anticipate as well as meet user needs. It should encourage user awareness of the potential of information resources to fulfill individual information needs.	The goal of Semantic Web project x is to provide the information sought by agents (computer and human). The Semantic Web service should anticipate agent needs. It should facilitate agent awareness of the potential the services' its information resources can fulfill to individual needs.
RUSA Statement 1.3	SWPS Statement 2
The library should strive to provide users with complete, accurate answers to information queries regardless of the complexity of those queries.	Semantic Web project x should strive to provide agents (computer and human) with complete, accurate answers to information queries regardless of the complexity of those queries.
RUSA Statement 1.6	SWPS Statement 3
The library should actively publicize the scope, nature, and availability of the information services it offers. It should employ those media most effective in reaching its entire clientele or selected segments of that clientele, as appropriate.	Semantic Web project x should actively publicize the scope, nature, and availability of the information services it offers. It should employ those media most effective in reaching its entire clientele or selected segments of that clientele, as appropriate.
RUSA Statement 1.7	SWPS Statement 3
The library should survey and assess the information needs of its community and create local information products to fulfill those needs not met by existing materials.	Semantic Web project x should survey and assess the information needs of its community and create local information products to fulfill those needs not met by existing materials.

*RUSA's *Guideline for Information Services* (2000). Information in left column used with permission from RUSA and the American Library Association.

TABLE 2. Library Reference and Semantic Web Project Evaluation Policy Statements

Library Reference Service Statements*	Semantic Web Project Evaluation (SWPE) Statements
RUSA Statement 5.1	SWPE Statement 1
The library should regularly evaluate its information services to ensure that the service furthers the institution's goals and that the goals reflect the needs and interests of the community served.	Semantic Web project x should regularly evaluate its information services to ensure that the service furthers the initiatives goals and that the goals reflect the needs and interests of the community served.
RUSA Statement 5.2	SWPE Statement 2
The library should integrate the perspectives of staff and community in the overall evaluation procedure for information service.	Semantic Web project x should integrate the perspectives of managers, staff, and user agents (computer and human) in the overall evaluation procedure for Semantic Web service.

*RUSA's *Guideline for Information Services* (2000). Information in left column used with permission from RUSA and the American Library Association.

"Chat-Reference" or "Ask-a-Librarian." Digital technology and the Web have had an impact on the overall reference activity, leading to the development of "digital reference," which includes new challenges, such as interface and architecture design, and requires new ways of marketing, evaluation, and collaboration. IFLA's Digital Reference Guidelines (2005) provides guidance for addressing these new digital reference challenges. The IFLA guidelines and other resources on digital reference (e.g., Lipow, 2005) may prove useful for articulating more detailed *Semantic Web service* plans. Finally, these resources may also assist with *Semantic Web outreach projects* promoting community events and use of a Semantic Web service. For example, the creation of a community bulletin board listing local concerts as explored by Graves (2003).

Circulation

Library Circulation

Circulation is the last primary library function to explore in this inquiry of the applicability of library functions to Semantic Web development. Circulation policies document collection access and use procedures. These policies are created to promote healthy collection use and protect library collection holdings. Users often want access to the same collection materials, of which there may be limited copies, or rare materials that are fragile. Circulation polices identify who may use a collection and who has borrowing privileges; they define loan time periods and present renewal polices so that all interested users can have access to library materials. Circulation polices generally state fines and procedures for late returns, lost and damaged items, and other problems associated with delinquent use. Circulation policies also identify non-circulating materials, such as very costly collection holdings, resources needed daily (e.g., a reference resource), or fragile and rare materials. For an example of a thorough policy see the University of Rochester's circulation policy.[21]

Semantic Web Resource Use

In examining circulation in the context of the Semantic Web, it is important to point out that digital libraries have eliminated basic circulation challenges tied to physical collections. For example, multiple users can access a digital resource at any time, and for extended time periods, eliminating the need for a loan period. Notwithstanding these developments, basic circulations challenges are still applicable to Semantic Web projects on a fundamental level. Table 3 indicates how several basic circulation issues may translate to a *Semantic Web resource use policy*.

On one hand, much of the sprit of the Semantic Web is open–open access, open information, and open source–and it seems a bit restrictive to consider something like a Semantic Web resource use policy. On the other hand, it is important to recognize that a "use policy" can promote resource use and protect the integrity of a project's resources, including semantics. It is important to point out that not all libraries are "open," and not all user services are free. A user fee is generally required for access and searching certain online databases (e.g., Dialog and LexisNexis), and corporate and private libraries are not open to just anyone. Additionally, there are general operational and collection development and maintenance costs with any library that are related to all the functions addressed in this article. Similarly, the Semantic Web initiative includes a range of partners from both the academic/research and industry sectors, and there already are Semantic Web services that have been initiated

TABLE 3

Library Circulation Policy Issues	Semantic Web Resource Use Policy (for computer and human agents)
Who has access	A policy could state agent access procedures. A policy might involve an application procedure, where an agent would be given an access code. Agent status could then be verified via an identification number of digital signature.
Borrowing privilege	A policy could state if agents, with privileges, can borrow (or harvest) metadata/semantics to integrate with other applications to perform a task.
Loan period, Renewing loans	A policy could indicate how long an agent can access the project resources and how access privileges can be renewed.
Recalling checked out items	A policy might include a procedure for informing agents of new resources and semantic data updates, given the potential impact on ongoing, or previously conducted operations.
Recommending a library purchase	A policy could provide a venue for agents to request additional resources or semantics.
Locating items	A policy could indicate explain the arrangement of resources within a project.
Fines policy, Borrower blocks	A policy could state instances in which agents would be fined. For example, tampering with semantic data would results in fines or blocking agent use.
Record of use	A policy should inform agents of any tracking or recording of data use.

due to financial incentives. Despite financial motivation, the implementation of Semantic Web projects requiring fees need to be reasonable (and worthy of their cost) if they are to be as successful at the library.

THE SEMANTIC WEB/LIBRARY GAP

The Semantic Web and library communities are far from being healthfully integrated. On one side of this gap, the members of the Semantic Web community are not fully aware of the skills, talent, and knowledge that librarians (primarily catalogers) have, and which can help advance the Semantic Web.[22] This is evident by the absence of a metadata representation working group within the World Wide Web Consortium (W3C), and the severely limited participation of professional librarians on various W3C working groups. Granted, the W3C's Semantic Web activity has focused more on the development of enabling technologies, rather than processes or activities. Clearly, librarians could become Semantic Web advocates by engaging in W3C discussion groups and participating in Semantic Web conferences, if they want to be involved in this initiative. Even so, I am able to confirm only one professional librarian active and chairing a W3C task force that has relevancy to the Semantic Web.

On the library side of the gap, librarians have been slow to embrace the Semantic Web and work with Semantic Web enabling technologies and standards (e.g., RDF, OWL, etc.) in comparison to the way in which computer scientists, engineers, and ontologists (who are often formerly trained as linguists, psychologists, or scientists) have. *Slowness* here is calculated in relation to today's fast paced and highly connected world with real time and instant processes for creating and disseminating information (e.g., blogs, e-mail, podcasting, Web sites, and instant messaging). Additional factors interfering with librarian participation in the Semantic Web are:

- Communication barriers stemming from the different languages used by members of the Semantic Web initiative and the library community.
- An absence of user-friendly applications for making digital information (documents to data sets) operative for the Semantic Web (although this is changing, with more user friendly tools, like Protégé for ontologies).[23]

- Heavy and demanding daily workloads for library operations, resulting in limited time to read and digest Semantic Web developments.
- Limited documentation on the processes, plans, and policies for building the Semantic Web.

Following on this last point, it is worth reiterating that the majority of Semantic Web documentation presents technical standards or hypothetical scenarios (e.g., Berners-Lee et al., 2001) currently not possible, which makes it difficult for librarians to determine where their skills and knowledge can aid Semantic Web development. True, examples can be found to counter each of the above listed obstacles. For example, Brooks (2002) reviews cataloging and information retrieval developments and presents *lessons of librarianship* that are applicable to the Semantic Web. A more recent development is the increase in panels and workshops addressing the Semantic Web at library and information science at professional conferences (e.g., American Society of Information Science and Technology (ASIST) and the Joint Conference on Digital Libraries (JCDL) have both offered workshops on ontologies and Semantic Web technology). Additionally, blogs and e-lists frequented by librarian show limited attention to the Semantic Web. Despite these examples, the link between the library and the Semantic Web is still limited.

The Semantic Web/library "gap," it seems, could be reduced if the Semantic Web initiative more heavily recruited librarians to participate in current projects, and if librarians could explore beyond their current enclaves and consider how their skills were applicable to the Semantic Web. This current article focused on one possible path by exploring the applicability of library functions and policies to the Semantic Web. There are other means of reducing the Semantic Web/library gap as alluded to here, and exploration is required if we are advance and accelerate Semantic Web development.

CONCLUSION AND FUTURE RESEARCH

This paper explored the applicability primary library functions to the Semantic Web. The inquiry was a discussion based on rudimentary deduction and was supported by an analysis of various library guidelines and policies. An exploration of similarities between the library institution and the Semantic Web served as a base. All four of the primary library functions proved applicable to the Semantic Web. Each library function translates to a Semantic Web function. The translation (or redefinition) of each library function for the Semantic Web follows:

- *Collection development* → *Semantic Web selection.*
- *Cataloging* → *Semantic Web "semantic" representation.*
- *Reference* → *Semantic Web service.*
- *Circulation* → *Semantic Web resource use.*

This paper is an initial inquiry, and the results illustrate that primary library functions are applicable to the Semantic Web. The functions, redefined in the context of the Semantic Web, may improve and accelerate Semantic Web development. Development, implementation, and evaluation of Semantic Web policies, underscoring these functions, is required if we are to determine the true impact of library functions on Semantic Web development. As a first step, the results presented in this article indicate that the functions are applicable to the Semantic Web, and invite more research. In conclusion, continued efforts may bridge the Semantic Web/library gap and lead to new opportunities for both communities.

ACKNOWLEDGMENTS

The author wishes to thank Robert Losee and Francis Miksa for their thoughtful comments and editorial input.

NOTES

1. Semantic Web layer cake: http://www.w3.org/2004/Talks/0412-RDF-functions/slide4-0.html.
2. Flickr: http://www.flickr.com/.
3. Del.icio.us: http://del.icio.us/.
4. Facebook: http://www.facebook.com/.
5. South Western State University: http://www.gsw.edu/~library/Libmission.htm, Georgetown Law Library: http://www.ll.georgetown.edu/about/mission.cfm, and Seattle Public Library: http://www.spl.org/default.asp?pageID=about_mission.
6. Madeleine Clark Wallace Library, Wheaton College: http://www.wheatonma.edu/Library/Info/home.html.
7. Seattle Public Library: http://www.spl.org/default.asp?pageID=about_mission.
8. Semantic Web homepage: http://www.w3.org/2001/sw/.
9. Semantic Web Activity Statement: http://www.w3.org/2001/sw/Activity.

10. Resource Description and Access (RDA): http://www.collectionscanada.ca/jsc/rda.html.

11. Semantic Web Best Practices and Deployment Working Group: http://www.w3.org/2001/sw/BestPractices/.

12. It is important to note that the Internet has penetrated less than 10% of the populations in African and the Middle East, and less than 15% of the population in Asia and Latin America/Caribbean [viewed Sept. 1, 2006]: http://www.internetworldstats.com/stats.htm.

13. Iola Village Library: http://www.owls.lib.wi.us/ivl/Collection_Development_Policy.htm, Tempe Public Library Collection Development Policy: http://www.tempe.gov/library/admin/colldev.htm, Bobst Library, Mathematics, New York University, http://library.nyu.edu/collections/policies/math.html, and Cornell University, Archeology: http://www.library.cornell.edu/colldev/cdarchaeology.html.

14. MusicBrainz: http://musicbrainz.org/.

15. Semantic Web Environmental Directory: http://www.swed.org.uk/swed/index.html.

16. MARC Standards Website: http://www.loc.gov/marc/.

17. Cataloging Documentation: Yale University: http://www.library.yale.edu/cataloging/ccc/catpol/catpolhome.htm#documents; University of Illinois at Urbana Champaign: http://www.library.uiuc.edu/committee/charges/cataloging%20policy.htm.

18. American Library Association, Library Bill of Rights: http://www.ala.org/ala/oif/statementspols/statementsif/librarybillrights.htm.

19. American Library Association, The Freedom to Read Statement: http://www.ala.org/ala/oif/statementspols/ftrstatement/freedomreadstatement.htm.

20. Code of Ethics of the American Library Association: http://www.ala.org/ala/oif/statementspols/codeofethics/codeethics.htm.

21. University of Rochester, Circulation Policies, "Who Can Borrow,": http://www.lib.rochester.edu/index.cfm?PAGE=1324.

22. Librarians is used loosely in this article to refer to information professionals working in custodial agencies or institutions that is identified as a library, or includes similar functions (e.g., museum, archives, or data centers).

23. Protégé homepage: http://protege.stanford.edu/.

REFERENCES

Berners-Lee, T. (1999). *Weaving the Web: The Original Design and Ultimate Destiny of the World Wide Web by its Inventor*. San Francisco: Harper.

Berners-Lee, T., Hendler, J., and Lassila, O. (2001). The Semantic Web. *Scientific American*, 284(5): 34-43. Also available online at: http://www.sciam.com/article.cfm?articleID=00048144-10D2-1C70-84A9809EC588EF21.

Brooks, T. A. (2002). The Semantic Web, Universalist Ambition and Some Lessons from Librarianship. *Information Research*, 7(4): http://informationr.net/ir/7-4/paper136.html.

Bush, V. (1945). As We May Think (1945). The Atlantic Monthly, 176(1): 101-108. Also available at: http://www.theatlantic.com/doc/194507/bush.

Chepesuik, R. (1997). The Future is Here: America's Libraries Go Digital. *American Libraries*, 2(1): 47-49.

Cutter, C. A. (1904). *Rules for a Dictionary Catalog*, 4th ed. Washington, D.C.: Government Printing Office.

Dartmouth College. (2000). *Guidelines for Writing Collection Development Policies*: http://www.dartmouth.edu/~cmdc/bibapp/cdpguide.html. [Original publication 1998, latest update, 2000.]

Functional Requirements for Bibliographic Records: Final Report. (1998). München: K. G. Saur: http://www.ifla.org/VII/s13/frbr/frbr.htm.

Graves, M. J. (2003). *Concert Event Metadata: Describing Concerts Effectively in a Digital Environment.* [A Master's paper for the M.S. in L.S. degree.] Also available at: http://ils.unc.edu/MSpapers/2830.pdf.

Greenberg, J. (2005). Understanding Metadata and Metadata Schemes. *Cataloging & Classification Quarterly*, 41(3/4): 17-36.

Greenberg, J. and Robertson, D. W. (2002). Semantic Web Construction: An Inquiry of Authors' Views on Collaborative Metadata Generation. *DC-2002: Metadata for e-Communities: Supporting Diversity and Convergence. Proceedings of the International Conference on Dublin Core and Metadata for e-Communities, 2002,* Florence, Italy. October 13-17. Firenze University Press (ISBN: 88-843-043-1), pp. 45-52. Also available at: http://www.bncf.net/dc2002/program/ft/paper5.pdf.

Greenberg, J., Sutton, S., and Campbell, G. D. (2003). Metadata: A Fundamental Component of the Semantic Web. *Bulletin of the American Society for Information Science and Technology*, 29(4): 16-18. Also available at: http://www.asis.org/Bulletin/Apr-03/BulletinAprMay03.pdf.

IFLA Digital Reference Guidelines. (2005): http://www.ifla.org/VII/s36/pubs/drg03.htm.

International Federation of Library Associations and Institutions. (1963). Report: international conference on cataloguing principles, Paris, 9th-18th October, 1961. London: Organizing Committee of the International Conference on Cataloguing Principles, p. 91-96.

Koivunen, M. and Miller E. (2001). W3C Semantic Web Activity. E. Hyvönen (Ed.). Semantic Web Kick-Off in Finland: Vision, Technologies, Research, and Applications. Helsinki Institute for Information Technology (HIIT), Helsinki, Finland. May 19, 2002, pp. 27-43. Also available online at: http://www.cs.helsinki.fi/u/eahyvone/stes/semanticweb/kick-off/proceedings.pdf, and http://www.w3.org/2001/12/semweb-fin/w3csw.

Lipow, A. G. (2003). *The Virtual Reference Librarian's Handbook.* New York: Neal-Schuman Publishers.

McGuinness, D. L. (2003). Ontologies Come of Age. In Dieter, F., Hendler, J., Lieberman, H. and Wahlster, W. (Eds.) *Spinning the Semantic Web: Bringing the World Wide Web to its Full Potential.* Cambridge: MIT Press, 2003, pp. 171-194.

McIlraith, S.A., Son, T.C., and Zeng, H. (2001). Semantic Web Services. *IEEE Intelligent Systems.* [Special Issue on the Semantic Web]. 16(2): 46-53.

Miksa, F. (1996). The Cultural Legacy of the "Modern Library" for the Future. *Journal of Education for Library and Information Science* 37(2): 100-119. Also available at: http://www.gslis.utexas.edu/~landc/fulltext/LandC_35_1_Wiegand.pdf#search=%22Fran%20Miksa%20modern%20library%22.

Miller, P. (2006). Coming Together around Library 2.0: A Focus for Discussion and a Call to Arms. *D-Lib Magazine*, 12(4): Also available online at: http://www.dlib.org/dlib/april06/miller/04miller.html.

Office of the Associate University Librarian for Public Services and Communications. (2006). *Public Services Policy Memo 1. Access to Library Resources and Services*: http://www.libraries.rutgers.edu/rul/about/pub_serv_policies/pspm_01.shtml.

RDA–Resource Description and Access Objectives and Principles [Draft]. (2005): http://www.collectionscanada.ca/jsc/docs/5rda-objectives.pdf.

Rolfe, J. M. and Staples, K. J. (1986). *Flight Simulation*. Cambridge University Press, London.

RUSA Access to Information Committee. (2000). *Information Services for Information Consumers: Guidelines for Providers*. Prepared by the Standards and Guidelines Committee, Reference and User Services Association. Approved by the RUSA Board of Directors: http://www.ala.org/ala/rusa/rusaprotools/referenceguide/guidelinesinformation.htm.

Snow, S. (2004). *Center of Knowledge versus Center of Information: A Comparative Study of the UK Academic Library with the US Academic Public Library*. [A Master's paper for the M.S. in I.S. degree.] Also available at: http://ils.unc.edu/MSpapers/2965.pdf.

University of Texas at Arlington. (2006). *Information Service (Reference) Guidelines*: http://library.uta.edu/policies/reference/.

Wilson, A. (2000). *Libraries FAQ*, 2.1(9/10): http://www.faqs.org/faqs/books/library-faq/part9/.

doi:10.1300/J104v43n03_12

Social Bibliography:
A Personal Perspective on Libraries
and the Semantic Web

Stuart L. Weibel

SUMMARY. This paper presents a personal perspective on libraries and the Semantic Web. The paper discusses computing power, increased availability of processable text, social software developments and the ideas underlying Web 2.0 and the impact of these developments in the context of libraries and information. The article concludes with a discussion of social bibliography and the declining hegemony of catalog records, and emphasizes the strengths of librarianship and the profession's ability to contribute to Semantic Web development. doi:10.1300/J104v43n03_13 *[Article copies available for a fee from The Haworth Document Delivery Service: 1-800-HAWORTH. E-mail address: <docdelivery@haworthpress.com> Website: <http://www.HaworthPress.com>* © 2007 by The Haworth Press, Inc. All rights reserved.]

KEYWORDS. Semantic Web, Web 2.0, Library 2.0, social software, social bibliography

Talk of the Semantic Web is reminiscent of the artificial intelligence (AI) rage of two decades ago. There is compelling jargon, hyped prom-

[Haworth co-indexing entry note]: "Social Bibliography: A Personal Perspective on Libraries and the Semantic Web." Weibel, Stuart L. Co-published simultaneously in *Cataloging & Classification Quarterly* (The Haworth Information Press, an imprint of The Haworth Press, Inc.) Vol. 43, No. 3/4, 2007, pp. 227-236; and: *Knitting the Semantic Web* (ed: Jane Greenberg, and Eva Méndez) The Haworth Information Press, an imprint of The Haworth Press, Inc., 2007, pp. 227-236. Single or multiple copies of this article are available for a fee from The Haworth Document Delivery Service [1-800-HAWORTH, 9:00 a.m. - 5:00 p.m. (EST). E-mail address: docdelivery@haworthpress.com].

doi:10.1300/J104v43n03_13

ise, over-arching expectation, large sums of money, conferences, grants, and grand research programs. Will we see a reprise of the collapse of expectations, the so-called *AI-winter*, as well? AI research suffered not so much from lack of ideas, resources, and enthusiasm, as from a plethora of all of these, without a sufficient intellectual foundation to support them. Before we enquire as to the role of libraries in the Semantic Web revolution, it is fair to ask the question: Déjà vu all over again?

Part of the problem is . . . well . . . semantic. The *Semantic Web* isn't primarily about semantics at all. From the W3C Semantic Web activity pages (W3C, 2001):

> The Semantic Web is about two things. It is about common formats for interchange of data, where on the original Web we only had interchange of documents. Also it is about language for recording how the data relates to real world objects. That allows a person, or a machine, to start off in one database, and then move through an unending set of databases which are connected not by wires but by being about the same thing.

There is a hint of semantics there (the notion of being about the same thing), but philosophers have struggled with identity longer than computer scientists, and the struggle isn't over yet. The challenge of encoding that *same-thingness* is not so obvious when you get past simple string comparison. *Same-thingness*, though, reverberates strongly with classic and new problems of identity in our own library environs.

The heart of the W3C Semantic Web Activity is the bit about *data*. Specifically, interchange of data, rather than documents. It's a little less exciting than swinging around the weightiness of the term *semantics*, but on the other hand it is without question both useful and tractable in a way that the AI movement never really achieved.

Still, it would be nice to have confidence that we're not repeating the fool's errands that led to *AI winter*. What evidence might we bring to bear?

COMPUTING POWER

We have orders of magnitude more, it is low cost, and ubiquitous. My colleague Thom Hickey is fond of the quote "quantity has a quality all its own" [extra credit for finding the surprising source]. The enormity of computational cycles we have to bring to bear on these problems is wildly improbable and growing steadily. Except it is eminently probable. Moore's law[1] has served us well for decades, and there seems to be no let up in sight, but it doesn't really help us understand how we're going to use those ever-cheaper-cycles. The availability of such computational largesse is, however, an important difference from 1985.

PROCESSABLE TEXT

The combination of born-digital and retrospectively-captured text changes what can be done. Two decades ago the AI domain had small data sets–mostly toys–which substantially constrained what was possible. In the information sphere, we are steadily approaching the state of *that-which-is-not-on-the-Web-does-not-matter*. While a great deal (perhaps the most important part) remains behind databases or other impediments to access, the machine processability of the global textual corpus changes what is possible from a computational linguistic point of view, and this has already altered the business cases for the use of textual materials, search, and classification.

For example, Amazon's bibliometric feature set is now commonplace, and in most respect eclipses that which library catalogs offer:

- Statistically Improbable Phrases
- Capitalized Phrases
- Search Inside™
- concordance data
- text statistics

Add to this the social bibliographic benefits of customer reviews, editorial reviews, *people-who-bought-X-also-bought-Y*, customer forums, customer-added-tags, and you have a rich and formidable resource that outperforms most library systems. The wide availability of everything-textual is another important difference from 1985.

A Ubiquitous Architecture for the Expression of Resource Relationships (the Web)

The graphic nature of the Web–nodes and arcs self-organized in ever-more-articulated graphs of emergent semantics–is new. In fact, it has spawned a perspective that has rapidly become a discipline of its own, and is deeply embedded in both the technology and the business propositions of digital information. Barabasi's *Linked* tells us why hyperlinks are the currency of significance, and helps us to understand the essential part that hyperlinking must play in every aspect of our relationship to data, information, and knowledge (Barabási, 2003).

The very existence of semantic graphs enables exploration of theories, products, services, and systems that could scarcely be imagined when libraries began their own march towards digitization 40 years ago. The recent passing of Henriette Avram reminds us that libraries planted a major foundational stake in the ground of sharable data. Is there any more successful example of such in existence than the MARC record?

This early leadership notwithstanding, librarianship has been slow to embrace the rapid advances of data mining, linking, social networking, and the myriad, intricate opportunities that spring, weed-like, in the fertile fields of the entrepreneurial Web. The Web, then, is perhaps the most significant difference of all from 1985, and it is chasing us even as we chase it.

None of these factors is conclusive, but together they afford greater confidence that the technology and approaches growing up around the Semantic Web will have a lasting impact.

SOCIAL SOFTWARE AND WEB 2.0

If the Semantic Web is a sulking adolescent, then social software, *ala* Web 2.0, is a manic preschooler. Librarians are the clueless grownups, knowing the kids are hip, and only vaguely cognizant of their potential on either side of the ledger.

Le buzz du jour is social software and Web 2.0 (which inevitably and quickly led to *Everything 2.0*), as if all digital reality was a first release. Like it or not, we have *Library 2.0* to understand and wrestle to the mat. Start with Tim O'Reilly's article on Web 2.0 (O'Reilly, 2005). Then perhaps have a gander at Paul Miller's article in the April *DLib Magazine* on Library 2.0 (Miller, 2006). Along the way, you may want to read Walt Crawford's deconstruction of what the librarian blogosphere had to say about Library 2.0 through early 2006 (Crawford, 2006). I commend his thoughts to anyone trying to come to grips with these ideas. His definition follows:

> Library 2.0 encompasses a range of new and not-so-new software methodologies (social software, interactivity, APIs, modular software . . .) that can and will be useful for many libraries in providing

new services and making existing services available in new and interesting ways.

The tone of this informative piece is that of elder statesman and adult supervisor, and his call to *take a deep breath* is almost certainly a good idea. But while I respect his circumspection, I have a stronger sense of urgency about libraries needing to embrace the revolution (or evolution) that is overtaking us.

Crawford's assertions about a large component of the library constituency as being voting adults who still want buildings with books on shelves is well founded and important. It behooves us to remember, though, that the *Gamers* among us will not become those bond-issue-passing adults without a stake and a perception of value in what our community does. We must fight for the next generation as well as support the last. Libraries need to support not the Semantic Web, but the semantic lives of our users, and our users are, on average, more connected, more online, more mobile, and more digital than ever. We must bring together the infrastructure, the applications, and the content in practical ways that support their rapidly changing needs. I'm pretty sure Walt would agree.

My colleague, Lorcan Dempsey, synthesized O'Reilly's Web 2.0 ideas as follows in his Computer's in Libraries 2006 talk (Dempsey, 2006):

- Flat applications (lightweight base applications)
- Rich interaction
- Data is the new functionality
- Participation

Lorcan's presentation highlights a variety of OCLC research projects that fall in these categories, including the audience level prototype, which capitalizes on the distribution of materials across different classes of WorldCat libraries to identify the probable audience level of a resource, and the Fiction Finder prototype, which showcases the usefulness of FRBR algorithms in bringing order to large result sets. Another project illustrates the usefulness of the Dewey Decimal System as a browsing framework, bringing the power of a legacy knowledge organization system into the context of the Web. These projects illustrate the power of data, and the value that can be released from that data when used appropriately in a new technological context. These projects and more are accessible through the Research Works Website at OCLC.[2]

The archetypical Web 2.0 applications are now well known to most of us. Google Maps was perhaps the first ubiquitous splash, giving us a high quality, richer interaction with data through a Web Browser than we were accustomed to. Such applications are becoming commonplace, and themselves are calling forth new business models for software functionality. Tools to create such applications are growing simpler and easier, lowering the barriers to widespread adoption of such applications. The Google Code site is one example of a growing model for shared code building blocks that help developers bring up sophisticated, data-rich applications easily.[3]

As attractive and interactive as are the user interfaces, it is the data that is at the heart of the value. If the Semantic Web is indeed about data interchange, we can find encouragement in our past. MARC cataloging remains one of the most successful structured data exchange standards in use (and one of the most long-lived, as well). If the Semantic Web is about structured data–"common formats for interchange of data"–then we should be optimistic about the place a half-century aggregation of semantics-laden data. OCLC's Open WorldCat program[4] represents an important step towards making such data part of the Web, rather than expecting users to come to our portals or OPACs. The marketing slogan "weaving libraries into the web" is apt and exemplary of a strategy that will serve to bind libraries more tightly into the daily workflows of our constituents.

The Dublin Core, another example of encoded common semantics, has justifiable claims to library lineage as well, informed by strong participation by librarians from many countries. DC is the best-known metadata brand on the Web, helping as it does to connect open Web applications with structured description for knowledge organization and management. Both of these standards are influential in embedding semantics in the Web.

The Semantic Web and Web 2.0 are not the same, but they are intertwined technologies that, taken as a whole, support the expression of semantics from both a bottom-up and a top-down direction.

RDF, the W3C's Resource Description Framework, is the foundation technology for the Semantic Web. It evolved from recognition that an earlier tagging scheme (PICS, or Platform for Internet Content Selection) would be more useful if it were generalized. PICS was an early response on the part of the W3C to the problem of identifying content unsuitable for general viewing. RDF became a modular metadata architecture for declaring and reusing semantics that can help to make metadata standards from many sources more compatible and inter-changeable.

The Dublin Core community was a prominent early consumer of RDF, and hence had a significant impact on its evolution. RDF provides the syntactic carrier for metadata elements, and a model for other communities as well. It is infrastructure to support bottom-up metadata from many sources, rationalized with the use of RDF schemas.

The OWL (Ontology Web Language) family of technologies provides formalisms for terminology, grammars and the declaration of semantic relationships, and represents a top-down approach to building semantics into systems. The specification of an ontology implies thorough understanding of the scope and structure of a knowledge domain. Semantic coherence of this kind is rare outside a tightly constrained domain, and leads one to wonder whether ontologies are likely to play a practical role on the open Web.

Semantics is in the mind of the beholder, the reader, the user. Sharing meaning across the gulf of machines and symbolic languages is harder than sharing it face-to-face. Controlled vocabularies reply to exactly this problem. As hard as controlled vocabularies are to use and maintain, the many-to-one mapping problem they address is at least a step forward from the many-to-many problem of human semantic interchange.

Enter *folksonomies*: an up-welling of community-generated semantics that is expected to (compete with? . . . augment? . . . complement?) formal taxonomies. It is too early to tell whether the information landscape becomes more coherent or more chaotic because of them, but as I write these words, LibraryThing.com has just introduced a feature that may help to elucidate these answers.

LibraryThing[5] embodies a lot of what we want to see in Library 2.0 applications:

- It does data (thanks largely to LC cataloging data and the Amazon API).
- It links . . . books, reviews, users, catalogs.
- It has recommender services . . . several.
- It supports tagging as well as traditional use of subject headings (see below).
- It supports community.

As of May, 2006, LibraryThing provides categorization using both Library of Congress Subject Headings and user-generated tags. This is an exciting development that should help the community understand the benefits to users of each and perhaps explore how they might be effectively hybridized.

SOCIAL BIBLIOGRAPHY AND THE DECLINING HEGEMONY OF CATALOG RECORDS

Online customer reviews of products, including books, are popular throughout the Internet. Book reviews represent significant intellectual products that can help readers find and choose appropriate resources to meet their information needs. Recognition of the intellectual property embodied in book reviews strengthens the incentives for such contributions, and hence the fabric of social bibliography.

Most reviews today are contributed to sites such as Amazon.com, authors having surrendered their copyright and control over the disposition of their content. In fact, reviews should be discrete content in their own right–they should be *first class objects*:

- Endowed with persistent identity–such content should have identifiers that are long-lived and reliable, and hence useful for citing and managing their content.
- Harvestable on the open Web–by being harvestable on the Web, search engines will encounter and index them so that they contribute to the linking richness of social bibliography, thereby raising the visibility of their referents (and thus making library assets a more visible and findable part of the Web).
- As managed intellectual content in their own right, such reviews should be curated so as to assure their continued role in social bibliography, which includes linking to content, but also "citability," such that they may be claimed by their authors, referenced, and perhaps refuted as well.

Linking is the currency of attention, and attention is the essence of success on the Web (cf. Walker, 2006). If we are to "Weave Libraries into the Web" then it must be, in part, through ever-richer linkages among the intellectual products that we create and those we curate.

As curated, harvestable, persistently-identified content, well-crafted reviews can play a role in resource discovery as well as reader advisories. The catalog record will continue to be the lynchpin of bibliography, but thoughtful reviews will assume greater importance in the bibliographic spectrum. The creation and curation of persistent book reviews is a worthy complement to traditional cataloging. Library administrators should recognize (and provide incentives for) contributions by staff to creating and maintaining such resources.

Allyson Carlyle, in a recent discussion group on the Semantic Web at the University of Washington Information School, observed that we must not lose sight of the strengths that libraries bring to the table–the hard stuff, with details that bottom-up social collaboration is unlikely to get right. The challenge we face is the creation of a new social bibliography that embodies these strengths of traditional cataloging and embraces the emergent richness of social collaborative networks as well. In so doing, we'll strengthen the contribution of librarianship to the Web, and help enrich semantics where it counts the most–in the minds of our constituents.

NOTES

1. Moore's Law. Entry in Wikipedia: http://en.wikipedia.org/wiki/Moores_law.
2. ResearchWorks: OCLC Research Project Prototypes and Demonstrations: http:// www.oclc.org/research/researchworks/default.htm.
3. Google Code: http://code.google.com.
4. Open WorldCat: http://www.oclc.org/worldcat/open.
5. LibraryThing.com: http://librarything.com.

REFERENCES

Barabási, Albert-Laszló (2003). *Linked: how everything is connected to everything else and what it means for business, science, and everyday life.* (New York: Plume) 2003: http://www.worldcatlibraries.org/wcpa/oclc/52315903.
Crawford, Walt (2006). Library 2.0 and "Library 2.0." *Cites & Insights: Crawford at Large*, Midwinter 2006, Vol. 6, n. 2, (Whole Issue 72). Available online at: http://cites.boisestate.edu/v6i2a.htm.
Dempsey, Lorcan (2006). Structured data, Web 2.0, libraries (PPT: 2.7MB/44 slides). *Computers in Libraries* 2006, 23 March 2006, Washington, DC (USA). Available online at: http://www.oclc.org/research/presentations/dempsey/cil06.ppt.
Miller, Paul (2006). Coming Together around Library 2.0: A Focus for Discussion and a Call to Arms. *D-Lib Magazine*, April 2006, Vol. 12, n. 4. Available online at: http://www.dlib.org/dlib/april06/miller/04miller.html.
O'Reilly, Tim (2005). What is Web 2.0: Design Patterns and Business Models for the Next Generation of Software. *O'Reilly Net*, 09-30-2005. Available online at: http://www.oreillynet.com/pub/a/oreilly/tim/news/2005/09/30/what-is-web-20.html.

W3C (2001). *Technology and Society Domain: Semantic Web Activity.* World Wide Web Consortium, 2001. Available online at: http://www.w3.org/2001/sw/.

Walker, Jill (2002). Links and Power: The Political Economy of Linking on the Web. Presented in June 2002 at the ACM Hypertext conference in Baltimore. Available online at: http://huminf.uib.no/~jill/txt/linksandpower.html.

doi:10.1300/J104v43n03_13

Index

9 780415 541565